A New Capitalist Order

Pitt Series in Russian and East European Studies

Jonathan Harris, Editor

A New Capitalist Order

Privatization & Ideology in
Russia & Eastern Europe

Hilary Appel

University of Pittsburgh Press

Published by the University of Pittsburgh Press, Pittsburgh, Pa., 15260
Copyright © 2004, University of Pittsburgh Press
All rights reserved
Manufactured in the United States of America
Printed on acid-free paper
10 9 8 7 6 5 4 3 2 1

Library of Congress Cataloging-in-Publication Data

Appel, Hilary.
    A new capitalist order : privatization and ideology in Russia and
Eastern Europe / Hilary Appel.
        p. cm. — (Pitt series in Russian and East European studies)
    Includes bibliographical references and index.
    ISBN 0-8229-5855-4 (cloth : alk. paper)
    1. Privatization—Russia (Federation) 2. Privatization—Czech Republic.
3. Russia (Federation)—Economic policy—1991– 4. Czech Republic—
Economic policy. I. Title. II. Series.
HD4215.15.A8 2004
338.947′05—dc22
                            2004011318

Contents

Acknowledgments   vii

Part I. Bringing Ideology Back In

 1. The Ideological Determinants
     of Post-Communist Economic Reform   3

 2. The International Dimension of
     Post-Communist Privatization   22

Part II. Probing the Czech and Russian Cases

 3. The Origins and Design of Czech
     Large-Scale Privatization   39

 4. The Origins and Design of Russian
     Large-Scale Privatization   71

Part III. Elaborating the Theoretical Framework

 5. The Beliefs of Leaders and the Content of Reform   109

 6. Power, Interests, and the Ideological Context   127

 7. The Ideological Foundations of Building Compliance   157

 8. The Ideological Fit and the Cost of Compliance   172

     Notes   181
     Bibliography   225
     Index   241

Acknowledgments

I am grateful to many individuals and institutions for their support of this project. This book could not have been written without generous funding from the Social Science Research Council, the American Council of Learned Societies, the Fulbright Commission, the Kennan Institute at the Woodrow Wilson Center, the Harriman Institute at Columbia University, and the Institute for the Study of World Politics. I would like to thank these organizations as well as the Benjamin Z. Gould Center for Humanistic Studies, the Keck Center for International and Strategic Studies, and the Dean of Faculty's research fund at Claremont McKenna College for their research support. This book has also benefited from the substantial research assistance of my students at Claremont McKenna College, especially Michael Albertson, Elizabeth Hillman, and Annie Lee.

I am extraordinarily grateful to the many political actors and government officials in the Czech Republic, Russia, and Poland who sat down with me and shared their experiences and impressions. The book has benefited enormously from their generosity and openness. I would also like to heartily thank numerous friends and scholars who have commented on either parts or all of the manuscript at various phases of the project. For their suggestions, comments, and insights, I would like to recognize the thoughtful feedback of Herbert Levine, Peter Rutland, John Gould, Mitchell Orenstein, Juliet Johnson, Anna Grzymala-Busse, Mark Blyth, Zdenka Mansfeldová, Stephen Hanson, Srirupa Roy, Alev Cinar, and Meredith Hyman El Nems. I also want to express my gratitude to M. Steven Fish for his years of generous and insightful feedback and his tireless attention to my work. Having carefully read and meticulously commented on numerous drafts of this manuscript, he deserves recognition for substantially improving the clarity of my ideas and the rigor of my argument. I am also greatly indebted to Thomas Callaghy, who sparked my interest in political economy and has provided careful guidance and friendship since my days as a graduate student at the University of Pennsylvania. I would like to thank my colleagues and friends at Claremont McKenna College for providing a supportive environment in which to complete this project. Furthermore, I would like to thank Nathan Macbrien, Deborah Meade, and Jonathan Harris at the University of Pittsburgh Press for their conscientious and efficient handling of my manuscript. I am grateful for their hard work and support.

Finally, and most important, I would like to thank my husband, Vincenzo Quadrini, for his patience and encouragement. My greatest debt is to my parents, Marjorie and Jeffrey Appel, to whom I dedicate this book. Anything I have ever accomplished I owe to them.

Part I. Bringing Ideology Back In

1. The Ideological Determinants of Post-Communist Economic Reform

When the new democratic leaders of Russia and Eastern Europe initiated the capitalist transformation of their command economies, many expected the transfer of public property to the private sector to be one of the more popular measures to implement. Indeed, when the movement to privatize state-owned industries through widespread distribution gained momentum in Great Britain in the 1980s, it was as much a populist measure to build support for Margaret Thatcher's government as a means to revitalize sluggish industries under state control.[1] More important, considering the pain associated with other early transition programs in post-Communist Europe—such as price deregulation, reducing industrial subsidies, imposing wage caps, or increasing the retirement age—privatization seemed to offer the greatest potential for building rather than diminishing public support for the government's promarket agenda. In this vein, the proponents of liberal economic reform championed the ability of large-scale privatization to produce a broad base of capitalists overnight who, given their vested interests, could serve as reliable defenders of the new capitalist order.

Rather than providing a dependable source of legitimacy and support, however, privatization has served as a focal point for the public's frustration with the corruption and economic disappointments of the post-Communist period. Though supported in the early phase of transformation, both the program and its promoters were later demonized at home, breathing new life into the nineteenth-century French socialist idea that ownership is theft. In many contexts, post-Communist privatization became synonymous with collusion, corruption, and material deprivation.

Some of the frustration with privatization in the region revolved around the pain of economic transition in general: the disappearance of life savings due to inflation, the decline in the standard of living of large sectors of the population, and the general feeling of material uncertainty.[2] There was also considerable anger, however, with the way that privatization programs were designed and with the consequences of property distribution. First, privatization did not bring about the revitalization of most economies in the region, at least not as quickly as many were led to expect. Second, the new incentive structure did not lead to broad-based enterprise restructuring in the short run and instead left many enterprises vulnerable to asset stripping. Third, while the results vary across countries, formal mass privatization programs— also known as voucher privatization programs[3]—did not generate an equitable distribution of property ownership among the citizenry. Rather, it exacerbated the general trend of *nomenklatura* enrichment that had been intensifying during the Gorbachev period by providing a legal means to transfer the title of state assets to the well-connected few. Mass privatization is also maligned for bolstering popular expectations of personal material gains, only to disappoint them when companies failed, investment funds folded, and small shareholder rights were violated. Even many of those who were initially committed to the logic of mass privatization were critical in retrospect of the decision to distribute property at low prices or for free, since it forfeited an opportunity to raise revenue for social safety nets and gain new technologies and investment for domestic firms.

The critical light in which post-Communist privatization is often now viewed[4] is curious when one recalls the breadth of support for mass privatization during the early years of transition among the general population, local government officials, and foreign advisers across numerous states.[5] The early momentum behind mass privatization in the 1990s and its popularity among government officials are especially surprising given the lack of historical precedent for privatization on an economy-wide scale. That is, leaders energetically embarked upon mass privatization without any real precedent to guide policy design or to reassure them that this novel course of property rights reform would be feasible and effective. The European and North American privatization experiences of the preceding decade concerned the transfer of individual enterprises, or perhaps industries, but not the privatization of an economy. East European policy makers faced the daunting task of designing from scratch programs to transfer nearly the entire wealth of the state to private hands. With few exceptions, the officials appointed to this task concluded that standard privatization methods relying upon piecemeal sales of enterprises to private investors would be too slow and unwieldy. In many post-Communist states, a mounting economic crisis discouraged a more gradual reform process and justified the use of ambitious unprecedented approaches. Consequently, officials chose to rely significantly on the free and popular distribution of property, followed with or supplemented by conventional techniques like the sale of strategic blocs or residual shares in leading enterprises.

Even though there was no historical precedent, East European officials could take comfort in knowing that there was near universal consensus in the international policy and lending community in support of mass privatization. Shortly after Czechoslovakia initiated the first voucher privatization program, the international community uniformly and enthusiastically embraced the notion of the rapid and widespread distribution of national wealth to private hands. Legions of Western advisers and lenders visited the region, advocating mass privatization, among other liberal policy prescriptions.

Many of these past advocates of mass privatization are much less sanguine in their support today, given the poor economic performance of most of the post-Communist region during the 1990s. As one senior economist from the World Bank, Harry Broadman, explains, "In the earlier years of Russia's (and other countries') transition, there was a sense in the policy community that ownership change from public to private—however it comes about—is necessarily welfare improving, even in the short-run. We know better today."[6] In a similar vein, John Nellis, Broadman's colleague at the bank, writes, "The international financial institutions must bear some of the responsibility for the poor outcomes, since they so often insisted on the primacy of economic policy (or uncritically followed the lead of intensely committed reformers). That is, they requested and required transition governments to privatize rapidly and extensively."[7] More dramatically, David Ellerman from the World Bank writes, "The Western advisers were marketing themselves as the intellectual saviors of the benighted East by putting the scientific prestige of neoclassical economics behind one of the most cockamamie social engineering schemes (voucher privatization) of the twentieth century." Ellerman contends, "Only the mixture of American triumphalism and the academic arrogance of neoclassical economics could produce such a lethal dose of gall."[8]

Accounting for Privatization's Early Popularity

Serious criticism of the policy choices within post-Communist privatization began to appear often in the late 1990s and beyond—that is, once mass privatization had run its course in most countries. Only then did members from prominent institutions, like the World Bank or USAID, begin to reflect seriously upon the wholehearted embrace of mass privatization and the formidable momentum behind this common prescription for property reform.[9] Reconsidering this overwhelming support for post-Communist privatization, officials like Nellis at the World Bank began to ask the question of why privatization "swept the field and won the day" and (quoting others) moved "from novelty to global orthodoxy in the space of two decades."[10] After all, there was little theoretical or empirical evidence for rapid and extensive property transfers and yet large-scale privatization took the region by storm.

No one answered this question more forcefully or with greater controversy than the maverick former vice president and chief economist of the World Bank, Joseph Stiglitz. Economics professor, Nobel laureate, and former economic adviser to President Clinton, Stiglitz unequivocally argued that the widespread adoption of post-Communist privatization, and of shock therapy more generally, was driven by "free market ideology," "market fundamentalism," and special interests.[11] In his controversial 1999 World Bank address "Whither Reform?" he refers to the advisers in Washington as "market Bolsheviks" who were possessed by a "moral fervor and triumphalism left over from the Cold War."[12]

According to Stiglitz's perspective, the wide-scale adoption of neoliberal reforms in post-Communist states can be explained largely by recognizing that a free-market ideology dominated the international community, and this ideology was aggressively pushed on post-Communist governments. To some extent this is true, but as this book will show, the role of ideology is much more nuanced than that, and the beliefs and preferences of actors on the ground deserve much more recognition than Stiglitz allows for.

In seeking to uncover the complex role of ideology in post-Communist economic policy making, this volume explores in detail the determinants of large-scale privatization in the Czech Republic and Russia, among other East European countries. The specific task of this study is to show that ideology accounts for the choice of *how* to privatize in these states—rather than to explain the choice of *whether* to privatize more generally. The book begins by investigating the role of the West in the international spread of a particular privatization paradigm in Eastern Europe. It argues that ideological factors drove the privatization process in Eastern Europe in ways much more complex and profound than the West's promotion of a neoliberal privatization agenda. The book also demonstrates how ideology shaped the perception of individual and group interests within the privatization process, created expectations regarding the efficacy of various approaches, informed leaders' attitudes toward building public support for a new ownership regime, and affected the realization of a leader's privatization approach.[13]

How Ideology Drove Privatization

There are three main channels in the domestic sphere through which ideological variables determine the design, revision, and implementation of new ownership arrangements. First, the beliefs of policy makers and the ideological foundations of the theories they espouse determine the initial design of new property rights reforms. Second, the beliefs of actors in society (non–policy makers) shape the definition of interests and the distribution of power among groups in society. This in turn shapes the nature and potency of interest group demands within the property rights reform and determines the version of reforms that leaders can ultimately pursue. Third, the beliefs of policy makers influence the implementation process—namely, they shape how policy makers attempt to build compliance to a new property rights arrangement. These first three channels together generate a final mechanism of ideological influence on domestic policy making. Namely, the compatibility between the ideological foundations of privatization policies and the beliefs of societal actors affect the ease of implementation and the distortion of privatization programs over time.

Ideology and Policy Design

Given the multiple uses of the word "ideology," it is necessary to make explicit how it is understood in this study. As a rule, the term "ideology" seems to invite controversy irrespective of the definition; and for this reason many scholars (Stiglitz aside) avoid the term entirely. As a case in point, Nobel laureate Douglass North noted in an address to the American Political Science Association that he prefers the term "belief system" to "ideology," since the latter word is not worth the trouble.[14] Several political scientists studying the impact of economic theoretical constructs (like developmentalism, Keynesianism, and economic liberalism) on policy making choose to study the influence of "ideas" rather than "ideology."[15] Within this literature, the choice to study ideas rather than ideology can be a stylistic or a substantive choice, depending on the particular analysis. However, the intention of such enterprises is similar to this one: to uncover the role of nonmaterial, ideational phenomena in the policy-making process.

The definition of "ideology" in this book is borrowed from one student of ideology, Malcolm Hamilton. After identifying more than twenty-seven conceptual elements or "definitional criteria," Hamilton isolates the essential core around which all definitions are built. He defines ideology as "a system of collectively held normative and reputedly factual ideas and beliefs and attitudes advocating a particular pattern of social relationships and arrangements, and/or aimed at justifying a particular pattern of conduct, which its proponents seek to promote, realize, pursue or maintain."[16]

Hamilton's definition is useful for several reasons. First, this definition makes explicit that ideologies are first and foremost mental constructs espoused by individuals, rather than discursive constraints or patterns of behavior. Second, Hamilton's definition stresses that ideologies provide an interpretation of the world both as it is (a weltanschauung) and *as it should be.*[17] That is, ideologies prescribe an ideal and thereby advocate a particular formula for change. Hamilton notes that ideologies "seek to persuade. . . . they make claims, present an argument, state reasons, for or against some plan, programme, behavior, action, conduct, value, attitude, preference, view and so on."[18] Given that the goal of this book is to identify the mechanisms through which ideologies recommend and shape privatization strategies, the term "ideology" has advantages over the more limited term "ideas," which may or may not be interpreted as advocating certain approaches or responses to political problems.[19]

Moreover, in referring to the term "ideology," this book adopts a Hayekian notion of ideology, in that it is a neutral term. That is, "ideology" here does not imply a Marxian false consciousness—it simply is a belief system with nothing pejorative intended in its usage.[20] Furthermore, references to both ideology and ideas do not imply the idiosyncratic beliefs of individual leaders, but instead a set of beliefs held by the individual but *shared by many*—such as economic liberalism, nationalism, anti-Communism, or pro-Westernism. As this list suggests, negative ideologies (that is, belief systems based on the rejection of a set of principles or constructs) is a subset of the broader category of shared ideologies. Thus, anti-Communism is as much an ideology as Communism.

Finally, and most important, Hamilton's definition highlights the multiple constitutive elements within an ideology, referring to ideas, beliefs, and attitudes individually. This brings us to a central issue in the growing "literature on ideas," as this strand of research can be called. Many contributors to this literature have been criticized either for studying a vast array of nonmaterial variables, all of which get called "ideas" (norms, paradigms, values, beliefs, identities, etc.), or for lumping together different types of politically relevant actors (such as policy makers, organizations, and members in social groups) who subscribe to various ideologies and ideas.[21]

There are different ways of coping with this difficulty. One is to take a small subset of ideational phenomena—like norms—and limit the study to this piece of the puzzle. This approach would capture only part of the nonmaterial forces informing the consideration of privatization options or the perception and formation of interests. While this might avoid one of the pitfalls attributed the literature on ideas, this narrow approach would lead to the same fundamental flaw of most material studies: Namely, for the sake of parsimony, it would exogenize key components of the process of preference formation at the expense of explanatory power.

Since analyzing one narrow type of ideational phenomena would exclude many interesting and important determinants of privatization policy making, this book takes a different tack. Avoiding the conceptual confusion associated with exploring various levels or types of ideological factors under the general rubric of "ideology" or "ideas," this book analyzes by chapter the different functions and levels on which ideological variables operate. That is, each chapter addresses one piece of the puzzle, analyzing one path by which an ideological variable influences the development of a new property rights regime. Moreover, the book distinguishes the types of ideas and beliefs that circulate in society and are espoused by members of societal groups from those of political elites in positions of policy-making authority.

Standard Determinants of Privatization

Characterizing privatization as ideologically driven, à la Stiglitz, is exceptional (and even then focuses narrowly on the advising community). The mainstream empirical literature on post-Communist privatization more commonly focuses on the material interests of key actors in order to account for the design and development of these reforms. In short, standard explanations for post-Communist privatization typically revolve around economic and political "stakeholders" who sought to impose their material preferences on the policy makers responsible for designing institutional reforms. Analyzing the special benefits for groups such as managers, labor, and entrepreneurs, among others, empirical studies have tended to emphasize the economic interests and the political resistance of groups and actors in the evolution of privatization programs. Notable examples of this line of argument can be found in the numerous works of Åslund; Boycko, Shleifer and Vishny; Nelson and Kuzes; and others.[22] For example, Shleifer and Vishny contend that privatization in general develops "in response to political pressure on the government."[23] In their analysis of the Russian case, they argue that when privatization officials tried to advance a particular program of mass privatization the demands of powerful actors in society constrained government officials and altered the course of liberal economic reform. At the time, Boycko, Shleifer, and Vishny explained, "the workers and particularly the managers are extremely influential, but the local governments and the branch ministries also play a role. . . . Unless the[se] stakeholders are appeased, bribed or disenfranchised, privatization cannot proceed."[24] According to this formulation, the distribution of power in society accounts for the ability of various groups or "stakeholders" to acquire special ownership benefits within a privatization program. Åslund similarly looks to the power of various groups to account for the distribution of benefits within Russian privatization. He explains the extensive privileges for managerial elites in Russian privatization by arguing that the Russian *nomenklatura* elite was "bigger, richer, more powerful . . . and far more prepared to fight" than in other country cases.[25] Studies of East European privatization similarly account for the design of privatization programs by emphasizing the strategies of government officials to use economic policy as a way to co-opt groups in society.[26] This common tendency in the post-Communist literature replicates trends in earlier research on privatization in Europe and North America in the 1980s, which similarly emphasizes power struggles and material interests over nonmaterial factors.[27]

Theories of Property Rights Change

The standard empirical findings of post-Communist privatization are consistent with the trends in property rights theory. That is, the theoretical literature on property rights change, which is not specific to the post-

Communist context, similarly looks to either power or economic interests to account for new ownership arrangements.[28] For example, by linking the insights of interest group theory to the formulation of property rights, Gary Libecap asserts that property rights are, first and foremost, the products of political bargaining among competing interests groups.[29] Like many interest group approaches, Libecap does not attribute any interests to the state per se. Serving the neutral role of arbiter, the state acts primarily as mediator between the competing claims that are brought forth by various societal groups.[30] Margaret Levi also looks at the formation of property rights systems as a product of bargaining between the state and societal actors, each constrained by resource endowments and other factors.[31]

Taking a wholly state-centered approach, Douglass North shows that since the premodern period the state or the sovereign constructs a system of property rights according to its own economic interests. North's emphasis on the calculation of economic interests by the agent specifying property rights builds upon the earlier interest-based work of Harold Demsetz and others.[32] Demsetz's work posits that private and exclusive property rights emerge when actors' calculations reveal that new property arrangements will yield material gains that exceed the costs of transformation.[33] However, North's work differs from earlier work because the previous studies rely exclusively on the rational calculation of known interests—the perception of which is unproblematic— as the determinant of property rights arrangements. Instead, North shows that the specification of property rights according to economic or material interests has historically been contentious for state actors (or the sovereign) since they are faced with different paths of reaching their objectives.[34] North's general theory of property rights captures much of the complexity in designing a new system of property rights by problematizing the state's pursuit of its economic interests, a complexity that is crucial to understanding post-Communist property regime change for reasons explained below. However, in stressing the state's dilemma between creating an efficient system of property rights and drawing immediate rents (predation), North does not address how state actors decide which property arrangements are efficient. Of equal concern is that North provides little analysis of power, considering state power as no more than a means to material extraction.[35]

More recently, political-economists have sought to widen the focus of interest-based property rights analysis by identifying the accumulation of political power as an end in and of itself. For example, Riker and Weimer argue that when governments seek to create an efficient ownership arrangement, it is not efficiency per se that may interest the rulers, but rather the political benefits that an efficient economic system accrues to the leaders.[36] In other words, the rulers of the state create an efficient property rights system such that it maximizes their personal *political* fortunes.[37]

Rethinking Theories of Property Rights and Privatization

Both the empirical and the theoretical literature stress the importance of powerful agents calculating their material self-interest in analyzing property rights development and change. Returning to the role of ideological factors in privatization, the crucial shortcoming of standard materialist and power-based analyses in both empirical and theoretical literatures is *the inadequate attention to the forces (1) shaping how the preferences of state and societal actors form and (2) determining how the distribution of power is perceived.* Instead, the interests and power of various groups are assumed from the outcomes.

Why is this problematic in studying post-Communist privatization? For one, given the high degree of uncertainty following the post-Communist change in governments, state actors may have no clear way of deciding which property structures or transformative mechanisms best advance particular goals or, as in the Northian property rights model, best facilitate material extraction. North's model does not speak to the possibility that comprehending the economic consequences of various property rights arrangements may be an ideologically charged process. In privatizing states, post-Communist leaders had to choose among competing prescriptions for promoting economic efficiency and defer to technical specialists—specialists who disagreed among themselves over ideal strategies. North's efficiency-predation dilemma, while problematizing the perception of economic interest, does not elucidate why one group of technocrats was chosen or why one form of privatization prevailed over another, especially in the case when the prevailing form does not appear to favor revenue extraction or economic efficiency. That is, the standard theories of state predation (material extraction) offer little in the way of explaining state divestiture through the nearly free distribution of property. Some contributors to the literature on property rights, such as Margaret Levi, directly acknowledge the difficulty of employing a predatory approach to analyze leaders who do not seek to maximize revenue. Unfortunately, state predation theorists do not offer any alternative for such cases and have no pretense of doing so for what they consider exceptional cases.[38]

The limitation of theories relying exclusively on the power and material interests of individuals or groups vis-à-vis the state to explain property rights is that they cannot account for the constraints on policy choice sets, the priorities of leaders and societal actors, or the nonmaterial resources of participants in policy debates. While the weakness of interest-based and power-based theories of privatization will be analyzed later in greater detail, consider briefly here the problem of explaining variation based on traditional variables in Russia and the Czech Republic:

An explanation consistent with the mainstream property rights literature would claim that the inclusion of extensive employee ownership privileges in Russian mass privatization, and their absence in Czech mass privatization, could be understood by analyzing the power and interests of managers and labor vis-à-vis the state in each country case. According to this logic, however, we should have expected equivalent privileges and benefits for management and labor in Russia and the Czech Republic. Managers and labor appear to be in equivalent lobbying positions in Russia and the Czech Republic. After all, both states emerged from relatively similar industrial structures and property rights structures (with around 95 percent of GNP stemming from the state sector). In both states, managers and labor should have had, in principle, equivalent material interests and prior claims to property. Yet the patterns of resistance to privatization and the lobbying for benefits vary enormously between cases. In the Czech Republic, enterprise managers and labor received essentially no benefits at all, while in Russia they had the opportunity to become majority owners in over two-thirds of the firms included in the mass privatization program, as discussed below. Without bringing ideology and legitimacy into our analysis, we would only realize the differing bargaining positions of these groups vis-à-vis the government post hoc—namely, with the benefit of knowing subsequently how property was distributed. In such a case, the distribution of property would act as both an independent and dependent variable: it would identify the relative power and interests of groups in society and be a product of that power or interest, thereby resulting in tautology.[39]

While the bargaining between the state and interest groups matters crucially in the formation of property rights systems, it is edifying to focus on the process through which interests and preferences form. It improves our understanding of post-Communist economic reform. It also forces us to pay greater attention to the assumptions that underlie rational choice analysis.[40] In focusing on the perception of interest, however, it is necessary to clarify that the assumption of self-interested behavior among actors in the political-economy literature is not directly at issue here, but rather the inattention to the process of defining those interests in highly unstable environments. More specifically, in a revolutionary context, the formation of interests—even those that are purely materialist in nature—is extremely complex and dynamic. During such a period of great uncertainty and change, judging which policies best advance one's parochial self-interest, or even the greater economic good, is highly challenging for politicians, industrial specialists, and economic advisers, not to mention workers, managers, or anyone else whose welfare is affected by the process. This complexity problematizes a methodological approach that exogenizes preference formation when attributing policy outcomes to the resistance and pressure of stakeholders, especially stakeholders who are simplistically characterized as pursuing objective and self-evident interests.[41] Similarly, it weakens arguments based on the pursuit of material interests when the ability to recognize and pursue those interests is highly precarious.

Posing similar challenges, property rights theory based on power ignore the degree to which the positions of actors in the existing hierarchy of power turn on dynamic human and material resources as well as highly malleable, subjective perceptions of authority and legitimacy. Power is constantly under negotiation, especially during revolutionary moments. Since perceptions of power determine the kinds of demands interest groups make during privatization and the government's willingness to accommodate those demands, the forces shaping the perception and redistribution of power deserve close consideration.

In revolutionary and postrevolutionary environments, determining one's self-interest and the way to advance that interest for most, if not all, economic actors requires thoughtful analysis.[42] For this reason, we must not start with a theory that explains regime change by beginning with an assumed distribution of interests and power, especially if we want to understand variation across cases. Rather, we should take a step back and explore the ways economic preferences form and how the distribution of power is perceived during economic regime change. To do so, we must bring ideological variables back in to social science analysis and explore the nuances and subtleties of ideological forces in regime change.

Much of this book pursues a direct comparison of the Czech and Russian mass privatization experiences, supplemented by an extensive discussion of other country cases, especially Poland and Slovakia. Despite the obvious differences in size and nature of the economies of the two major cases, the Russian and Czech privatization experiences are well suited for comparison, owing to important political similarities and equivalent policy starting points. In both examples, a small coterie of liberal economists achieved key positions in the government and from there developed similar mechanisms to break with the past Communist system. While both countries underwent privatization relatively early, they did not design their programs independently from each other. Russian officials borrowed from the prior Czech experience in property reform. Aside from the brief period separating the initiation of mass privatization in each country, both Russia and the Czech Republic initiated their programs within a similar international context, with relatively equivalent property rights structures and degrees of state ownership. For example, in 1990 in both Russia and the Czech Republic, approximately 5 percent of the gross domestic product (GDP) constituted private-sector output. In Hungary, private-sector output as a percentage of GDP was nearly four times greater and in Poland nearly five times greater.[43]

The Czech and Russian programs, moreover, were among the earliest mass privatization programs and together shaped the course of public sector reform in the region. They demonstrated to other transition countries that mass privatization could quickly transfer an enormous amount of property without causing an economic shock or political instability in the short-term. Moreover, the *proposed* Russian and Czech programs initially resembled each other closely as well, especially when compared to those of other privatizing states, even among neighboring postsocialist privatizing states.[44] Both Russia and the Czech Republic quickly carried out a mass privatization program that distributed property to the population nearly for free, using vouchers. In contrast to Hungary, Poland, Romania, Bulgaria, Ukraine, and other countries, privatization in Russia and the Czech Republic occurred rapidly, shortly following a change in government, with speed being an overarching priority for privatization officials.

The Ideological Determinants of Post-Communist Privatization

The ideological dimension of privatization that has received attention by scholars relates to the role of the international advising community, as noted above. To what extent did external lenders and advisers push local actors on the ground to adopt a specific approach to property rights reform? Did "market fundamentalists," as Stiglitz calls them, impose a privatization paradigm on unwilling East European officials, or were East Europeans themselves largely responsible for the evolution and dissemination of an economically liberal approach to property rights reform? I contend in chapter 2 that foreign advisers and policy specialists contributed to the evolution of thinking on public sector reform and created conditions that strongly favored the adoption of a liberal economic paradigm in many country cases. However, rather than crudely imposing privatization on unwilling officials, they promoted leaders already predisposed to liberal economic reform and many of the ideas on how to privatize evolved from the exchange of ideas among actors in the region. Using the spread of the post-Communist privatization paradigm can serve as a useful proxy for the spread of economic ideas and help identify the paths by which ideology proliferates across borders.[45]

Chapters 3 and 4 examine property rights reform from the late Communist period through the first decade of the capitalist transformation in each country. Each chapter looks at the rise of a small cohort of previously unknown academic economists and elucidates how they gained access to policy-making arenas and succeeded in advancing a particular vision of the new post-Communist economic order. These two chapters not only affirm that most of the development of mass privatization occurred in country, they also provide the historical background for the subsequent analysis of the role of ideology.

Elaborating the Theoretical Framework

To understand how ideology determines economic regime change, it is necessary to explore separately the key ideological factors. The first way that an ideology can shape property rights development is when those individuals who subscribe to it gain positions of power and draw from their beliefs to design transformative policies. Chapter 5 argues that in both Russia and the Czech Republic the urgency to privatize was largely motivated by the liberal economic belief of leading policy makers that economic recovery and revitalization could only be achieved through the immediate creation of a private ownership regime.[46] Ideological beliefs determined the choices and set the priorities of key leaders during the early years of reform. Indeed, economic beliefs colored their expectations of the economic efficiency gains that would ultimately flow from a capitalist system of ownership—much as it did decades earlier when Marxist-inspired economic principles recommended public ownership (and "scientifically based," state-led allocation of resources) over private ownership (and "arbitrary" market allocation). Moreover, leaders' ideological beliefs made appealing the development of a speedy, broadly distributional mechanism for industrial privatization. Second, the ideological beliefs of societal actors directly influence how they perceive their interests and their bargaining position within the property rights system. Furthermore, the sum of the ideas held by members in society find expression in the political discourse and in formal institutional mechanisms, thereby creating an ideological context.

Chapter 6 begins with the Czech post–Velvet Revolutionary ideological context in which anti-Communism was pervasive. The ideological context weakened the power of certain industrial groups to lobby the government to revise the legislation on privatization. Specifically, anti-Communism in both institutionalized and spontaneous forms heightened the professional insecurity of the politicians and industrial managers and made them reluctant to pursue changes to the privatization legislation. Due to the Czech lustration law (an anti-Communist screening law)[47] and due to unorganized protest by midlevel managers and the worker collectives to past politically motivated managerial appointments, large numbers of top managers were forced out of their enterprises. While many of those who left found a comfortable home in new private start-ups or foreign ventures, those managers remaining in the traditional domestic industries felt their positions to be too precarious to challenge the new regime. Therefore, midlevel managers who survived the forced exodus from industry considered the protection of their jobs a higher priority than achieving greater benefits within privatization.[48] Similarly, the pervasiveness of anti-Communist sentiment impaired workers in advancing claims to property within privatization. When the legislature debated large-scale privatization, Czech labor groups failed to secure support to revise the privatization program. The impotence of labor is highlighted by the workers' inability in practice to acquire the ownership rights to even the limited amount of property allotted to them by law.

In contrast, post-Soviet Russia did not see equivalent formalized expressions of anti-Communism as in Czechoslovakia following the Velvet Revolution. Russian privatization officials were working within a different ideological context and thus confronted a legislative arena that contrasted sharply with that faced by the Czech leadership. Unlike in most other post-

Communist states in Eastern Europe, there were no new elections called in post-Soviet Russia; and those politicians elected under the previous system were deemed legitimate within the new polity. Similarly, those managers in top posts in Russia (many of whom obtained their positions for political reasons in the past) kept their jobs. Hence, when the Supreme Soviet began to debate privatization, a large proportion of the deputies were Communist.[49] They were ideologically sympathetic toward employee-share ownership and felt compelled (at the very least to appear) to support employee rights.[50] Hence, Russian managers could easily form alliances with members of the federal legislature and pressure the State Property Committee to increase their ownership stakes in privatization under the banner of employee rights. In essence, the *lack* of professional insecurity of parliamentarians elected under the Communist regime or managers appointed under the past system enabled managers to make bold claims for property.

In sum, widely held beliefs in society can determine the distribution of power and shape the perception of material self-interest. Czech anti-Communism discredited the demands of labor, and Czech managers, in contrast to their Russian counterparts, preferred minimizing the risk of losing their jobs to becoming proprietors of their firms. In Russia, anti-Communist sentiment was less prevalent and was not manifested in formal institutions to anywhere near the same extent. As a result, many groups who had benefited under the communist regime saw their legitimacy and thus their power project into the new regime, which in turn affected their ability to advance their claims to property during the reformulation of Russia's ownership regime.

The Ideological Foundations of Compliance

The ideological beliefs of leaders and societal actors not only influence policy design, they also affect the way leaders approach the task of eliciting support for and gaining compliance to newly designed privatization policies. To examine how leaders go about winning acceptance from groups in society, chapter 7 borrows from the work of Amitai Etzioni to identify three mechanisms that can be employed to gain compliance: coercive, remunerative, and ideological.[51] Coercive compliance mechanisms involve the credible threat or the use of force to gain compliance, such as the threat of physical violence or imprisonment. Remunerative compliance mechanisms rely upon economic incentives to garner support, such as special enterprise share-holding privileges, bribes, and monetary transfers.[52] Ideological reinforcing mechanisms use ideational and normative appeals to bring legitimacy to a program in order to achieve the necessary compliance.

The usefulness of Etzioni's framework in a theoretical discussion on the role of ideology is not simply to assert that post-Communist governments employed ideological legitimization. Although ideological justification is a common practice in politics, this function is intuitive as well as consistent with mainstream theories of property rights and policy making more broadly.[53] Rather, Etzioni's framework is relevant because it can illuminate how leaders' ideological beliefs inform which among the three reinforcing mechanisms they employ. This choice does not merely represent an intellectual exercise by political strategists. Instead, this choice can determine the intensity of political resistance as well as the content of a policy program—especially when remunerative mechanisms are chosen that require the incorporation of material benefits within a program.

While both the Russian and Czech leaders employed remunerative reinforcing mechanisms, such as the free distribution of property through vouchers, Czech leaders *also* relied extensively on anti-Communist and pro-European ideas to develop highly effective ideological reinforcing mechanisms. An effective technique was to insist upon the historical appropriateness of liberal property reform. The voucher program would "return" the country to its rightful historical place as a member of the Western or European community. This pro-European emphasis dovetailed with Klaus's pro-Czech orientation.

In Russia, rather than develop ideological legitimating mechanisms in the Czech tradition, Yeltsin's economic team relied heavily upon material incentives to individuals and groups to implement privatization. Although issues of fairness were certainly addressed, the Russian privatizers paid scant attention to promoting mass privatization on an ideological basis. The writing and public statements of Russian privatization officials reveal their scorn for ideological reinforcement and political slogans and their preference for tangible material incentives. They chose not to employ Russian cultural symbols or historical referents to "sell" the privatization program due to their commitment to their own liberal economic ideas and professional identities.

A lack of compatibility between the ideological basis of a reform program and the ideas of members of the elite and mass groups increases the cost of political reinforcement. And, depending on the will and skill of leaders, this incompatibility can determine the extent to which liberal economic reform is distorted. In this regard, the compatibility between a people and a program relates directly to the political resistance that leaders face when implementing reforms. The less the ideas underpinning a program fit effortlessly with the ideas of different economic and political groups, the greater the cost of developing reinforcing mechanisms. Chapter 8 shows that it was relatively easy for the Czech reformers to portray privatization as anti-Communist (such as with the property restitution laws), pro-European (with the institutionalization of private system of ownership), and thus essentially Czech by emphasizing that the Communist system was imposed and enforced from without and needed to be replaced by a system more appropriate to the Czech context— that is, a European system. Given prevailing cultural and territorial referents, it was rather straightforward for property reformers to make the creation of a new property system part and parcel of the formation of a new Euro-Czech identity.

However, given the difference in ideological contexts and existing territorial referents in Russia, a similar strategy would have been much more challenging for privatization officials. Since the end of the cold war, the rejection of the communist past in favor of a new Western liberal orientation was often interpreted in post-Soviet Russia as a rejection of oneself and demeaning to one's past. And while perceptions of history are subject to distortion and reinterpretation, portraying persuasively the adoption of capitalism (and private property) as a return to a former self would have been exceptionally difficult. Russian politicians could not easily reject Communism as alien or overlook the foreign connotation of a liberal property system. Furthermore, it would have required both the willingness and the skills of Russian liberals to promote such a campaign effectively.

More than a dozen years have passed since the countries of Eastern Europe and the former Soviet Union embarked upon a transition to democracy and capitalism. It is only now that scholars are able to look back at this period and begin to evaluate the paths taken for creating markets in each country. Many questions deserve careful reflection: In retrospect, did these governments have more time to undertake fundamental market reform? Why did the speed of transformation dominate other priorities? Why did domestic officials and foreign advisers place so much emphasis on privatization as the hallmark and the benchmark of capitalist transformation? Could the state have used alternative means to transfer property to private hands that would have avoided intense controversy and public disillusionment? What kind of ideological reinforcement could have brought greater legitimacy to the privatization process? Why was so little attention paid in Eastern Europe to developing the public sector as a credible actor in the restructuring of industry, in the enforcement of contracts, and in the financing and monitoring of capitalist economic activity? In answering these questions, this book argues that choice of strategies in post-Communist privatization cannot be understood either as economic policy optimization or as politics as usual, but instead should be understood as an ideologically driven program of regime change.

2. The International Dimension of Post-Communist Privatization

B eginning an analysis of ideology and privatization with a discussion of the international diffusion of ideas makes good sense if one accepts the premise that leaders in various East European and post-Soviet states did not develop their ideas and beliefs about privatization entirely independently. Indeed, the repeated use of a novel mass privatization approach across numerous countries with varying conditions suggests that privatization was not exclusively an individual response to domestic political and economic concerns, but was also an interrelated international phenomenon.[1] After all, private property reform topped the policy agenda for most governments in the region, with over a dozen pursuing a version of a Czech mass distributional program.[2] This raises the question of why a radical approach to property reform—with the free distribution of shares and an emphasis on speed—prevailed in so many countries at once. Moreover, why was large-scale privatization seemingly more urgent than other transition measures in post-Communist Europe?

Some critics suggest that the similar approach to privatization across numerous countries results largely from an aggressive effort by the Western policy community to promote a specific privatization paradigm. In fact, many scholars and pundits have expressed anger with the international community for allegedly imposing a narrow model of reform on weak states.[3] The role of external actors and institutions in the spread of a post-Communist privatization paradigm, however, is easily overstated. While the international community proactively and even aggressively promoted liberal ideas about property reform in several different capacities, East European policy makers themselves generated privatization models and disseminated the ideas supporting these models by interacting with, and emulating the practices of, their counterparts abroad.

Positive Incentives or Material Coercion?

What role did the international community play in the diffusion and promotion of liberal economic ideas about property rights reform in post-Communist countries? It is well known that institutions such as the International Monetary Fund (IMF), the World Bank, the European Bank for Reconstruction and Development (EBRD), as well as donor organizations and governmental institutions within the advanced industrialized states were active in post-Communist economic reform and privatization in particular. There are at least four ways in which they promoted the spread of privatization and the dissemination of neoliberal ideas about property reform: using lending conditionality, providing financial support for reform measures under way, altering the domestic political balance, and funding the ideological reorientation of economics education and research. Each will be considered in turn.

Lending Conditionality

The most coercive way that the Western policy community could promote privatization and other neoliberal policies involved linking access to financial credits to progress in market-oriented structural reforms. To what extent could and did lenders invoke conditionality? Since 1968 the IMF and the World Bank have regularly made a member country's access to loans contingent upon fulfilling a set of policy conditions.[4] That is, if a government wants to borrow from these institutions, it must agree to the terms they outline. In the current international lending regime, these terms may involve the adoption of policies that are economic, social, and even political in nature. The primary instrument to force countries to adhere to a set of policy conditions is through the phasing of loans. For instance, in a standby agreement, the lending institution makes financing available at specified intervals, with disbursement conditional on implementing certain policies and satisfying basic performance criteria. The IMF reached standby arrangements with Armenia, Azerbaijan, Belarus, Croatia, Estonia, Georgia, Kazakhstan, Latvia, Macedonia, Moldova, Poland, Romania, Russia, Slovakia, Ukraine, and Uzbekistan.[5] Over the past decade, the international financial institutions have typi-

cally included property rights reform as a basic condition for subsequent disbursements in their standby agreements or structural adjustment loans when
formulating the conditions associated with their loans to former Communist
countries. That is, it has been standard for the World Bank and the IMF to
officially require governments to privatize in order to receive future disbursements of loans. Sometimes these provisions are of a general nature, but frequently they specify privatization targets. For example, in April 1997 the IMF
approved a standby agreement with Romania for $430 million. The first in-
stallment was immediately granted, but four future installments were subject
to policy implementation and the observance of performance criteria. In the
loan negotiations, the Romanian government agreed to privatize three thousand enterprises plus two banks and to close ten large loss-making state-
owned enterprises.[6] In the negotiations over the IMF standby agreement with
Russia in 1999, the privatization targets were similarly specific. The government pledged to privatize shares in seven major enterprises by the end of
1999, including Gazprom, Lukoil (Moscow), and Svyazinvest, among others.[7]
In addition, the Russian government agreed to remove increasing percentages
of small and medium firms from protected "strategic" status and advance
their privatization.[8] In the European Community's 100 million ECU loan to
Lithuania in March 1993, the second tranche of the loan was dependent on
progress in privatization.[9] In the World Bank 1991 loan to Poland, 50 percent
of nine thousand state-owned enterprises were identified for privatization
over three years.[10]

Without a doubt, the use of credit to compel governments to privatize either in general or to withdraw state control and ownership of specific enterprises holds the potential to be highly coercive. Did the World Bank and the
IMF deny states credit in a way that constrained the policy autonomy of these
governments? In some instances it did, but less than might be assumed. Any
analysis of coercive potential of the international financial institutions absolutely must acknowledge that the degree to which the financial institutions
could push for privatization depended on the bargaining power of the countries involved. And the bargaining position of each country turned on its
geopolitical power and its ability to borrow from private lenders. For example, the Czechs were able to maintain policy autonomy from the IMF by paying back a loan in advance and by resisting future credits. Moreover, the government could maintain policy autonomy due to its low level of foreign debt,
its ability to accumulate foreign exchange revenues from an inflow of foreign

direct investment and tourism, and its access to credit from private capital markets. As a general rule, however, the further east a country was located, the more constrained it was in attracting foreign investment or loans, thereby exacerbating its dependence on the World Bank and the IMF.

In addition, a country's geopolitical power affected its bargaining position and policy autonomy. For instance, the geopolitical position of Russia meant that the international community was more committed to providing resources independent of its ability to meet performance criteria enumerated in structural adjustment programs and standby agreements. Randall Stone's analysis of Russia's negotiations with the IMF over monetary policy illustrates this point well and supports the contention that Russia maintained autonomy in the face of external lending pressure.[11] Indeed, whenever Russia appeared to be at risk of a domestic political crisis, the Group of Seven (G-7), and the United States and Germany in particular, would pressure the fund to ease its conditions for granting loans or for releasing a disbursement.[12]

That said, the international financial institutions did sometimes manage to use their financial might to compel weaker borrowing countries to pursue a liberalizing agenda in property rights reform, trade policy, and price deregulation. At times lenders delayed disbursements due to sluggish progress in privatization in specific areas, such as in the case of the 1997 World Bank $800 million loan to privatize the Russian coal industry. In 1999, the bank threatened to withhold the remaining $400 million worth of this loan due to inadequate progress in privatization. While the bank subsequently released half of the remaining disbursement to provide social supports for those hurt by coal restructuring, it refused to release the final $200 million due to the lack of privatization.[13] Similarly, disbursements from the $184 million IMF loan to Ukraine were suspended several times for not meeting economic reform targets.[14]

While it is difficult to identify specific examples in which the IMF and the bank delayed loan disbursements due to poor performance *in privatization and only privatization,* this should not suggest that international lenders were neutral regarding a country's fulfillment of privatization targets. As one key privatization official at the World Bank explained, when a country made progress in other areas, "it could get away with not privatizing rapidly. We [at the World Bank] would say 'that in the next loan you must privatize,'" but for the time being they were "not harassed." He explains further:

Poland, Hungary and Estonia eschewed mass privatization through vouchers but we did not give them a hard time because they made progress on other issues. Estonia adopted a currency board and there was a bias toward foreign owners. Hungary had strong bankruptcy laws and this helped to compensate for the lack of mass privatization ... sort of privatization through bankruptcy. Hungary privatized banks in 1995 and its infrastructure in 1995–1996 and this was the salvation of Hungary's economy. And Poland had liberal entry laws, a tough macroeconomic front. So other progress was being made.[15]

This frank response reveals both the bank's determination to promote privatization, as well as its flexibility in measuring a country's progress in terms of a broader commitment to advancing a liberal policy agenda.

One additional caveat should be mentioned in discussing the potential for coercion in IMF conditionality. Although standby arrangements were drafted to link loans to progress in privatization, this does not necessarily signify that privatization targets were being imposed on countries against their wishes. Standby arrangements could be negotiated between the IMF and the proponents of privatization already in government as a way to disempower the local opposition to rapid property rights reform. That is, government officials could use the targets established in structural adjustment loans and standby agreements *as excuses* to move forward with extensive property transfers. For example, although Russian privatization official Alfred Kokh claims in reference to the Russian loans-for-shares scheme that he felt a general pressure to reach privatization targets from the international financial institutions, it is clear Kokh had several domestic political reasons to push through the privatization of select properties to well-connected bankers. Among other motivations (not mentioned by Kokh), the loans-for-shares program served to enrich a small group of bankers who later supported President Yeltsin's 1996 reelection campaign.

Supporting Privatizing Programs Under Way

A related path by which the international financial institutions could promote privatization and other liberal economic programs was by providing the funding for governments to carry out existing privatization policies. Financing privatization was a central task of the international financial institutions. Indeed, post-Communist privatization was a key reason for the creation of the EBRD in 1991.[16] By making vast sums available, the IMF, the World Bank, the EBRD, and other institutions did not require governments

to privatize as a condition for general lending. Instead, they provided the resources to help fund existing privatization policies that the government was
pursuing of its own volition. Whether characterized as imposing pressure or
as simply facilitating with resources, the finances allocated to fund privatization's implementation in post-Communist countries are staggering.

One might think that privatization could be a relatively inexpensive type
of reform, in contrast to currency stabilization or infrastructure development. In fact, considering that the state was giving away the title to property,
sometimes for money and sometimes for free, the program could potentially
have even paid for itself. However, Western credits and grants to support privatization did not encompass tens of millions or even hundreds of millions of
dollars, but reaches into the billions of dollars, as shown below. The provision
of large amounts of credit certainly facilitated the realization of privatization
and necessarily contributed to the breadth and depth of the privatization
movement in the region.

Material support for privatization outpaced support in other areas of institutional reform. Consider the funding by the European Union (EU) for
privatization and private sector development. From 1990 to 2001, the EU
committed €1.44 billion to property rights reform, shared among a dozen
East European and Baltic countries through the PHARE program. The disproportionate emphasis on privatization funding is evident when one considers other commitments through the PHARE program, such as €160 million to financial sector reform, €263 million to civil society and
democratization programs, €175 million to humanitarian aid, and €95 million to public health programs. The only areas where the funding approached
or exceeded the funding for privatization were in infrastructure development
(€2.72 billion) and in education, training, and research (€1.21 billion). The
large allocation to the development of the infrastructure was intended to prepare the candidate countries for membership and integration in the European Union. Additionally, part of this figure includes the cost of preparing
certain sectors for privatization—such as the energy and telecommunications
sectors. The resources allocated to the area of education, training, and research are discussed further below.[17]

Although a more comprehensive (but by no means exhaustive) list is
posted on the World Bank's Web site, consider some of the following transfers
linked specifically to privatization. In Poland the EBRD provided a $50 mil-
lion loan to prepare municipal heating enterprises for privatization in 1991;[18]

the World Bank allocated $280 million (out of a larger $580 million loan) for enterprise restructuring and privatization in 1991;[19] and the World Bank approved a $750 million loan in 1993, with $450 million for financial restructuring and bank privatization and $300 million for reforming agriculture, including privatization in 1993.[20]

In Bulgaria the World Bank provided $30 million for privatization, enterprise restructuring, and safety nets for displaced workers;[21] the World Bank allocated $75 million to the reform of agriculture, including privatization, in 1999;[22] and the Japan Bank for International Cooperation and the World Bank together provided $50 million to promote financial reforms and privatization in April 2000.[23]

In Ukraine the World Bank provided a loan for $310 million for enterprise restructuring, privatization and postprivatization restructuring reforms in 1996. This was part of a larger loan of $835 million (for Ukraine and Russia).[24] The World Bank allocated $600 million for boosting privatization and restructuring of the banking sector in 1998.[25] And the European Union and the IMF have collaborated in providing resources for market reforms, in part including privatization: $260 million in 1996 and $184 million in 1999.[26]

In Russia the World Bank provided $600 million to support the first phase of privatization in August 1992 and $90 million for establishing the Russian Privatization Center and for policy consultants in December 1992.[27] USAID allocated $58 million to support the Russian voucher privatization program[28] and $45 million to support the institutionalization of the Russian Privatization Center. The European Bank for Reconstruction and Development also provided loans to the Russian Privatization Center for $43 million.[29] In addition, the center received grants from the British Know How Fund and the governments of Japan and Germany and World Bank. The World Bank committed $90 million in 1996[30] and $85 million in 1997[31] to support privatization and postprivatization programs in Russia.

Altering the Political Balance

A further way in which the international community contributed to the diffusion of a liberal economic paradigm—especially as it related to privatization—was by channeling resources to policy makers in the region who already demonstrated a commitment to private ownership and free markets. In part, this has already been raised in the caveat above. Namely, conditionality could be used as an excuse by the local leaders supporting privatization as a way to advance their goals within a domestic political context that was inhospitable to privatization. However, foreign lenders could also direct financial aid such that it tipped the political balance in favor of leaders with a particular ideological orientation. Once again, this would help explain—albeit only in part—why so many Western-oriented liberals became powerful in the region over a short period of time.

The provision of moral and material support to local actors is emphasized by multiple writers on privatization. In a controversial book on aid to Eastern Europe, Janine Wedel looks at the cases of Russia and Poland specifically in order to illustrate the transfer of resources to sympathetic well-placed individuals in order to promote the capitalist transformation. She quotes the Department of State's top aid official, Richard Morningstar, speaking to this strategy directly. He states, "If we hadn't been there to provide funding to Chubais, could we have won the battle to carry out privatization? Probably not. When you're talking about a few hundred million dollars, you're not going to change the country, but you can provide targeted assistance to help Chubais."[32] Even those supportive of the provision of Western funding stress this political tactic. For instance, Boycko, Shleifer, and Vishny make explicit in *Privatizing Russia* that American aid was used to shift the political balance in favor of the Chubais free-market team. Andrei Shleifer, an adviser who oversaw the disbursals of USAID contributions via the HIID (Harvard Institute for International Development) writes with his coauthors, "Aid can help reformers by paying for the design and implementation of their projects, which gives them greater capacity for action than their opponents have. . . . It helps the reformers in their political battles."[33]

Funding Educational Reforms

A further practice facilitating the spread of liberal economic ideas involved the funding of the ideological and theoretical reorientation of economics faculties at universities and research institutes in post-Communist countries by Western lenders and foundations. Research and education reform was the most indirect (but potentially the most long-lasting) way that the West contributed to the widespread embrace of liberal economic programs of reform. This occurred in several ways: Numerous foundations created fellowships for East European and former Soviet students to study economics in American and West European universities—specifically to educate them in Western economic theory and analytical techniques. One of the main goals of these programs was to identify and train students who intended to become economics teachers when they returned to their home countries. Although the retention of these students in academia proved difficult given competition from foreign companies investing in the region, the selection of future teachers (or policy makers) remained a primary selection criterion as a way of extending the reach of the program beyond the individual fellowship student.[34]

In order to provide an enduring means to transform the study and teaching of economics, Western foundations and financial institutions also allocated vast resources to reorient existing, Soviet-style economics departments to be better equipped to teach Western-style economics. Where resistance from or indifference among the existing economics faculty for retraining proved to be too great, donor organizations and multilateral institutions funded the establishment of new departments, programs, schools, and research centers in the region. Examples of such institutions are the New Economic School (NES) in Moscow, the European University at St. Petersburg and the Higher Economic School in St. Petersburg, the Warsaw School of Economics in Warsaw, the Center for Economics Research and Graduate Education (CERGE) in Prague, and the Central European University in Budapest.[35] The primary tasks of such programs are strengthening the "greater knowledge and understanding of market-based economic systems" and "building sustainable in-country institutions that will help reform education and policy-related research over the long term" as one such program, the Economics Education and Research Consortium (EERC) explains in its literature.[36]

The seed money for new educational institutions and programs was provided by a variety of sources: the United States Agency for International Development, the Pew Charitable Trusts, the George Soros's Open Society Institute and International Renaissance Foundation, the Carnegie Corporation of New York, and the Ford Foundation, among others. The resources involved in transforming the field of economics are considerable. The EERC's programs for economics education in Russia and Ukraine spent over $9 million from 1996 to 2001, with the most recent annual budget reaching approximately $3 million.[37] Most striking are the sums allocated by the World Bank for economics reeducation. For example, in the 1997 World Bank's $1.7 billion loan to Russia, $71 million was set aside "to help higher education institutions reorient their teaching of economics and social sciences toward market economy conditions" in Russia.[38]

Implications

Taking these four practices into consideration, what role should be attributed to the international community—especially the international financial institutions and Western aid organizations—in an analysis of the international diffusion of ideas? Were these organizations employing their financial resources to coercively promote privatization? Or were they facilitating the reform agendas of policy makers already in place on the ground? While it would be easy to exaggerate the power of these institutions to force local governments to privatize against their preferences for the reasons outlined above, it would be equally misleading to suggest that they did not play an active role in promoting privatization in the region. This occurred by funding privatization consultants, privatization conferences, privatization centers, privatization proponents, and privatization research. Very seldom, however, did the funding institutions freeze loan disbursements in response to inadequate performance in privatization specifically. This suggests that external lenders rarely used the most coercive instrument available to compel governments to privatize, and then in only exceptional circumstances.

Ultimately, the international community was extremely proactive in promoting the diffusion of neoliberal ideas and facilitating privatization across the entire region. Rather than imposing privatization on unwilling officials, it more commonly promoted leaders already predisposed to rapid and extensive privatization. In other words, Western aid organizations and lending institutions provided crucial financial and moral support to those East European political actors who embraced a neoliberal agenda and a Westward economic trajectory. Thus, by tipping the political balance in favor of neoliberal leaders, the provision of aid in part explains the sheer number of governments undertaking a novel privatization approach in the region over the span of a few years.

The Spread of Economic Liberalism

The international diffusion of liberal policy ideas should not always be characterized in terms of the West's provision of incentives and disincentives. Even without material incentives, privatization ideas were diffused due to policy emulation and policy transfer across borders. Policy emulation refers simply to the process by which one government or a few key leaders follow the example of another government after judging the latter's experience to be successful.[39] That is, if a government reasons that an observed policy approach could also respond appropriately and effectively to its own problems or could advance its own goals, then it emulates another's approach. As a result, a new policy paradigm spreads from one country to the next. Policy emulation, referred to alternatively in some studies as bandwagoning, policy transfer, or the demonstration effect, may consist of either a wholesale adoption of a policy agenda or only select aspects.[40]

In the case of large-scale privatization in Eastern Europe, the spread of mass privatization across the region was accelerated by the apparent success of the Czech experiment with vouchers—or at least the lack of any shocks following the initial implementation. As the first country to design and implement a voucher privatization scheme, the Czech example widely shaped the direction of property rights reform in the region when several governments followed with a version of the Czech voucher program, such as in Russia, Lithuania, Bulgaria, Belarus, and others. In various countries, privatization officials were explicit in acknowledging their emulation of the Czech approach and even outlined which elements of their voucher privatization program they borrowed directly from the Czech experience and which innovations they added de novo.[41]

The diffusion of the Czech model was facilitated by the fact that some Czech privatization officials became privatization advisers themselves. That is, they served as the hired hands of the IMF and World Bank to advise other countries in the ways of property reform. For instance, Václav Klaus's main coauthor of voucher privatization, Dušan Tříska, consulted in a half dozen countries on voucher privatization.

Indeed in several cases, governments adopted a Czech-style voucher approach before anyone understood or knew the outcome of the Czech experiment. In such instances, it was not the *proven* success that led to the emulation of the voucher approach. Rather, leaders could see that in the short run the voucher program neither generated a shock to the Czech economy nor produced destabilizing political forces. Thus, even if the economic consequences were still far from certain, adopting a similar strategy appeared less daunting after observing the Czech voucher experience.[42]

In addition to hiring East European policy makers as consultants, privatization officials could also learn from the experiences of their counterparts abroad by attending international workshops and conferences. Since many of these meetings were donor sponsored, Western organizations were importantly involved in who was invited and who would speak. Policy makers would meet each other by participating in regular meetings, such as the Central and Eastern Europe Privatization Network (CEEPN) annual meetings. One senior World Bank official explains that at the CEEPN, representatives of the countries more advanced in privatization would speak and representatives from countries like "Ukraine and Bulgaria would go to listen to the success stories or [those that] seemed so at the time."[43]

Not only high-level privatization officials attended international meetings funded by Western organizations and the financial institutions; lower-level bureaucrats working in regional privatization centers participated in separate workshops and attended practically oriented international meetings. For both groups, but especially for the latter group, traveling to the foreign-funded meetings was often considered a perk of their job. As public employees working for modest salaries, they could seldom afford foreign travel.[44] Only in this capacity might Western support for international conferences be seen as providing incentives for the adoption of a program of reform. The most significant international diffusion effect, however, was the exchange of policy options among the practitioners of different states.

Ideological Trends in the International Policy Community

In a similar vein, new ideas spread across different countries due to shifts in the theoretical trends or ideological orientations of transnational groups of policy experts. These experts were influential given their recognition as having competence in specialized, technical areas. That is, policy makers in different countries gained access to, and acted upon, new theoretical insights or new policy-relevant information available in international policy circles when formulating their own responses to policy dilemmas. As knowledge about a type of economic problem accumulated and circulated among recognized specialists, a pool of information became available to leaders who were in search of policy solutions. In both this and the previous practice of policy emulation, national leaders were responding to new information. However, in this case, leaders were drawing from a new body of knowledge around which a consensus has formed rather than strictly mimicking the approaches of other leaders.

This type of practice has been analyzed for other regions in the political science literature on "epistemic communities."[45] According to this literature, specialized theories, by virtue of their acceptance by a transnational group of widely recognized technical experts (that is, an epistemic community), shape policy making in complex issue areas. In particular, when a consensus among authoritative elites is reached, new policy ideas can spread either through direct advising by specialists or through their appointment to powerful bureaucratic or governmental positions.[46]

In the case of post-Communist privatization, the group of academics, lawyers, and financial consultants advising East European governments on privatization bears some resemblance to an epistemic community given its role in the international dissemination of neoliberal policy ideas. However, it was not an epistemic community in the strict sense for several reasons. As already mentioned, many advisers were members of the government apparatus of early privatizing states rather than members of an independent, scholarly, research community. Second, although the community advising on privatization was transnational in nature and had reached a high level consensus on the importance of extensive and immediate property transfers to the private sector, its membership was too large to be unified, coherent, or consistently endowed with genuine expertise. The community of advisers on property rights reform (and liberal economic reform more generally) was so enormous that it included both novices and experts with competing interests and perspectives. A common complaint among locals was that foreign funding agencies did not hire their consultants very carefully. While some Western consultants had advanced academic credentials or firsthand policy-making experience in their own country, others had only recently graduated from American universities and had little experience in the subject matter and limited knowledge of the region.

In characterizing the community of privatization advisers, however, it becomes clear that, even though there was no epistemic community per se, new information about privatization was accumulating and exchanged on an international level, Western incentives aside. These liberal economic ideas became available to governments considering their own need for property rights reform. Indeed, the status and the resources of specialists advising in mass privatization, the uncertainty following the moment of revolutionary change, and the inexperience of many new post-Communist leaders contributed to the widespread deference to ideological trends and an emulation of existing privatization approaches.

These policy ideas from the transnational community of specialists influenced East European leaders' specific choices in designing privatization programs. They offered a road map to follow in order to reach certain technical goals.[47] Moreover, these ideas offered a path for many East European leaders to advance their larger vision of breaking with the post-Communist past and building a Western-style capitalist economy.

While many Westerners from aid agencies, financial institutions, academia, and think tanks contributed importantly to the evolution of the post-Communist privatization paradigm, there is a tendency to overstate the role of the West in the generation and the promotion of privatization ideas. The specific techniques of mass privatization were worked out with substantial, if not primary, input from economists from the region, as will be outlined in the following two chapters. Thus, *both* the political leaders on the ground and the officials in advising and lending capacities offered new ideas to the policy debate and contributed to the momentum surrounding privatization.

Understanding the role of the West in privatization has direct implications for the study of the role of ideas in policy making. Specifically, the magnitude of Western financial and moral support may lead some to assume that self-proclaimed, neoliberal leaders in Eastern Europe adopted a mass privatization scheme, not due to their ideological commitment to economic liberalism, but in response to incentives and disincentives provided by the international community. Was this the case?

The answer to this question would vary not only by country but also by individual leader. Certainly some political leaders may have felt a sudden surge of ideological conviction when financial factors were taken into consideration. However, it would be cynical and facile to dismiss the individual convictions of leaders in general at this revolutionary moment. After all, liberals prevailed even in states where external financial pressure was low, such as in the Czech Republic, where the government remained exceptionally free from the financial influence of the World Bank and the IMF. In fact, when Václav Klaus and his associates first lobbied the World Bank in 1990 for a loan to support their novel privatization approach—an approach born out of the Czechoslovak context—they were turned down, but pressed on with mass privatization nevertheless.

Economic liberals prevailed in Russia as well, where financial dependence on the international community was greater, but where geopolitical power offered an alternative source of policy autonomy. To state it unequivocally, Russia's thousands of nuclear warheads meant that it could not be easily manipulated by the bank or the fund. In the case of powerful or strategically important countries, national governments stepped in to ensure that a country's geopolitical significance remained prominent in IMF lending deliberations. Thus, while it is true that lenders and donors provided considerable material incentives to privatize quickly and extensively, these incentives do not explain why leaders with strong bargaining positions energetically pursued large-scale privatization.

Rather than undermining a "power of ideas argument," the international dimension supports the role of ideas. After all, the international community helped economic liberals and their aggressive privatization strategy to prevail. Not only did it provide financial support, it also offered moral support for large-scale privatization, which in some cases lent credibility to privatization's proponents and bolstered their chances of success. In sum, emboldened liberals in the region exchanged information and techniques of rapid and extensive privatization—some of which they borrowed from foreign lenders and consultants and others they generated themselves. A detailed study of the key privatization actors and the evolution of their approaches reorients the study of ideology and privatization to the domestic sphere. The following chapters demonstrate that the ideological appeal, not the coercive pressure of international lenders, accounts for the spread of a similar version of large-scale privatization throughout the post-Communist region.

Part II. Probing the Czech and Russian Cases

3. The Origins and Design of Czech Large-Scale Privatization

The Empowerment of the Liberal Economists and Their Programs

Private ownership in the Czechoslovak economy was extremely limited under the Communist regime, with approximately 95 percent of the gross national product in 1988 still being produced in the state sector. In the late 1980s, Czech and Slovak scholars had only just begun to publicly discuss the possibility of introducing ownership reforms, in contrast to economists in Poland and Hungary. That is, only during the last year or two of Communism did Czechoslovak economists benefit from a new state tolerance for nontraditional economic analysis and from the circulation of ideas about private ownership in academic and research institutions. Moreover, the scholarly freedoms in 1988 and 1989 in Czechoslovakia paled in comparison to those allowed in the late Gorbachev period in the Soviet Union and were weaker than those enjoyed in the months preceding the Soviet-led invasion of Czechoslovakia in August 1968.

That said, the Czech form of *perestroika*, known as *přestavba,* led to the reinstatement into the Academy of Sciences several economists who had been expelled during the 1970s. A newly formed, semiofficial think tank called the Institute for Economic Forecasting offered research positions to a diverse group of economists. This institute had recently invited back into the Academy of Sciences an older generation of economists who had participated in designing economic reforms in 1968 but had been pushed out of the academy during the period of "normalization." Unique in that its founder and director, Valtr Komárek, enjoyed significant freedoms in hiring, the institute housed a group of younger economists with some Western training and technical skills. In the past, research institutes and official think tanks needed prior approval by the secret police for each individual hire. It was alleged, however, that Komárek was free to hire whomever he wanted because he had obtained an exemption from the government through his strong ties (and some say fraternal ties) with the Czechoslovak secret police.

Václav Klaus was among the group of younger scholars invited to join Komárek's institute. Klaus, an economist with some training in the West (a semester at Cornell University in the late 1960s), had been expelled in 1970 from the Academy of Sciences for allegedly harboring antisocialist views. As a member of Komárek's institute, Klaus organized seminars in the new institute and at the School of Economics in Prague, speaking at times on monetarism and, more generally, on economic reform. In 1988 the group of scholars at the Institute for Economic Forecasting, along with some economists from the Prague Economics Institute, began to debate and publish—albeit with some caution—their views on how economic structures should be altered.[1]

The flourishing of new ideas in the academic community had very little effect, if any, on policy making during the Communist period. For the most part, liberal ideas regarding property structures failed to influence the attitudes of decision makers in the Communist Party. Some reform was undertaken within the system of central planning, but the state's monolithic control over property was untouched by the ideas of the liberal-oriented economists. Any willingness to reform industrial structures seemed to stem not from a burgeoning of intellectual activity in research institutes, but from the changes in attitude toward economic reform in the Soviet Union. Indeed, in the second half of the 1980s, internal battles among the Czechoslovak party elite raged over whether to pursue the political and economic restructuring along the lines of Gorbachev's perestroika and glasnost. At first, hard-line Czech and Slovak Communists refused to follow the Soviet Union's example. Gradually, though, the more pragmatic Communist leaders led by Prime Minister Lubomír Štrougal prevailed. In late 1987, Gustav Husák, the party's general secretary of two decades, ultimately conceded the need for economic reform.

At the same time, Husák did not accept that economic reforms should drastically alter the ideological basis of the existing system, nor did he allow political liberalization to accompany economic reform. Owing in part to his age (seventy-four) and in part to his ideological disposition, Husák declared himself unable to lead the reform process. He stepped down as general secretary on December 17, 1987, and assumed the largely ceremonial post of

Czechoslovak president. In his place, the Central Committee elected Miloš Jakeš, who until then had served as chairman of the Central Committee's National Economic Commission. As general secretary, Jakeš's willingness to undertake economic reform was minimal. Prime Minister Štrougal himself resigned the year following Jakeš's appointment due to the former's insistence on more far-reaching reforms. Despite Jakeš's announcements to Western journalists that he would follow Gorbachev's example on economic reform and despite his public statements that excessive economic centralism should be abandoned in order to make the economy more efficient,[2] Jakeš primarily pursued the type of reforms implemented under Brezhnev's Soviet Union that tied material incentives to industrial productivity. He allowed minor increases in trade with the West and the division of large state industrial concerns into smaller state industrial units.[3] In the area of property reform, Jakeš never supported the need for private ownership, as advocated by certain academic economists, such as Lubomír Mlčoch or Pavel Kysilka.

During Jakeš's administration, the only reform directed toward the ownership of productive property was the legalization of joint ventures between state-owned enterprises and foreign private enterprises (Act 173/1988 Coll.).[4] When the government adopted legislation on joint ventures in 1988, the party had hoped to encourage foreign investment in the Czechoslovak economy and to gain access to new technologies. It should be stressed that this law in no way represented a reconsideration of the efficiency or appropriateness of existing property relations. And although this law formally altered the monolithic structure of state ownership, in practice it mattered little since few joint ventures were formed. Due largely to unfavorable terms for foreign investors, such as limitations on the use of profit and a high level of taxation, only fifty-five joint ventures were established under this law by the end of the decade.[5] The weakness of this reform measure is underscored by the contrast between the low level of foreign participation under this law and the jump in the number of joint ventures formed after the post-Communist government passed an amendment to the law five months later (Act 112/1990 Coll.). By the end of 1990, more than 1,200 joint ventures formed, with that number doubling in the following six months.[6] As amended, the law offered greater protection to foreign investors and abolished limitations on the foreign share. More important, it allowed Czechoslovak private persons to participate in forming joint ventures. Thus, while Act 173/1988 Coll. was passed within a monopoly system of state industrial ownership (and indeed occurred before the Velvet Revolution), neither individual private ownership of productive assets nor substantial changes within the structure of state ownership were legislated until after the Velvet Revolution.[7] Only after the revolution did the Institute for Economic Forecasting's economists, in cooperation with the powerful Czechoslovak political dissidents, advocate new ideas regarding property structures and promote liberal economic reform more generally.

Essentially none of the liberal economists who studied market economics in the late Communist regime openly supported the dissident movement. Klaus, like many intellectuals, researchers, and scholars was mildly acquainted with the dissidents over the two decades preceding the Velvet Revolution but had interacted little with them.[8] Their collaboration did not begin until mid-November 1989 when the dissidents invited a group of economists from the Institute for Economic Forecasting to join Civic Forum and provide it with an economic program.

Rita Klímová served as the link between the two groups, making the cooperation between the economists in Prague and the dissidents possible. Klímová, an active dissident and an economist by training, worked as the translator for Civic Forum and as the editor of the economic page of *Lidové noviny*, Civic Forum's then-underground newspaper. She knew the economics community and the reputation of Václav Klaus, Valtr Komárek, and others. In November 1989, she brought Klaus and several others from the Forecasting Institute to the attention of Václav Havel, the most prominent dissident at the time and the first post-Communist president.

Considering the future tensions between Klaus and Havel, it is ironic that Klaus's initial ascent to power occurred due to Havel's overtures to Klaus. After Havel became president of the interim government, he appointed several economists of the Forecasting Institute, such as Václav Klaus, Vladimír Dlouhý, Karel Dyba, and Valtr Komárek to lead the key economic ministries in the first post-Communist government in 1990.[9] It is often said that, even in these early days after Klaus joined Civic Forum, Havel sensed that Klaus would be difficult, due to the latter's aggressive personality and strong ambitions. Yet despite the dissident's reservations, he needed the economists at the time. The confident demeanor of the economists from the Forecasting Institute convinced the dissidents that they could provide the economic components of Civic Forum's general platform. One leading dissident, Jan Urban, describes the utility of the economists to Civic Forum as follows: "We, the dissidents, were all semi-conscious after 20 years in the underground. . . . In came Klaus and Dlouhý saying 'look, we know what the problems are, we've been studying them for 10 years, we've got the analyses ready.' We were all just so relieved."[10]

From the early moments of the revolution, Klaus was hard working, outspoken, and eager to shape the platform for Civic Forum. During the most heady days of the revolution, Klaus drew up an unsolicited document for the organization entitled "Programmatic Principles of the Civic Forum," and on November 29, 1989, he presented it to the overwhelmed and exhausted dissidents who had been organizing and leading the revolution.[11] In these three typewritten pages, he outlined a vision for the post-Communist system: He called for the rule of law guaranteed by an independent judiciary, free elections at all levels, a market economy, social justice, respect for the environment and for cultural life, equality of all forms of property, and a "normal country" in the center of Europe.[12] As described by the firsthand accounts of British journalist Timothy Garton Ash of the November meetings of Civic Forum, there was little agreement among the diverse group of participants in Civic Forum over even the most basic structures of the new polity. However, the economists from the Forecasting Institute were effective advocates within this diverse and contentious coalition group, and through their determination they shaped the coalition's platform and hence the course of Civic Forum.

Prior to an alliance between the advocates of new economic reform ideas and the former-dissident political elite, new ideas circulated among economists in several research institutes and academic centers, but the intellectual activity of Czech and Slovak economists had little effect on the course of reform. The Communist government undertook only the most modest steps to improve economic performance.

This reluctance to pursue systemic change should not be surprising. In contrast to the Soviet economy, the Czechoslovak economy showed little sign of a pending crisis. Despite low to zero growth, unemployment was nonexistent, inflation was stable at around 2 percent per year, and foreign debt was relatively low at approximately $8 billion. Exports were high, and, relative to most of its Communist allies, the stores were well stocked.[13] Since the decline in output had been gradual and goods were still readily available to the population, the Czechoslovak Party elite did not feel their backs up against a wall—as could be said for Soviet elites during the same period. Not until the

Velvet Revolution changed the previously stagnant political environment to one that was open to new ideas did a movement for systemic reform gain any real force.

The November revolution brought about a turnover in personnel at the very apex of power. The post-Communist dissident leadership wanted new thinkers for both substantive and symbolic reasons. On a substantive level, when the elites changed so did the point of reference. While the former Communist elite looked to the economies of other Eastern bloc countries and concluded that the need for reform was hardly urgent, the new political and economic elite looked to the Western world and insisted that the polity and the economy needed reform. For example, economists pointed to Czechoslovakia's decline in world rankings of gross national products (GNP), noting that before the Second World War, its level of development approached that of most West European countries, with a GNP only slightly lower than that of Austria.[14] The new comparisons pitting the Czechoslovak economy against the economies of the West promoted a perception of economic failure in the public discourse.[15]

The entry of new actors and new reform approaches, however, did not result from an acute sense of economic crisis, as is commonly emphasized in the literature on economic ideas.[16] While the dissident leadership certainly hoped to improve the material well-being of Czechs and Slovaks, they simply were not confronting an economic crisis. This would be overstating the sense of urgency of economic reform in Czechoslovakia in early 1990. As noted above, the Czechoslovak economy had been performing better than others in the post-Communist region and the stores were stocked with consumer goods at the time of the November revolution. Rather, Klaus and other new entrants gained access to policy-making circles because the revolution's leaders were looking for a plan and a set of advocates that would underscore the government's break with the past. This break was of great symbolic value to the dissidents.

Indeed, the dissidents found value in collaborating with a group of economists who had not been part of the past party elite or political *nomenklatura*. None of these economists had worked in government posts, and all (except Komárek) had studied, if only briefly, in the West. Klaus was particularly appealing because, unlike the other economists, he had never been a member of the Communist Party. Klaus's nonparty status was important because when the dissidents and the Communists together appointed the in-

terim government following the November revolution, they explicitly identified and counted the number of ministers who were Communists and non-
Communists.[17]

Reviewing this background on Klaus and his liberal cohort at the Institute
for Economic Forecasting helps to elucidate how Czechoslovakia's future privatizers became national policy figures during the initial period of transition.
In short, they were talented, articulate, ready to provide the dissidents with an
economic program, and lacked any association with the past Communist
leadership. Although the inclusion of Klaus in Civic Forum at a crucial moment afforded him direct access to decision makers in the post-Communist
political system, it still does not explain why his radical liberal ideas prevailed
over others and why he became the most prominent politician in the Czech
Republic. After all, even if Klaus was given the important post of finance minister in the interim government, he was still junior to his more moderate, former boss at the institute, Valtr Komárek, who was appointed first deputy
prime minister. To account for the dominance of Klaus's ideas, we must consider more deeply Klaus's ascent to power.

During the interim government, Klaus worked to distinguish himself and
his program from competing economists and their alternative proposals for
economic reform. In early 1990, Klaus expended a great deal of energy to shift
the reform debate to the right and to position himself as the leading supporter of right-wing liberal reform. Although frequently forgotten, economists disagreed strongly with each other about the type of property rights
system that should be established in the post-Communist era. Public docu-
ments reveal the support for various forms of ownership systems as late as the
summer of 1990—that is, after the first free elections.[18] During the days of the
revolution and the drafting of the "Programmatic Principles," Klaus's position encountered opposition from several members of the Civic Forum coalition who were not willing to privilege private property. One observer notes
how Klaus had to compromise his original version in order to placate coalition members who, as self-conceived social democrats and reform Communists, still supported state and cooperative forms of ownership.[19] As a result of
these compromises, the final "Programmatic Principles" document spoke of
"real competition" coming about on the "the basis of the parallel existence,
with equal rights, of different types of ownership and the progressive opening
of our economy to the world."[20]

While Klaus worked to shift the debate from the equality of different types of ownership to the development of the new private property system, the first proposal for creating a private property system did not come from him. In early February 1990, several economists held a crucial meeting on economic reform in the Koloděje castle outside of Prague. The ministers and deputy ministers of the interim government, along with other domestic and émigré economists, met to discuss price liberalization, currency convertibility, and privatization. At this meeting, Jan Švejnar, a Czech émigré economist, then teaching at the University of Pittsburgh, presented a recently published paper proposing the rapid privatization of productive property.[21] While some prominent Czech economists, such as Lubomír Mlčoch, had focused on privatization previously, Švejnar's paper became credited with introducing a version of mass privatization into the Czech economic reform debate. It proposed a different formula for mass privatization than the version ultimately adopted, but Švejnar's paper provided the basis for ensuing discussions over property rights reforms.[22]

During the spring of 1990, the main debate focused on how to create the institutions of a postsocialist economy. The issue dividing the early debate over economic reform was the speed with which the process should proceed. In the spring of 1990 there were two dominant concepts for systemic transformation that grew out of the debate. The two concepts were often referred to as the Klaus concept and the Komárek concept.[23] The Klaus concept called for rapid privatization, the abolishment of central planning, and full price liberalization.[24] The Komárek concept advocated gradual price liberalization and the restructuring of particular sectors of enterprises followed by a gradual program of privatization.[25]

The debate between Komárek and Klaus was extremely important because, first, it set the stage for the long debate to follow between two groups of economists, the gradualist economists and the radical liberal economists, over the future of economic reform. Second, it represented the passing of power from the old to the new. As noted above, Komárek had been senior to Klaus in the Forecasting Institute and the Czech government. He had recruited Klaus and resuscitated the careers of many politically fallen economists from 1968. Klaus and many others owed their recent careers to him. While Komárek was open-minded and progressive, he lacked the analytical and technical skills to adapt to the new environment. In contrast to Klaus, he was unable to propose a cohesive reform program and was soon seen by many as incompetent.

The debate between Komárek and Klaus fascinated the public; the press followed it closely and dramatized it.[26] According to Czech sociologist Zdenka Mansfeldová, what became important were not only the technical proposals of these protagonists but also who these men were and the people they represented.[27] The economists surrounding Komárek, and the leaders supporting his ideas, tended to be more conservative. Furthermore, many of his supporters had some previous affiliation or connection with the Communist Party, either as recent members or as 1968 members of an elite coterie of reform economists. In Klaus's circle, there tended to be younger economists with some Western economics training whose experience primarily came from the progressive research institutes and the banking sector. When Klaus's program prevailed over Komárek's, the press portrayed it as a victory of the new over the old or capitalism over reform-Communism.[28]

Komárek's place in the government did not survive this debate. After being upstaged by Klaus, Komárek's professional reputation declined. Furthermore, he was criticized sharply for being more interested in talking to foreign reporters and traveling abroad than in working on a coherent proposal.[29] Despite his top post as deputy prime minister of the federal government, Civic Forum did not appoint him to any position after the June elections, whereas Klaus maintained his post as the minister of finance.

The Evolution of the Reform Debates

The issue of the speed of privatization continued to dominate the debate even once Komárek left the spotlight. In June, the Federal Assembly (the parliament) tentatively approved the government's proposal for rapid economic reform, conditional on the government's ability to elaborate a step-by-step plan to achieve systemic change by the fall session. During the summer, the discussion on economic reform intensified between the radicals and the gradualists. Klaus, as a radical, developed his program of rapid liberal economic reform, including a program of mass privatization. With the support of a small group of economists,[30] Klaus argued that state property must quickly be transferred to private owners in order to create an effective system of incentives to restructure enterprises. It was neither necessary nor possible to restructure enterprises before finding private owners, because only private owners would use resources in the most efficient manner. Characteristic of Klaus's liberal beliefs on the role of the state in the economy, he summarizes his position: "We have no doubts that it is the new [private] owner, not the

government, who will find ideas, time and resources for the necessary restructuring. . . . The government of a transforming country is the worst
imaginable agent to undertake restructuring tasks."[31]

The way in which Klaus and his team envisioned the process of privatization rested upon the urgent and speedy distribution of enterprises shares to
the population at large—without a formal valuation or restructuring of individual enterprises. The government proposal developed that spring and summer of 1990 became known as the Scenario for Economic Reform (hence-
forth referred to as the Scenario). In this document, mass privatization—or
voucher privatization—was first proposed in a general form to the Federal
Assembly.

The radicals' program of mass privatization faced opposition from all
other economic institutes as well as from many political elites.[32] For example,
in October 1990 five major economics research institutes were surveyed: the
Institute for Economic Forecasting in the Academy of Sciences in Prague and
in Bratislava, the Economics Institute of the Academy of Sciences, the Prague
School of Economics, and the Czechoslovak Economic Forum. All five institutes favored large-scale privatization using standard methods—in other
words, nonvoucher methods. Only one institute, the Economics Institute of
the Academy of Sciences, gave partial support for voucher privatization.

The opponents to voucher privatization were diverse. But for simplicity's
sake, the press often grouped them into one category, referring to them as
graduálové, or the gradualists. Despite their diversity, the gradualists as a
group became characterized as older economists since many opponents had
previously held important positions in the government or the Academy of
Sciences in 1968 (such as František Vlasák, Otakar Turek, and Zdislav Šulc).
Virtually all had been expelled from the academy after the Soviet invasion of
Czechoslovakia. In addition to the 1968 reformers, the gradualist camp included younger economics professors and researchers in the Prague School of
Economics and in the Academy of Sciences. In the initial debate between
Komárek and Klaus, the gradualists tended to support the ideas of Komárek
even if many of them would not care to be associated with Komárek, due to
his reputed incompetence as an economist.[33]

While the radicals were formulating the Scenario, the gradualists were developing an alternative program in which industries would be denationalized
and corporatized—that is, broken into subunits or shares. Subsequently, the
shares would be placed in a fund controlled by the state. This fund, to be

called the National Property Fund, would restructure the firms as their owner. Only once an enterprise had been restructured would new private owners be found. Through the initiative of Miloš Zeman, then chair of the budget committee, the Federal Assembly commissioned the most prestigious economic institutes to analyze and to propose alternatives to the Scenario. Representatives from five institutes testified before the Federal Assembly but nothing came of their alternatives. Greater attention, instead, was paid to a proposal brought forward in the Czech parliament by František Vlasák. Vlasák's proposal was called the Czech Plan since it had been formally proposed to the Czech parliament (rather than the Federal Assembly). The Czech Plan's program of privatization centered on the creation of a National Property Fund that would function like the German Treuhand. The state-led fund would separate enterprises into groups according to their potential profitability and viability. Weaker enterprises would either be restructured or liquidated and sold in parts. The fund would then hold auctions or contact potential direct investors to transfer the shares of the profitable and restructured enterprises.

Given the extent of resistance to radical mass privatization among specialists, one would expect the Czech Plan to have prevailed. The Czech Plan enjoyed the support of the gradualists and many Czech parliamentarians, as well as foreign advisers, members of the dissident community,[34] and industrialists from Svaz průmyslu (the Union of Industry), a powerful organization of industrial elites and enterprise managers.[35] The gradualist position, as represented by the Czech Plan, was more conservative and would pose less of a shock to the status quo than the radical program. Further, there was a precedent for the standard privatization techniques that the gradualists recommended involving the sale of property through a central state agency. Yet despite its more conservative nature and the widespread support for gradual privatization, the Scenario proposing the voucher method prevailed. The Scenario was formally presented to the Federal Assembly for consideration on September 17, 1990, and, after a brief debate, was adopted and put into force on January 1, 1991.

Although certain ideas and some of the language of the Czech Plan were incorporated into the federal program of rapid privatization, the substance of the latter program clearly triumphed. One poignant example is the case of the National Property Fund. The gradualists first proposed the establishment of a National Property Fund (FNM) to restructure property and to locate new owners. Although the gradualist plan was rejected, an institution called the

FNM ultimately was established under the radicals' plan as a concession. However, this institution assumed only the name rather than the function as specified by the Czech Plan. The radicals legislated that the FNM would only act as a temporary holder of enterprise shares after enterprises had been corporatized (turned into joint stock companies) but before they had been privatized. According to the mass privatization legislation, and according to actual practice, the FNM would remain a passive owner and would not restructure enterprises.[36]

It should be noted for reasons of clarity that the Czech Plan never directly competed with Klaus's proposals in that there was never a formal choice made between Vlasák's gradualist plan and Klaus's radical reform program by any one legislative body.[37] One politician explains the adoption of the Scenario rather than the Czech plan in institutionalist terms.[38] The Scenario was presented to the Federal Assembly, a body that had more authority at that time than the national (republic-level) parliaments and governments. In general, support from the federal parliament typically carried more weight than support from the national parliaments. Yet, in the area of privatization this generalization is less applicable since privatization was specifically not a federal issue. In order not to aggravate Czech-Slovak relations, property decisions were decentralized according to the two republics. Thus, instead of creating a Federal Ministry of Privatization, the first government established two separate institutions: a Czech Ministry and a Slovak Ministry for Privatization.[39] Hence, privatization was no less the domain of the national governments than the federal government.

Given the support of the gradualist program by a greater portion of the economics community, by the Czech parliament and by leading dissidents, and given the unprecedented, potentially risky nature of mass property distribution through vouchers, the triumph of the radical program is puzzling. In large part, Klaus's ideas prevailed due to the skills and deep commitment of their carrier. Klaus's keen political instincts and his understanding of the dominant concerns and beliefs in Czech society enabled him to promote his specific ideas on liberal economic reform. First, he recognized that the country's power was concentrated in the umbrella organization Civic Forum. Thus, in order to advance his program, he would have to increase his prominence in the organization. This was not a straightforward task since former dissidents led Civic Forum. Because he could make no pretensions of having been a dissident during the Communist period, Klaus had to look elsewhere to amass power within the organization. Much to Klaus's good fortune, President Havel decided in the spring of 1990 that it was no longer appropriate for Civic Forum to be an amorphous organization without a transparent structure of leadership, and he proposed that all of the Civic Forum cells meet to elect one chairperson.[40] At that time, Civic Forum was run by four dissidents from Prague: Olga Havlová, Martin Palouš, Petr Kučera, and Vojtech Sedláček. Klaus seized the opportunity. After the parliamentary elections in June 1990, Klaus traveled to more than three hundred towns outside of Prague in order to galvanize personal political support.[41]

As an outsider in the Prague dissident community, Klaus had to locate sources of support outside the capital. As Jan Sokol, a former leader among Civic Forum's parliamentary deputies, describes it, Klaus had ambition and acute foresight. During the summer of 1990, Klaus undertook a formal campaign in which he visited virtually all of the local cells of Civic Forum throughout the Czech Republic to gain their confidence. In fact, at the time, Klaus was sharply criticized by his superior, Deputy Prime Minister Václav Valeš, for traveling too much that summer and leaving his work to his deputies at the Ministry of Finance. In speaking to local cells, Sokol explains that Klaus understood which ideas would resonate with the Czech people. That is, Klaus had recognized and exploited a divide that was beginning to take shape in Civic Forum:

> The split then was . . . generational, and more importantly, countryside people versus Prague people. The known dissidents were generally older, with many reform communists from 1968. Then there were a lot of ambitious countryside people who felt like second class citizens in Civic Forum. This created tension . . . and presented itself as the Left and the Right. The Left was the Prague people, the former [reform] communists, who were cautious in their ways and a bit condescending to the country folk. . . . All of the country folk saw [Klaus] as the right man. The countryside people really liked him, and the dissidents less so. Maybe like is not the right word, rather they had confidence in him. People believed he would run the country well, and clean out the old communists.[42]

Klaus played on the countryside resentment of the Prague dissidents and on pervasive anti-Communist sentiment, relating them to his economic program.[43] He claimed that the resistance of the Prague dissidents to the Scenario was without technical foundation. He emphasized the link between the ideas of those economists who criticized his radical approach and their efforts in the distant past to reform—rather than replace—the Communist economic system in 1968. In contrast, Klaus presented himself as a realist, a pragmatist, and ideologically neutral, all the while preaching liberal economic reform. Klaus emphasized that he had never been a Communist, nor a dissident, just a practical-minded technician. Interestingly, Klaus's symbolic identity appealed to mass groups and midlevel political officials for many of the same reasons that he initially appealed to the dissidents; he appeared unconnected and even untouched by the past regime.

Judging from the results of the election, Klaus had identified an effective way to pique the prevailing concerns of post–Velvet Revolutionary society. On October 13, 1990, all of the local cells from around the Czech Republic gathered at the Civic Forum Congress to elect a single chairman. Most observers expected the leading dissident and current leader, Martin Palouš, to win since he was the candidate favored by Havel. However, Palouš lost to Klaus by a landslide. Much to everyone's surprise, 115 out of 170 delegates voted for Klaus, and only 52 voted for Palouš.[44]

This was the first—but certainly not the last—time that Klaus won an unexpected victory by exploiting the ideological and political context. Without a doubt, Klaus's remarkable political talents catapulted him to the top of the political arena and enabled him to pursue a particular reform trajectory. Klaus's ascendancy demonstrates how individuals, or human agency, matter immensely for the emergence of new ideas. Without his commitment and skill, it is unlikely he could have overcome the odds stacked against the prevailing of the radical approach. Reading the popular mood, Klaus claimed that his victory represented nationwide mandate for his bold reform proposals and the society's move to the right of the political spectrum.[45] In the media's coverage of his election at Civic Forum Congress, several major Czech newspapers described the election of Klaus as signifying the Czech leadership's move to the right and the pending realization of Klaus's liberal market reforms.[46] In a nationwide poll taken later that month, as many as 70 percent of the people surveyed expected Klaus's election as chairman to give him sufficient support for his radical economic reform.[47]

At his first Civic Forum press conference after becoming chairman, Klaus announced that, as a result of recent developments, Civic Forum must "narrow its spectrum" and that "it is not enough for Civic Forum to play the role of an umbrella organization covering an endless quantity of different views." Within two weeks, Klaus announced that the Civic Forum Council had decided to expel the Left Alternative (a group led by the well-known dissident Petr Uhl) and Obroda (the movement of reform Communists were also co-founders of Civic Forum).[48]

Despite the landslide, Klaus's election was controversial. Many members of Civic Forum felt that a dissident who had actively resisted the past regime should lead their movement.[49] Others felt that Klaus would be amassing too much power if he served as both finance minister and the chairman of Civic Forum. Yet despite rumors of Klaus's pending dismissal by Havel as finance minister, Klaus remained in both positions until the forum split into formal parties.

As chairman of Civic Forum, Klaus could use the dissidents' own organization to bolster him. His landslide victory made him largely immune to criticism by domestic and foreign economists. Within the following six months, the Federal Assembly passed a half dozen laws calling for rapid privatization, ensuring the speedy transformation of property rights systems. From his early days of political campaigning, Klaus had positioned himself clearly on the right and in support of radical liberal economic programs. Additionally, his political tactics, his use of language and symbolism, and his choice of public persona were ingenious. He expertly recognized and exploited prevailing concerns in society, such as the Prague-countryside split and anti-Communist sentiment. He painted himself and his program in a way that appealed to these concerns in order to realize his ideological vision and to push ahead with his liberalizing economic agenda.

The Evolution of the Design of Czech Large-Scale Privatization

Despite the political turbulence and heightened tension of the first year following the June 1990 elections, post-Communist Czechoslovakia saw the rapid adoption of legislation that fundamentally altered the country's political and economic structures. With the Scenario passed and Klaus at the helm of Civic Forum, the government quickly drafted, proposed, and pushed radical reforms through the Federal Assembly. During late 1990 and 1991, Klaus and his cohort of economists constructed the general framework for transforming property relations.

Although the Federal Assembly had already passed the Scenario, the bill had called for the use of a voucher mechanism alongside other techniques, without specifying how vouchers would be used or which property would be included. Not only were the details of privatization undecided as of yet, but the most crucial issues remained to be solved, such as how much of the economy would be privatized; to what extent the voucher method would be used versus other techniques; who would become the new private owners; who would decide how industries or specific firms would be privatized; and so forth. All of these choices and decisions were derived from Czech considerations and deliberations, and with very little exception were they ever shaped by foreign advisers pushing a particular model of reform.

The privatization of large-scale industry was much more controversial and complex than other areas of property rights reform. A detailed blueprint was needed. The complexity of the problem of large-scale privatization stemmed from the absence of a clear, applicable precedent. Past experiences with privatization, for instance in Western Europe, encompassed only a limited number of enterprises and occurred within a preexisting capitalist economy with well-developed market institutions. Privatization in post-Communist countries had to be designed in conjunction with other key institutional reforms and carried out on a much larger scale.

Work on developing the program of large-scale privatization began in the federal Ministry of Finance in the spring of 1990. Klaus worked closely with his deputy, Dušan Tříska, and his adviser, Tomáš Ježek, in developing the ideas behind voucher privatization. In November 1990 (after the Federal Assembly had already approved privatization acts no. 403/1990 Coll. and no. 427/1990 Coll., the basic legislation for restitution and small-scale privatization respectively),[50] Klaus and Tříska proposed the bill on large-scale privatization to the Federal Assembly.[51] Once passed in February 1991, Klaus and Tříska's proposal, the Act on the Conditions of Transfer of State Property to Other Persons (no. 92/1991 Coll.), became known as the large-scale privatization law.

The large-scale privatization law's ease of passage was largely aided by Klaus's political mandate but also by its high degree of generality. In order to limit resistance, this law outlined only the basic structure of large-scale privatization, enumerating several potential methods according to which large enterprises could be privatized. According to this law, the privatization of each firm would depend upon the submission and approval of a "privatization project." The project would include basic information about the firm, such as the name, the book value, how the state had previously acquired the enterprise, and information regarding any pending restitution claims. Furthermore, the project would suggest a method of privatization, noting, for example, the percentage of enterprise shares to be privatized through vouchers or the conditions and price for the sale of enterprise shares. All firms would be corporatized, and subsequently up to 97 percent of the shares could be included in voucher privatization. Otherwise firms could be partially or almost entirely sold through public auctions, public tenders, or direct sales with special approval. Large-scale privatization would include the relevant ministries in the process by requiring the founding ministry (for instance, the Ministries of Agriculture or Industry and Trade) to evaluate and recommend one project to the Ministry of Finance or the Ministry of Privatization for approval, depending on the type of enterprise. In addition, this act outlined the process by which adult citizens could participate in the privatization process, explaining how they obtained investment vouchers and exchanged vouchers for shares in enterprises.[52] Furthermore, the law called for the establishment of the National Property Fund to act as the owner of enterprise shares following the corporatization of enterprises, but preceding the privatization of the shares. Given the breadth of the bill, it neither required nor favored the use of vouchers over other methods and thereby displaced much of the conflict and tensions surrounding large-scale privatization to future nonlegislative arenas.

The economists involved in formulating the large-scale privatization law —namely, Klaus, Tříska and Ježek (the Czech "privatizers")—all supported the extensive use of vouchers. The privatizers hoped to transfer to private hands as much of the economy as possible and agreed among themselves that a voucher mechanism could serve this purpose with the greatest speed and certainty.

Once speed was identified as the underlying priority in the design of the program, the reformers set out to determine which among the seemingly fast approaches would be politically acceptable and sufficiently effective in building the kind of economic and social structures that the privatization officials envisioned for a post-Communist society. Programs relying primarily upon the immediate sale of property were quickly rejected for several reasons. First of all, given the priority of speed, the government would need to sell enterprises without a lengthy valuation process. As a consequence, enterprises would need to be sold without providing the public with even the most basic information. This approach would favor the previous class of *nomenklatura* managers—as the only group with access to information on the true value of firms. Second, very few Czechs had access to financial resources, and those who had accumulated sufficient financial assets were often assumed by the mass public to have acquired them by suspect means.[53] If firms were instead sold to foreigners through auctions and tenders, this would be a protracted process. More important, the extent to which the population would tolerate a mass transfer to foreign investors was uncertain. There was also some concern that foreign participation would be dominated by short-term speculation rather than by long-term investment commitments. In sum, the widespread, free transfer of property qualified as a speedy approach and avoided the problem of selling the "family silver" to foreigners, the mafia, or former Communist elites.

In the early discussions over mass transfers, there were several groups advocating the free or nearly free transfer of shares to employees within the program of mass privatization. During small-scale privatization, the employees in shops undergoing privatization demanded special privileges in purchasing the small businesses in which they worked, and they held a series of minor strikes in order to press the government for priority sales and interest-free credits for the purchase of "their" shops.[54] Despite these demands, the privatizers formally rejected their suggestion on the basis of fairness. Officials argued that the new economic system must not perpetuate inequalities and privileges of the past Communist system. Everyone should begin with an equal chance.

The government's resistance to granting special privileges during small-scale privatization set the precedent for large-scale privatization. During the early large-scale privatization discussions, the media and the parliament gave some attention to proposals including privileges for employees. Employee share ownership plans (ESOP) were supported by several famous Czech economists, such as Ota Šik, the most prominent economist from the 1968 reform period, and political parties, such as the Social Democratic Party and the Czechoslovak Peoples Party.[55] After conflicts within small-scale privatization regarding the privileged access to property, the privatizers could more easily reject any suggestion of employee benefits in large-scale privatization.

Despite the privatizers' consensus that vouchers should dominate the process, they disagreed over the extent to which a voucher method could be employed. They disputed among themselves over whether entire industries should be privatized solely through vouchers or whether other mechanisms should be employed as well. In Deputy Finance Minister Tříska's initial proposal, virtually all of Czechoslovak industry would be privatized through vouchers: 97 percent of the shares would be included in voucher privatization, with only 3 percent of shares remaining to compensate those applicants to the restitution program who could not be paid in kind for confiscated property. Tříska advocated the transfer of shares through vouchers as quickly and extensively as possible to individual private citizens. The "97+3 proposal," as Tříska's proposal was called, was strongly supported by Klaus, who also wanted to include as many enterprises and the greatest percentage of shares as possible in voucher privatization.[56]

However, Ježek thought that Tříska exaggerated the usefulness of privatizing solely through vouchers. Ježek instead argued for a mixed program in which vouchers would transfer only some of an enterprise's shares to the population. First, he believed that large-scale privatization should help accomplish other goals besides the transfer of property. For instance, in addition to creating a restitution fund, he wanted to buttress the pension and social security system by reserving shares for these institutions. Moreover, he wanted to use shares from voucher privatization to support a national fund to support nonprofit foundations.[57] Finally, Ježek also felt that certain industries would benefit greatly from outside strategic investors. Ježek vehemently resisted the 97+3 proposal and called Tříska a voucher-fundamentalist and his proposal a new kind of socialism.[58]

After a heated debate, Tříska and Klaus submitted to Ježek's demands and accepted Ježek's notion of a mixed program. Tříska claims in retrospect that Ježek had not convinced him that the 97+3 proposal was less than ideal, but he accepted the mixed design within the legislation as a concession to Ježek and the Czech government. Although the notion of 97+3 was not strictly included or fixed by the legislation, it survived in the form of direct pressure from the federal Ministry of Finance on enterprises and on other ministries to devote enterprises entirely to the voucher process. While Ježek insists that he resisted Tříska's proposal on his own accord, Tříska claims that the Czech government, under the pressure of dissidents and gradualist economists, pressured Ježek to oppose the extensive use of vouchers, implicitly denying ideological dissonance as a reason for their discord.[59]

Once the privatization process had begun, disagreements between Ježek and the Ministry of Finance continued, now over the competitiveness of the submission of privatization projects. Tříska and especially Klaus wanted only the top managers to submit the formal privatization project to the Privatization Ministry for approval. According to Klaus's formulation, the enterprise directors would submit a simple privatization project to the founding ministry within which the terms of the transfer would be outlined, as specified by the large-scale privatization law. Ježek opposed leaving the submission of projects solely to the management and instead insisted the process of submitting privatization proposals be competitive.

In accounting for his opposition, Ježek claims in retrospect that he was submitting in part to lobbying pressure by entrepreneurs who felt that small businessmen and businesswomen were in unfair positions vis-à-vis management. In particular, Ježek felt he needed to take into account the demands of the Association of Entrepreneurs, led by Rudolf Baránek. This association, founded in 1990 and boasting an enormous membership, lobbied Ježek to delay the voucher privatization process so that independent entrepreneurs would have time to draft alternative projects.[60] While acknowledging the efficacy of Baránek's lobby, Ježek asserts that his commitment to a competitive process also stemmed from his devotion to economic liberalism, which rendered competition an essential element.[61]

At the time, Klaus acknowledged that a competitive process held important advantages for efficiency but feared that the delay caused by the submission and evaluation of competitive projects would be considerable. Klaus's concern for speed was not limited to the issue of making the submission of projects competitive. In fact, his commitment to speed frequently determined his position on various reforms, such as the property restitution program. In this case, Klaus opposed restitution because he feared it would slow down industrial privatization.[62] In voucher privatization, Klaus contended that a competitive process would require an extension of the submission period by at least two months in order to allow outsiders to accumulate the necessary information to propose alternative projects and to enable the founding ministries to evaluate the additional proposals. Klaus claimed that this delay would "prove costly"—namely, that "extending the agony of many state companies will cause enormous economic losses," estimating that the "postponement of voucher privatization by a single month could cost as much as 100 million crowns."[63] Klaus commented further and more candidly, "what is even worse is that it will make the citizens lose trust in the government's ability to handle existing problems."[64]

While Klaus had emphasized the importance of speed throughout the process—as his entire team did—the reason motivating his position at this particular moment in the process requires some explanation. On the issue of allowing alternative proposals, Klaus's commitment to speed was pragmatic only in that it was a way to achieve a larger ideological goal. His goals remained ideological in nature, even if his means reveal political pragmatism and flexibility. Inspired by liberal economic theory, he wanted to seize the opportunity to ensure that private property, as a fundamental component of a capitalist economic system, was securely in place so that resources would be efficiently channeled. That said, why would a two-month delay matter if it meant a more efficient transfer of ownership rights? In this regard, Klaus's commitment to speed reflected multiple tactical considerations. By the second half of 1991, when the prospect of competitive projects was raised, speed mattered not only for ushering in the benefits of a capitalist form of ownership but also for political maneuvering and electoral politics.

Specifically, Klaus wanted citizens to have already started to place their bids for enterprise shares, thereby making the impending transfer of property feel more tangible. Klaus had envisioned that the bidding process (that is, the investment of voucher points) could begin on January 1, 1992. In order to maintain this schedule, he would allot only two weeks for the approval of all privatization projects. Ježek countered that this schedule was unrealistic, if not absurd. He insisted that this schedule was physically impossible given simple human constraints. After all, his staff had to approve the projects individually and personally rather than rely on some mechanized or automatic procedure.[65] In fact, even if the process were not made competitive, insisted Ježek, the privatization ministry could never accomplish such a feat. Ježek cited numerous reasons for the delay, such as complications stemming from restitution claims, increases in property prices due to new legislation, and delays in registering new joint stock companies. The conflict between Klaus and Ježek ultimately was resolved when the regional Czech government, revealing loyalty to Ježek, voted to postpone the deadline for the submission of alternative privatization projects.[66]

Ježek won this battle against Klaus. Consequently, any interested party could submit a privatization project. First, top managers had to submit a "basic privatization plan" and make the firm's basic information available to any interested party: midlevel managers, workers, foreign investors, or any other individual. In both waves of voucher privatization, competitive projects outnumbered the basic projects submitted by managers—with every enterprise on average receiving five privatization project proposals.[67] Although the government clearly favored those plans proposing the voucher method during the selection process,[68] the decision to accept competing projects nevertheless marked a clear victory for the Czech government over the federal Ministry of

Finance and a loss for top managers. Now managers had to compete with any interested investor in submitting privatization projects. Ježek paid a price for his victory, however. According to Ježek, his push for a competitive submission process was the reason for his dismissal as privatization minister when Klaus became prime minister the following year.

Outlining the debates and splits among the privatizers themselves helps to demonstrate that the general choices and the smaller decisions within the design of voucher privatization were products of the Czech context itself. Voucher privatization was not a model imposed from the outside, but was derived from the peculiarities of Czech circumstances and leaders. Its seeming success, however, led to its broader popularity in the region, as other states hoped to learn from this early policy success.

Assessing Czech Mass Privatization

Once the implementation of the first wave of Czech mass privatization came to an end and the second wave began to run its course, the popularity and the efficacy of the process were broadly recognized. The program was widely hailed a success throughout the international community, despite initial trepidation. Numerous governments in Eastern Europe emulated the Czech approach when designing their own privatization programs, and the World Bank employed members of the Czech privatization team as consultants to other governments to explain how to transfer state property. Frequently, Czech privatization officials took an authoritative position in international meetings, and Klaus and his coauthor of voucher privatization, Dušan Tříska, made keynote addresses at the internationally sponsored meetings of the Central and East European Privatization Network.[69]

At home, Klaus's mass privatization program was also well regarded initially, which Klaus attributes to his ability to explain to the population frequently and clearly the aims of the program.[70] During the first wave, 78 percent of the eligible adult population participated; in the second wave, 81 percent participated. Early public opinion toward the government and its program remained highly positive, with 63 percent of those surveyed expressing positive sentiment toward voucher privatization and 71 percent expressing positive sentiment toward the Klaus leadership.[71]

The smooth realization of the mass privatization program went unfettered even with the dissolution of Czechoslovakia. Negotiations over the breakup of Czechoslovakia occurred during the height of the first wave of privatization, with the final division occurring on January 1, 1993. For the most part, the so-called velvet divorce bore minimal consequences for Czech mass privatization owing to the existence of two republic-level privatization ministries. Since the beginning of economic reform, each ministry in charge of privatization was formally part of either the Czech or the Slovak government. Furthermore, because the economists involved in designing privatization were largely Czech and remained in the Czech government after the split, there was little disruption. The continuity in Czech privatization personnel and economic leadership more generally contrasts with Slovakia. In Slovakia, the Mečiar government canceled the second wave of voucher privatization after independence.

In the Czech Republic, the second wave of privatization not only took place as scheduled but also attracted even more participants and privatized almost as much property (specifically, the first wave included 988 enterprises and the second wave 861 enterprises).[72] By 1995, the government had announced triumphantly that it had transferred 80 percent of the economy to private hands (although other sources put the estimate closer to 70 percent). Never missing the chance for a symbolic statement, Klaus underscored the completion of the second wave, and of the mass privatization process more generally, by closing and eliminating the Privatization Ministry in 1996.[73] The gesture was intended to signify that the dearth of property remaining in state hands did not justify the existence of an entire ministry. In truth, however, the government simply transferred the ministry's remaining responsibilities to the National Property Fund and the Ministry of Finance.

Despite early praise, weaknesses in the Czech mass privatization program became apparent shortly following the completion of the second wave. Although the program was implemented more or less as it was planned, one aspect that was criticized by outside observers and even lamented by the architects of privatization themselves was the continuation of state ownership of large blocks of enterprise shares following voucher privatization. The continued ownership role for the state in enterprises resulted first from residual share holdings. Residual holdings included those shares for which the state could not find interested investors during either wave of voucher privatization.

In addition, the state maintained an ownership position indirectly in large numbers of nominally privatized enterprises as a consequence of the success of investment privatization funds founded by the main national banks. That is, the popularity (with ordinary Czechs) of investment privatization funds that had been founded by majority state-owned banks indirectly prolonged the state's ownership position in "privatized" enterprises. This occurred because the state maintained its controlling stake in those banks that had founded these voucher-rich investment funds that in turn held the shares of "private enterprises." Since these investment privatization funds ultimately attracted 71 percent of the available vouchers in the first wave and 64 percent during the second wave, the *potential* for state involvement in industry was enormous. By some estimates, the funds that were founded and controlled by the major Czech banks had attracted enough vouchers to control as much as 30 percent of the shares of privatized enterprises.[74]

The government had neither encouraged nor anticipated the success of investment privatization funds. In fact, the privatizers had created a complicated, centralized bidding process intended to socialize Czechs into the culture of the stock exchange and individual share ownership. However, during the spring of 1992, a young Czech entrepreneur named Viktor Kožený initiated a campaign to convince Czechs to invest their vouchers in his investment fund, Harvard Capital and Consulting. Promising tenfold returns in one year's time, Kožený changed the course of voucher privatization by heightening interest among Czechs to take part in the process and by encouraging many Czechs to invest their vouchers in investment privatization funds rather than using their vouchers to bid directly for companies.

Although Kožený's fund was not a bank fund (that is, a fund founded by a bank controlled by the state), the preference of participants to invest in funds, especially bank funds, encountered sharp criticism for two reasons. First, the new ownership structure undermined the meaning of private property by allowing a formal legal path for continued state control. Second, it distorted industrial-financial relations. The center-left opposition often zeroed in on the state's continued ownership position in the economy as a way to criticize the reform record of the center-right coalition. Members of the Social Democrats pointed to this development not only to account for the lack of restructuring in Czech industry but also to attack Klaus where he was otherwise on strong footing—that is, his image as the champion of economic liberalism. Indeed, emphasizing the government's failure to privatize banks—and by extension its continued ownership position in industry—enabled the Social Democrat Party to reposition itself as a European-style, left-of-center market supporter.

The attacks were symbolic rather than substantive, since the parties did not disagree in fact. Klaus and his party had wanted to privatize more of the banking sector in the first wave of voucher privatization, but in this exceptional case he bowed to international pressure not to include too much of the banking sector from this experimental form of privatization.[75] In fact, the limited banking privatization in the early years stands out as one of the few decisions within privatization motivated by foreign advisers. Curiously, the foreigners were calling for less privatization rather than more.

The opposition's criticism of the center-right's failure to privatize banks is not particularly damning, however. After all, once voucher privatization was completed, the center-right coalition actively tried to privatize the government's stake. For example, while still in power, Klaus approved the sale of 34 percent of Investiční a poštovní banka (IPB) and 51 percent of Československá obchodní banka (ČSOB).[76] In reality, Klaus failed to make as much progress as he had hoped due to a lack of interested foreign investors. For instance, in order to advance bank privatization, the Klaus government at one point lowered its asking price for IPB shares by half, hoping to attract greater interest.

Despite Klaus's insistence that his party wanted to privatize further the banking sector, some questioned whether the government was in fact exploiting its indirect ownership position in Czech industry as a way to prevent unpopular bankruptcies and to maintain high levels of employment. A debate emerged around the question of just how active the state had been in exercising its indirect ownership position. Although Klaus and his party, ODS, were unequivocal in asserting that they did not and would not intervene in the governance of companies, interviews with members in the Czech banking and industrial community at the time did not necessarily confirm this. What was clear, however, was that the interpretation of the government's role often divided along party lines. The supporters of ODS and its coalition partner, ODA, corroborated the government's formal position of passivity, whereas critics of the center-right coalition tended to offer examples suggesting state intervention.

Foreign observers were similarly mixed in their assessment of the Czech state's role as owner. One detailed World Bank study, commissioned specifically to analyze this question, argues that the ownership role assumed by the Czech state depended upon the type of enterprise concerned. The study's author, Andrew Schwartz, argues the state remained passive in nonstrategic enterprises—that is, in those enterprises in which the state maintained ownership stakes unintentionally through residual share ownership. In the case of strategic enterprises, however, the state was substantially more active in several capacities. It would attempt to restructure enterprises financially in order to make them more attractive to foreign investors—for instance, by assuming enterprise debt or by swapping debt for equity. Furthermore, when serving as a member of the board of directors, the state representative would actively discourage or prevent the payment of dividends so that profits would be reinvested in the firm (once again to make the enterprise more attractive to potential investors). In some instances, the report argues, the government would work with managers or even replace managers with the aim of enterprise restructuring. Finally, for the most strategically important enterprises—namely, for those employing large numbers of workers or those depended upon by numerous other enterprises in the economy—the state actively worked to prevent these enterprises from failing. Schwartz offers the example of the coal sector in which the state subsidized the acquisition of higher quality equipment and provided resources for downsizing through early retirement benefits. In the banking industry, the state used privatization revenues to assume nonperforming loans from the balance sheets of Czech banks, such as with Agrobanka. The state also limited the exposure of major banks to competition by limiting bank licenses.[77]

The second concern that the success of bank-controlled funds seemingly raised involved the distortion of industrial-financial relations. A common problem was that banks extended loans to undeserving companies listed in their fund's portfolio. As a result, a widespread pattern emerged in which banks would support large numbers of unprofitable enterprises and attempt to delay bankruptcies in order to protect their fund's assets or to safeguard the population's confidence in the bank. In other instances, distortions occurred such that relatively healthy companies were prevented from seeking out the best terms for a loan due to demands on them to borrow exclusively from the parent bank.[78]

In addition to distorted financial-industrial relations, a further structural weakness emerged following mass privatization. Legislation regulating the secondary market for privatized shares lagged behind the creation of private share ownership. And owing to the lack of transparency and low liquidity in secondary markets, financial speculators with minimal resources could surreptitiously obtain controlling blocks of shares by obtaining shares in the investment funds that controlled the enterprises. Investment groups could acquire shares without disclosing the emergence of a new block of ownership and without compensating small stakeholders. Once a new dominant ownership position emerged, minority shareholders lost any power to control the managers of enterprises and in turn their shares lost any resale value.

Controversy over minority shareholders' rights escalated during the spring of 1996 when several financial groups began to raid the shares of companies held in the investment funds of major Czech banks. A prominent example from this period was the Motoinvest group, which in late 1995 began raiding the investment fund of the largest commercial Czech bank. It quietly acquired approximately one-third of the shares of Komerční banka's investment privatization fund. Despite pleas for protection, the Finance Ministry refused to interfere in Motoinvest's stock market maneuvers—even despite the government's majority ownership stake in Komerční banka. Fearing a loss of control over its investment fund, Komerční banka lobbied the government and the Central Bank for permission to withdraw its shares from open trading, but the Stock Exchange Commission forbade it from protecting its ownership control through a moratorium on trade of its shares. As a result, Komerční was forced to pay Motoinvest dearly for its shares to avoid losing control over its fund. Throughout this period, the Klaus government and the Ministry of Finance refused to prevent the hostile takeovers of investment privatization funds of the major banks, including not only the fund of Komerční banka but also of several other major banks such as Živnostenská banka, Československá obchodní banka, and Credit Anstalt.[79]

The government's lack of response to the raiding has been interpreted in many ways. Some have understood the decision not to prevent corporate raiding as a sign that the state was a passive owner after all.[80] Alternatively, some members of the Czech media interpreted the government's inaction as a lack of concern for minority shareholder rights. In response to the fear that the government was indifferent to the fate of small shareholders, Tomáš Ježek (then chair of the parliamentary budget committee) undertook a campaign to improve the rights of minority shareholders. Thus, Ježek, the former privatization minister, decided to challenge Klaus's approach to property reform once again by forcing through new legislation to protect small shareholders. In May 1996 the Parliament adopted amendments to the commercial code that Ježek drafted requiring investors to announce if their ownership stake increased or decreased by 5 percent of the stock of an enterprise. If an investor became a majority owner, he or she was then required to offer to buy out minority shareholders. Some of the new constraints placed on investment privatization funds and investment groups, however, were easily avoided through legal maneuvers such as registering as joint stock companies or holding companies, which thereby enabled investors to dilute (and conceal) the percentage of ownership of one entity among several groups.[81]

The new ownership arrangement and the transfer of industrial shares preceded the development of a regulatory infrastructure and oversight bodies like a securities and exchange commission. The advancement of privatization with only minimal government regulation or private oversight was one casualty of the speed of the approach. Weak corporate governance structures and the resultant lack of managerial oversight enabled asset stripping by uncontrolled owners and managers. Once again, minority shareholders suffered losses in share value, now due to the phenomenon that Czechs call *tunelování*, or tunneling. Dominant shareholders or uncontrolled managers would "tunnel" (that is, channel) the assets of a privatized enterprise to a new and typically smaller enterprise with a narrower group of owners. In other words, an uncontrolled manager or a dominant owner would make an arrangement—such as selling part of the firm's capital equipment or inventory—on terms that greatly favored the smaller, newly created company at the expense of the larger group of minority owners. After repeated transactions, the larger firm would be stripped of its assets and the new smaller firm would either prosper under the new conditions or face liquidation, with the profits shared among its few owners—again at the expense of the former owners and the employees of the original enterprise.

These weak governance structures and the destabilizing industrial practices finally caught up with Czech economic performance in 1996 and 1997. After years of currency stability and steady growth, the Czech economy fell into recession. In May 1997 speculative pressure on the Czech crown forced the National Bank to float the national currency. Klaus responded to the recession with two austerity packages during April and May 1997. He also promised to progress with bank privatization as a way to cope with unhealthy industrial-financial practices in the Czech Republic. The perceived lack of restructuring in large-scale Czech industry—attributed not infrequently to the voucher program—bore much of the blame for the country's unexpected economic downturn in 1997. The once highly emulated approach to privatization lost some of its credibility. Surprisingly quickly, the Czech Republic lost its status as the model of post-Communist reform and in the second half

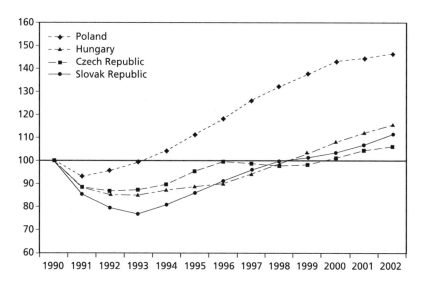

Figure 3.1. Real GDP Growth
Source: World Development Indicators (Washington, D.C.: World Bank, 2002).

of the nineties began to lag substantially behind some of its neighbors in terms of macroeconomic performance. See figure 3.1.

As in many post-Communist economies, the credibility of the privatization program in the Czech Republic was further undermined by allegations of corruption in several salient privatization decisions. There were a few important examples of corruption within mass privatization, most notably a scandal in 1995 that resulted in the imprisonment of the director of the Center for Coupon Privatization, Jaroslav Lizner. Lizner was caught leaving a restaurant with two participants in a privatization deal and a briefcase filled with over eight million Czech crowns (about $300,000).[82] For the most part, however, the privatization scandals involved direct sales and public tenders that occurred outside the voucher program. Among others, salient corruption cases included Crystalex (the Czech glassmaker), Karlovarská-Becherovka, and Čokoládovny.[83] A controversial privatization decision evoking repeated accusations of corruption throughout 1998 and 1999 involved the 1995 privatization of SPT Telecom, bought by the Dutch company TelSource, allegedly with the help of well-targeted bribes to government officials.[84]

While Klaus attempted to downplay the significance of corruption in privatization and deny his personal knowledge of corrupt practices involving the financing of his own party, the coalition government could not withstand the political pressure and collapsed on November 29, 1997. Yet despite the preponderance of corruption scandals allegedly linking illegal party contributions and secret bank accounts to favorable decisions in privatization by the center-right government, public support for these leaders and these parties remained relatively high. Therefore, even though the privatization process had fallen in esteem in the eyes of many Czechs due to corruption or the economic recession, the electoral consequences were virtually imperceptible. In fact, the center-right parties implicated in the scandals (including Klaus's own party, ODS) fared quite well in the June 1998 elections, increasing their overall representation in the parliament. Specifically, in the 1996 parliamentary elections, the center-right coalition had won a plurality but failed to reach a majority, winning 99 out of 200 seats. In 1998—after the government's collapse—the center-right parties reached a majority with 102 seats. In other words, the center-right gained enough votes to form a coalition and only failed to re-create a coalition due to the personal animosities between right-wing party leaders that emerged during the collapse of the coalition in November. Consequently, the Social Democrats, a center-left party that received the most votes in the elections, formed a minority government in cooperation with Klaus's ODS. Specifically, Klaus agreed not to vote down the government in exchange for key parliamentary positions.

Interpreting Czech public sentiment toward privatization and toward its architects is complex. For now, it is sufficient to consider the drop in support and the peculiar divide between mass and elite sentiment. According to one polling agency, approval ratings for privatization dropped from 63 percent in 1994 to 18 percent in 1998.[85] Another survey confirmed a substantial drop in support and also attempted to disaggregate negative public attitudes toward privatization in 1996 and 1998. The Public Opinion Research Institute (IVVM) reported that critics of privatization in 1998 were almost evenly divided between those who felt the process went too far (20 percent) and those who felt privatization did not go far enough (21 percent). Only 19 percent responded they were happy with voucher privatization, down from 43 percent in 1996.[86] Thus, in contrast to other cases like the Russian case, some of the disgruntlement with privatization was predicated on the understanding that *too little* property was included in mass privatization.

Although public approval of privatization declined dramatically, it is curious that the idea of expanding private ownership seemingly maintained its legitimacy among all major political parties. In fact, immediately prior to the 1998 parliamentary elections, all of the mainstream parties made explicit in their party platforms that they supported continued privatization. Only the Communist Party (KSČM) called for suspending privatization and examining suspect privatization decisions. Even the Communist Party, however, made explicit that it did not call for widespread nationalization or for the "unlawful interference" in ownership rights. Rather, it stated that the state should only uphold *legal* privatization.[87] The platform of the Social Democrats (ČSSD), the party that took power in 1998, formally supported privatization but noted that it favored privatization through employee ownership and through carefully negotiated contracts with foreign investors. In their support of employee ownership, a Western form of ESOP (Employee Share Ownership Plan) was their referent point, stating, "We consider purposeful a take-over or adjustment of Western European standards of employees' rights to participate in decision-making, suited for our conditions."[88] The new center-right party, Freedom Union, called for speedy privatization with foreign investment. As expected, the instigator of privatization, ODS, expressed support for continued property rights reform, stressing the need for bank privatization in particular.[89] Considering that the privatization process was faulted for the lack of industrial restructuring, tunneling, corruption, and the failure to protect minority shareholder rights, the continued support for privatization by all major parties is remarkable.

To a large extent, the elite support for privatization has been based on the continued understanding that privatization was and remains a necessary measure to strengthen the Czech economy. The Social Democrats claimed repeatedly that accelerating bank privatization was essential in order to strengthen the Czech economy; and, during late 1998 and early 1999, the Zeman government intensified its search for foreign investors in the financial sector.[90] Thus, continuing the trend of bank privatization from the Klaus government and the Tošovský government (the caretaker government appointed in January 1998),[91] the Social Democrats pushed through the sale of a 65 percent stake in Československá obchodní banka (ČSOB) to Belgium-based KBC Bank in the spring of 1999[92] and a 52 percent stake in Česká spořitelná banka to Austrian Erste Bank in the summer of 2000. In the end of June 2001, the government succeeded in privatizing its stake in Komerční banka as well. It also remained committed to its pledge to privatize other strategic industries during the ČSSD tenure in office, for example in the energy sector.[93]

The Czech privatization process is often criticized for corruption and for creating weak corporate governance structures. The well-respected IVVM in Prague finds that although the majority of Czechs surveyed (51 percent) are "convinced that privatization had been needed," most found its effects to be negative along many dimensions. Specifically, the IVVM survey conducted in August and September 1999 reports that 62 percent of the Czechs surveyed responded that the privatization process led to asset misappropriation (with 13 percent disagreeing); 54 percent responded that corporate management worsened after privatization (only 13 percent said it improved); 42 percent said privatization hurt Czech exports (16 percent said it helped); and 72 percent of the population linked the worsening labor market conditions to privatization (8 percent held the opposite opinion).[94] Indeed, given the economic hardship in the late 1990s, one can easily understand why the Czech public responds so negatively in survey research on large-scale privatization. Nevertheless, it is easy to overlook the successful aspects of Czech privatization, especially if one fails to consider privatization as part of a larger program of regime change. If evaluated in the context of the broader transition, then Klaus's privatization approach deserves recognition for its speed and certainty in transforming a planned economy to market capitalism. Private ownership as an institution is currently firmly entrenched in a country where a few years earlier the private sector accounted for only a small part of the economy.[95]

A detailed analysis of the evolution of Czech privatization reveals that the form of industrial privatization grew out of its own domestic context and the specific actions of skilled and committed economic liberals. In short, the Czechs themselves were central to the evolution of a mass distributive program, and very few decisions (such as the choice to exclude the bulk of bank shares from voucher privatization) were derived from the advice or pressure of Western donors and lenders. In turning to the Russian case, we see how the specific form of mass privatization is shaped not only by the Czech example, but also, more importantly, by the ideas and actions of Russian economic liberals.

4. The Origins and Design of Russian Large-Scale Privatization

The Limits of Reform under Gorbachev's Soviet Union

For several years prior to the introduction of Russia's mass privatization program, Russian economists had been analyzing policy options for revitalizing the economy, including changes to the Communist system of public ownership.[1] With Mikhail Gorbachev's ascent to power, a wide range of policy ideas gained new consideration. The worsening of relations with much of the outside world following the Soviet invasion of Afghanistan, the upward spiraling of the arms race, the depletion of hard currency and gold reserves, and a decline in production prompted Gorbachev to seek out solutions to domestic and foreign policy problems from scholars in elite research institutions.[2]

The Gorbachev leadership took an unprecedented step toward advancing structural economic reform in the summer of 1987 when the Communist Party's Central Committee and the USSR Supreme Soviet passed the Law on State Enterprises and Basic Provisions for Fundamental Perestroika of Economic Management. Taking effect January 1, 1988, these laws marked a retreat from the system of central economic control by offering greater autonomy to enterprise directors from the central branch ministries and by granting worker collectives the right to elect their managers, among other measures aimed at reorganizing industrial structures.[3] However, despite important reforms in industrial organization and the redistribution of control rights of productive property, the Communist Party remained firmly opposed to private property reform.[4] Before discussing the rise of those economists ultimately responsible for the change in Russia's system of ownership, it is useful to review the early attempts at transforming the Soviet system of property rights.

The first initiative by the Communist Party of the Soviet Union to reform the ownership regime occurred in May 1988, when the party's Central Committee and the USSR Supreme Soviet passed the Law on Cooperatives. This legislation granted citizens in groups of three or more the right to found cooperative enterprises. This legislation along with the full active support of Gorbachev and the political center encouraged entrepreneurship by guaranteeing the property rights of the owners of new cooperatives. Although as many as 85 percent of cooperatives were established by *state* enterprises,[5] this reform, in conjunction with the Law on Enterprises in 1987, allowed for the creation of a distinctly nonstate sector, with the development of many small cooperatives that resembled private family businesses.

In December 1988 additional property rights legislation provided the legal basis for individuals to sell a cooperatively owned apartment. Two additional laws altering the existing property rights code followed in late 1989 and 1990 that enabled workers to lease their enterprises and allowed families to lease small farms. In 1990 USSR Supreme Soviet passed the Law on Property, which allowed state enterprises to be converted into joint stock companies and sell their shares to other state enterprises.[6]

Although remarkable precedents at the time, these early laws mark only a slight weakening of the dominant system of state and cooperative ownership. Prominent economists during the perestroika period proposed more radical reforms in their scholarly work, including the privatization of state-owned enterprises.[7] For instance, as early as 1987, leading economists such as Oleg Bogomolov and Boris Kurashvili published essays that advocated turning state enterprises into cooperatives and allowing the workers to be the cooperative owners of their enterprise. Even more radically, in 1988 Nikolai Shmelev proposed the sale of shares in state-owned enterprises to citizens.[8] However, those academic proposals that addressed the overall structure of communist property rights, calling for a fundamental regime change, were not seriously considered until late in Gorbachev's tenure in office—that is, after the Berlin Wall had fallen, after Yeltsin had firmly established himself both as the premier Russian leader and as Gorbachev's clear nemesis, and after other East European governments had begun the process of designing techniques for large-scale privatization.

In early 1990 the Central Committee of the Communist Party invited academics to draft major systemic proposals to develop market structures within the Soviet economy. The first proposal for systemic transformation to receive broad public attention was drafted primarily by three economists, Grigory Yavlinsky, Mikhail Zadornov, and Aleksei Mikhailov in February 1990. Later that year, a second proposal for systemic reform also including a reorganization of property rights was presented by the widely respected economist Stanislav Shatalin. Shatalin proposed a radical plan to create a market economy within four hundred days. As part of this plan, he included a large-scale privatization program. Shatalin's proposal became the basis of a subsequent proposal by a working group, established by both the Russian and Soviet governments, to outline a path to transform the centrally planned system to a market economy in five hundred days.

Despite the contentious relations between the center and the Russia Republic—that is, between Mikhail Gorbachev as general secretary of the Soviet Communist Party and Boris Yeltsin as chairman of the Russian Supreme Soviet—a collaborative working group was formed on August 2, 1990, to develop a program of radical economic transformation. During August and September 1990, Shatalin and Yavlinsky joined forces to lead a group of liberal economists including Boris Fedorov (later minister of finance under Yeltsin) and Yevgeny Yasin (later minister of the economy) to draft a highly publicized program called the "500 Days Program" outlining a timetable for the swift creation of a market economy.

The 500 Days Program proposed three possible paths through which state-owned enterprises could be privatized: First, the government could transfer shares to enterprise workers at a symbolic price. Second, the government could distribute shares to the general population at a symbolic price. Third, the government could lease or sell state property to citizens in order to raise revenue for macroeconomic stabilization. Despite the length and density of the text, there was little elaboration of the mechanisms through which these methods would be applied. However, since the lead economists on the team opposed the free distribution of state property and considered macroeconomic stabilization their priority, they noted that the third option should dominate the first two options.[9]

The 500 Days Program attracted international media attention and widespread support at home and abroad.[10] Yet despite the initial tolerance and support for the proliferation of new ideas on property reform, proposals to privatize state-owned enterprises never gained party support. Shortly following the plan's adoption by the Russian Supreme Soviet, Gorbachev submitted to pressure from conservative forces in the Communist Party and deemed the plan too radical, subsequently rejecting it.[11] In November 1990, Yavlinsky, who headed the committee with Shatalin, resigned from his post as the Russian deputy prime minister in order to disassociate himself from any revised version of the economic program. He claimed that under the current conditions, the Russian leadership could not pursue meaningful economic reform and predicted that Gorbachev's revised program would lead to the collapse of the Soviet economy.[12] Yavlinsky accounts for the failure of the 500 Days Program by citing political instability and the politicians' lack of understanding of the need for radical measures. In an interview the following spring, he explains that the program did not take hold because "the politicians didn't sense the depth of the possible collapse."[13]

The strengthening of conservative forces in 1990 in the Soviet politburo weakened the willingness of the party's leaders to pursue a program of privatization and ultimately caused Gorbachev to retreat from systemic property reform. During 1990, Gorbachev vacillated between supporting radical reforms and expressing his opposition to private property.[14] Yet despite Gorbachev's not infrequent pronouncements of his opposition to private ownership, he never abandoned property rights reform entirely. He did take minor steps that suggested that the issue of property reform and privatization were still possibilities to be gradually explored. For example, on August 8, 1991, the USSR Supreme Soviet passed the Law on the Principles of the Destatization and Privatization of Enterprises, which called for the conversion of select state enterprises into joint stock companies and permitted the leasing of state enterprises by the end of the following year.[15] Despite some weak legislative activity expanding the opportunities for nonstate ownership, however, there is no indication that the Soviet leadership would have embraced the *broad* transfer of large-scale productive property to the private sector. Indeed, the extent of Gorbachev's interest and willingness to allow gradual private ownership of large enterprises will never be certain. Less than two weeks later (August 19–21), the Communist Party and the Soviet administration's authority collapsed. Gorbachev became a lame duck president as a result of the attempted coup by Soviet conservative forces and Yeltsin's decisive response during those crucial days.

In contrast to the Soviet government's slow progress in property rights reform, the Russian parliament had already begun to move forward with legislation to create a private property regime. Pursuant to the Russian parliament's declaration in June 1990 that its laws superseded any conflicting Soviet legal statutes, the Russian Supreme Soviet under the leadership of Boris Yeltsin began to draft policy independently from the Soviet Union. Thus, while property reform was stalled in the central apparatus, the Russian leadership established its own legal basis for private property. Its independent pursuit of economic restructuring was bolstered by the October 1990 decision of the USSR Supreme Soviet to formally grant the republics greater freedom to forge their own paths of economic transformation.[16] A series of systemic reforms shortly followed: On December 25, 1990, the Russian Supreme Soviet passed the Law on Enterprises and entrepreneurial activity, which rendered private property the legal equivalent to other forms of ownership (such as state ownership and cooperative or collective ownership) and provided the legal basis for all forms of private enterprises.[17] Further, in 1991, the Russian parliament adopted an additional measure importantly altering the structure of ownership—namely, the Law on Foreign Investment. This law allowed foreigners to form joint ventures with Russian enterprises and to own enterprises on Russian soil.

Despite the adoption of several acts allowing for the creation of private property, the acceptance of a program to privatize existing state-owned industry took more time. In November 1990, after the 500 Days Program was abandoned, discussions ensued on the privatization of one of the most controversial areas of property: land. Despite little progress in this area, a significant first step toward creating a legislative basis for privatization was taken in July 1991 with the passage of the Law on Privatization of State and Municipal Enterprises in the Russian Federation.[18]

This law outlined the potential methods according to which enterprises could be privatized. Enterprises would be privatized on a case-by-case basis, and several administrative or industrial bodies could propose a privatization plan to a designated property committee. A plan could call either for the auctioning or sale of an entire enterprise or for the corporatization and sale of shares to outside buyers or employees. An individual commission would manage the plan's approval process involving various institutions, including the workers' collective at the enterprise, the local Soviet, and in some cases the State Property Committee. If an enterprise were corporatized, the shares could be sold to outside investors or to employees at a 30 percent discount. The legislation did not stipulate the amount of shares that would be reserved for employees at this discount, but it did limit the percentage of shares that could be sold to juridical persons that were more than 25 percent state-owned, thereby preventing the redistribution of property within state structures in the place of privatization. Finally, Russian citizens could participate in the privatization of large-scale enterprises through privatization accounts in the state savings bank.[19]

The first Russian privatization law did not, however, provide the legal basis for Russia's eventual large-scale privatization program. Privatization according to this first law would have been a slow and cumbersome process. Furthermore, the first post-Communist government preferred to draft its own privatization legislation.

In sum, despite the Soviet and Russian political elite's pursuit of reform ideas for restructuring the ownership system, the actual transformative mechanisms and a new ownership regime were not decided upon until the Soviet government fell and until Yeltsin appointed a new set of economists to top posts in his administration. Thus, despite much activity in policy-making circles, the specification of transformative mechanisms to create a new ownership regime occurred in Russia only after its decisive break with the political center. The development of a mass privatization program awaited the formation of Yeltsin's new government. In November 1991, Yeltsin gave political sponsorship to a young group of promarket economists—most of whom had no role in drafting economic reform proposals during the Soviet period—and assigned them the task of restructuring Russia's economy.

The Rise of Russia's New Economic Team

Given that during the fall of 1991 Boris Yeltsin was at the height of his power, many expected the president to undertake bold economic and political initiatives immediately. But in contrast to Yeltsin's decisive action during the August coup attempt, he was slow to appoint a new government, deliberating for over two months before deciding on the members of his cabinet.

In early November, leaders of the Democratic Russia movement—a political movement that had supported Yeltsin and that had strengthened its alliance with him during the failed coup—pressured Yeltsin to appoint the highly respected, young economist Egor Gaidar to a leading position in the government.[20] Gaidar had no relationship with Yeltsin or the democrats prior to August 1991. Rather, Gaidar, after working as a researcher from 1981 to 1987 at Moscow State University, had become a member of the Institute for Systems Research at the USSR Academy of Sciences. In addition, he worked as a columnist for the journal *Kommunist* and as the editor for the economics section of *Pravda*. At the time of the August abortive coup, Gaidar was heading his own institute called the Institute of Economic Policy.[21]

Despite Yeltsin's strong loyalties to a number of more conservative politicians and longtime allies and friends, such as Russian deputy prime ministers Yuri Skokov, Mikhail Maley, and Oleg Lobov, the Russian president chose to appoint a close associate from his hometown of Sverdlovsk, Gennadii Burbulis, as first deputy prime minister, and Egor Gaidar, as deputy prime minister in charge of the Economics and Finance Ministry. Yeltsin assumed the post of prime minister himself while maintaining his position as the Russian president. Conservative reformers tended to dominate most branches of the government, except for the economic sphere, which was led by Gaidar and several young liberal-oriented economists from the Moscow and St. Petersburg intelligentsia.

Given the importance of Gaidar's position in the government, it is surprising that he had only recently become acquainted with Yeltsin and with those who had recommended him to the Russian president, including Burbulis and members of Democratic Russia. Similar to the Czech case where Václav Klaus had become involved with the dissidents only during the final days of the Velvet Revolution (in order to provide them with an economic agenda), Gaidar had begun his collaboration with Yeltsin and leading democrats during the days of the August 1991 putsch. On the first day of the coup, Gaidar and several of his colleagues went to the White House to announce their resignation from the Communist Party and to show their support for Yeltsin. The following October, the democrats asked Gaidar to draft the economic sections of Yeltsin's first, postputsch parliamentary address on the direction of the post-Soviet Russian state. It was through Gaidar's contacts with the economics community of Moscow and St. Petersburg that Yeltsin's team of market-oriented economists was later assembled. In fact, few of the new members had previously worked in prominent positions in the government.[22]

An economist from St. Petersburg and a colleague of Gaidar, Anatoly Chubais, was chosen that November to lead Russia's privatization process.[23] Like Gaidar, Chubais had never participated in the Democratic Russia movement but was known to espouse promarket economic views and had some administrative skill and municipal privatization experience. Having taught economics in the past, Chubais was working in 1990 and 1991 as a minor official in the St. Petersburg city government supervising early trials of small-scale privatization. Chubais brought in two likeminded economists: Dmitri Vasiliev as his deputy, who had also worked in the St. Petersburg pilot privatization program, and Maxim Boycko, who had studied in Moscow and briefly in Cambridge, Massachusetts, at the National Bureau of Economic Research.

Yeltsin's choice of which economists to sponsor was counterintuitive. Not only did he appoint young liberal economists over his trusted, more conservative allies, but he also chose relatively unknown, politically inexperienced academics when more visible and experienced liberal economists were available among the pool of potential government appointees. For example, missing from the list of Yeltsin's leading economic appointments were those economists who had come to the fore of national politics during the perestroika reform debates. Potential candidates were Shatalin, Yavlinsky, and their team of economists who drafted the 500 Days Program. Shatalin's absence in the government was significant, not only since he had led earlier reform efforts, but also since he had taught and mentored many members of Gaidar's economic team who had been chosen for important posts.[24]

Once again, there are interesting parallels to the Czech case. Like Valtr Komárek, Stanislav Shatalin had led economics research in new directions in the final years of the Communist period. Also heading a premier research institute with a similar title (the Institute of the Economics of Forecasting and Scientific-Technical Progress), Shatalin had been senior to most of the economists later appointed in Yeltsin's government. However, unlike Komárek, Shatalin remained highly respected in liberal economic circles. Thus, even though he was excluded from the new government, Shatalin was frequently consulted after his junior colleagues obtained key government posts.

More striking than Shatalin's absence was that of Yavlinsky. After all, Yavlinsky was of the same generation and same ideological camp as most of Gaidar's team. Moreover, he was nationally prominent, had a solid reputation as a competent economist, and enjoyed ties with the West.

What accounts for Yeltsin's sponsorship of the Gaidar team and for his preference for Gaidar, not only over longtime allies but also over other liberal economists? Why did he pass over the perestroika-era economists with more political experience and public exposure? Yavlinsky's absence was in part due to some personal animosity between him and Yeltsin, which intensified in the years to follow. During the final year before the dissolution of the Soviet Union, Yavlinsky chose to ally with Gorbachev over Yeltsin. He was also said to have undermined Yeltsin's role as a Russian reformer by trying to develop an economic reform program within the context of a Soviet structure, rather than within the Russian republic (that is, the level where Yeltsin wielded power). In fact, Yavlinsky supported the preservation of the Soviet Union as a federal state late into 1991.[25] Thus, when power shifted away from the center (and from Soviet structures) to the Russian republic, Yavlinsky paid the price for his political miscalculation.

While the animosity between Yavlinsky and Yeltsin certainly influenced the former's absence in the new Russian government, of greater importance was Yavlinsky's negative association with the failings of perestroika-era reforms, especially in contrast to Gaidar's untarnished reputation. In Yeltsin's own accounts of this period, he explains his choice of political unknowns over more prominent economists by explicitly noting his preference to find *new* economists to lead Russia's reform, as well as the strong impression Gaidar's team made on him. Yeltsin explains in his memoirs that he did not pass over Yavlinsky due to the substance of his ideas but because "psychologically it was difficult to return a second time to the same '500 Days' Program and its creators."[26] In particular, Yavlinsky's absence resulted from Yeltsin's desire to steer clear of any negative association with economic reform in the past and the unpopularity surrounding Gorbachev. Despite Yavlinsky's positive public image, his name was necessarily associated with the abandoned economic proposals under Gorbachev. Finally, Yeltsin considered Gaidar to be much more articulate and persuasive than Yavlinsky. Yeltsin elaborates his choice of Gaidar in his memoirs:

> Gaidar impressed me most of all with his confidence. . . . He would not hide his opinions, his reflections or his weaknesses. He would fight for his own principles and ideas to the end . . . Gaidar had a knack for speaking simply, which figured prominently in my selection. He—not I—would have to talk to opponents of reform sooner or later. He did not water down his ideas, but he knew how to speak plainly about complicated things. All economists try to do this, but Gaidar was able to do it the most persuasively. He was able to infect people with his ideas.[27]

Yeltsin further notes that Gaidar had a close-knit team of well-trained economists ready to tackle Russia's economic problems. Like the Czech dissidents in Civic Forum before the November revolution, the Russian democrats asserted that they had devoted their time to bringing down the Communist Party and not to designing what would follow in its place. This was less true in the Russian case than in the Czech case, given the development of systemic programs like the 500 Days Program, drafted under the auspices of the Soviet and Russian governments. But just as Yeltsin wanted new leaders for "psychological reasons," the Russian democrats wanted to follow a program without any association with the past reform efforts under Gorbachev. Gavriil Popov, a member of Democratic Russia and the mayor of Moscow at the time, explains that Yeltsin and "the movement [of Democratic Russia] as a whole . . . had not come up with a program that could become the starting point for the development of a government plan." Popov adds that the existing "programs—the 500 Days [Program], the law on privatization, etc.—were not programs developed by the democrats but programs developed by reformist apparatchiks . . . we lacked concrete programs in versions that were suitable for practical application."[28] The democrats wanted a new team and trusted Gaidar's team to draft Russia's new economic policy.

Popov's statements are reminiscent of those of the Czech dissident Jan Urban, who similarly notes the post-Communist leadership's need for coherent programs and for new confident individuals to carry out reform. Yet certain differences between the Czech and Russian early periods of transformation and between the economic elites are noteworthy. Although Gaidar's team won people over, as Klaus did, with their articulate, confident demeanor and their lack of association with the recent political past, Gaidar, Chubais, and other economists on this team did not see themselves as politicians but as technocrats. In addition, Gaidar, Chubais, and many others had been members of the Communist Party up until the abortive coup. So even though they were not associated with perestroika-era reforms, they had some association with the past communist academic elite. In further contrast to the Czech case, the revolutionary leader in Russia, Boris Yeltsin himself, was not strongly opposed to appointing individuals with links to the communist apparatus. Instead, he appeared more concerned with a person's association with the Gorbachev era.

The period when Yeltsin breaks most radically with the past—appointing unknown liberal-oriented economists rather than his old trusted allies—is striking but short-lived. As the economic crisis in Russia deepened in 1992, Yeltsin began to question the approach of the new team. A growing nervousness led him to turn to old friends and longtime allies to join his government.[29] Yeltsin replaced Gaidar with Viktor Chernomyrdin in December 1992.[30] Although Yeltsin reappointed Gaidar as first deputy prime minister to head the Economics Ministry in September 1993, Gaidar's tenure in office was short overall. He resigned on January 16, 1994, claiming to have had too little influence over government decisions.[31] By contrast, Anatoly Chubais, Gaidar's chosen economist to lead the privatization effort, remained in government until 1998, save a six month period in 1996. Chubais, unlike Gaidar, survived to see the realization of his reforms and went on to assume broader and greater responsibilities in the government.

The Evolution of Large-Scale Privatization

At the time when Anatoly Chubais was chosen to lead the privatization process in Russia, a legislative basis to transform the system of state ownership already existed, owing to the Russian Supreme Soviet's passage of the Law on the Privatization of State and Municipal Enterprises in the Russian Federation in July 1991. The 1991 law, however, provided only a general framework for large-scale privatization and required further specification by future lawmakers. It allowed for a wide range of techniques and called for the drafting of annual privatization programs.[32] It was through these annual privatization programs and several amendments to the 1991 privatization law that Chubais and the members of the State Property Committee (GKI) formalized their privatization approach into law.

Russia's new privatization officials inherited the responsibility of resolving several fundamental issues within mass privatization, such as whether property should be sold or given away for free, whether certain groups should be privileged over others, and whether any restructuring of enterprises should precede their transfer to the private sector. The earliest privatization decrees suggest the initial preferences of Chubais and his team as to how to resolve these issues; later decrees reflect those preferences but also include substantial concessions to various political and economic actors that represent a break with the original hopes of privatization's architects.

In late 1991 and early 1992, the government issued several privatization decrees, including two decrees concerning small- and large-scale industry, entitled the "Basic Provisions of the State Program for Privatization of State and Municipal Enterprises" and "Accelerating Privatization of State-Owned and Municipal Enterprises."[33] Although these early decrees focused primarily on small-scale property, they did stipulate that a group of large-scale enterprises would be transformed into joint stock companies and the shares would be *sold* publicly during 1992. Without rejecting the principle of the free mass distribution of shares, as stipulated in the 1991 privatization law, these decrees did postpone the launching of a privatization program using vouchers (or, as planned at the time, voucher savings accounts) until 1993. Furthermore, they included special privileges for employees: up to 25 percent of an enterprise's shares could be transferred for free, but those shares would not have voting rights associated with them. In addition, the decrees called for the establishment of property funds, which would be the temporary owners of shares. Clarification of ownership was considered necessary to stem the tide of what was called spontaneous privatization, or *nomenklatura* privatization—that is, the illegal appropriation of an enterprise's property by industrial directors.[34] Spontaneous privatization was a serious problem since many feared that managers in Russia were especially well poised to assume the ownership of the assets of their enterprises. If privatization of existing state-owned enterprises took too long, the expectation was that there would be little of value remaining in them. These decrees were essential starting points for formal privatization—that is, the adoption of the 1992 privatization program introduced later that spring.

The first privatization decrees reflected the hope of Chubais's team to transfer property extensively but to minimize the free transfer of shares to employees and the mass population.[35] In addition, members of the team at first considered auctions and tenders to be the preferable way to transfer substantial amounts of property to outsiders. Dmitri Vasiliev, Chubais's deputy, made explicit his preference for using sales over free transfers, arguing that property would only be valued if it were exchanged at a cost to the new owners.[36] He feared that the free allocation of property by the state would not be an effective way to channel resources to their most efficient owners.

The opposition to Chubais's initial approach to property reform mounted quickly from all sides. As was common throughout the 1990s, the liberals were not united around Chubais. For instance, liberal critics within the Moscow and St. Petersburg municipal administrations opposed the government's proposed *sequencing* of property reform. One key debate concerned whether privatization should precede or proceed price liberalization. An outspoken liberal economist working in Moscow's pilot privatization program, Larisa Piiasheva, proposed that instead of selling enterprises, the state should transform state enterprises into joint stock companies and give away shares for free immediately. Price liberalization could follow shortly thereafter.[37] Piiasheva and other promarket economists believed that this method of privatization would limit bureaucratic power within privatization and minimize corruption.[38] Another group of promarket economists argued in favor of sales, claiming that workers would only refrain from selling their shares if shares were purchased with savings.[39] Debates among liberals over the techniques of privatization thrived within academic circles and the popular press.[40]

The opposition to mass privatization that has received substantially more attention in the West, however, was that from the conservative factions in the Russian Supreme Soviet. In opposition to the proposals of the GKI, Ruslan Khasbulatov, the speaker of the Russian parliament, called for dramatically increasing the number of free shares for workers.[41] Preferring employee collective ownership to private ownership of large-scale productive property, he saw collective ownership as a "third way" for Russia, which would be more appropriate since it would not fully reject the ideas of socialism or capitalism. Khasbulatov's early opposition marks the beginning of a long series of demands by industrial groups and legislators to improve the terms for enterprise employees. Ultimately, the vision of Khasbulatov and others sympathetic to labor and managers prevailed.

Like Václav Klaus, Chubais recognized the importance of speed in the privatization process. As one journalist writes, "Chubais almost immediately identified a single, overriding goal: to transfer as much property, as quickly as possible, from the state sector into private control."[42] For both men, the sooner that property was privately held the sooner it would be put to more efficient use. Furthermore, there seemed to be an extraordinary opportunity for radical institutional change, and from the vantage point of the early 1990s they could not have known exactly how long that opportunity would last. Liberals in both the Czech and Russian contexts wanted to take advantage of the historical moment to establish as firmly and certainly as possible a private property system. Only in retrospect can we see that there was little real opposition to the creation of a private property system and that leaders (and economies) could have been better served by a more deliberate, careful, and legitimate transfer of property.

When the Russian debate over privatization began to heat up, however, and the resistance from various groups started to mount, Chubais and others in the GKI felt they were working under critical time constraints to advance the necessary legislation to transform the system as quickly as possible. From an economic standpoint, immediate and far-reaching change seemed imperative. In contrast to the Czech case, Russia's economy was rapidly deteriorating. Russian leaders were debating privatization under conditions of economic emergency: reports at the time estimated that in the first half of 1992, living standards had fallen by 25 percent, industrial output by 21.5 percent, and real incomes by 40 percent.[43] Yeltsin's team was anxious to begin reversing the economy's downward spiral. Moreover, they did not want opposition leaders to exploit the growing anxiety and popular fears of instability and famine in major Russian cities.[44] Given these political and economic conditions, Chubais understood that he must act fast to get the ownership reforms under way.

The following month, Chubais submitted a new version of the 1992 privatization program to the Supreme Soviet that he felt the legislature could not refuse.[45] In drafting this new version, the Russian privatizers emulated the Czech voucher method, hoping to transform the property regime quickly while ensuring the compliance of the mass population and the support of the industrialists. The revised version featured the distribution of property to the Russian people through a voucher mechanism. An important departure from the Czech model, however, was the substantially improved terms for employees, such that employees could become majority owners with very little investment in most large-scale enterprises.[46] It offered three variants by which enterprises could be privatized. In the first variant, employees could receive 25 percent of the shares of their enterprise for free; however, these shares would be nonvoting. In the second variant, employees could buy 51 percent of the voting shares for a negligible price. In the third variant, managers or a small group of workers could buy 20 percent of voting shares at the nominal price. The second variant was designed to placate workers and managers, and the third variant was specifically intended to satisfy managerial demands. The third variant was seldom applicable, though, owing to strict eligibility requirements that were obscurely written into the legislation.[47]

As already mentioned, Chubais and his privatization team initially scorned improved terms for workers. In a speech reviewing the results of voucher privatization, Chubais unequivocally states, "We were strongly against various attempts to divide the property between the workers. . . . We particularly were against the establishment of the so-called closed joint stock companies."[48] Nevertheless, Chubais's team recognized the value of using worker benefits as weapons against their left-oriented opponents in the legislature.[49] And while Chubais claimed that it was unfair for the program to privilege one group and should "reflect the interests of all groups of the population," he also understood that it would be politically difficult for the Supreme Soviet with a strong Communist Party presence to reject a plan that enabled workers to become the majority owners of factories.[50] In short, it was because of Chubais's priority to start the process of regime change, and to transfer as much property as possible, that he conceded enormous transfers to employees. Chubais, Vasiliev, and others recognized that this form was preferred by Khasbulatov and others in the legislature. Capitalist transformation was their overriding priority and they knew they faced serious economic and political constraints.

The concessions proved effective and the 1992 privatization program passed in its revised form without substantial delay on June 11, 1992.[51] Ultimately, these concessions meant a very different structure of ownership from that initially envisioned by Chubais, with employees in 72.5 percent of privatizing enterprises voting for the variant that would enable them to become majority owners.[52] Therefore, while the industrialists may have triumphed in terms of the initial distribution of property, Chubais succeeded in achieving his overarching goal: getting the process moving and denationalizing large bodies of state property quickly.

Despite substantial concessions to industrialist groups and labor, GKI officials continued to face strong opposition. Hoping to further strengthen popular support and weaken insider control, the government issued several decrees to ensure voucher holders access to enterprise shares. In May 1993, Yeltsin issued a decree to protect the right of citizens to participate in privatization by guaranteeing that enterprises would reserve at least 29 percent of their shares for voucher holders at auctions.[53] This measure again was fiercely resisted by the government's political opponents and declared unconstitutional by the Supreme Soviet despite its seemingly populist appeal.[54] According to Chubais and other GKI officials, the branch ministries along with conservative factions in the Supreme Soviet were attempting to block the creation of a private property regime by challenging the legality of the process. Attempts to halt Yeltsin's property reform occurred through legislative channels, with the parliament voting, first, to annul presidential decrees expanding privatization and, second, to transfer the administration of federal property away from the GKI to the central ministries.[55]

In response to the Supreme Soviet's declaration that the presidential decree guaranteeing citizen access to property was unconstitutional, Chubais threatened to resign. Playing up the conflict between the president and the

Communists, Chubais argued that sending the president's decrees to the Constitutional Court for review exemplified the parliament's attempt to obstruct privatization since the program would then be suspended until the Constitutional Court could review the parliament's claims.[56] Although this particular conflict was resolved with Yeltsin's intervention and support of Chubais, the sparring between deputies in the Congress, on one side, and Chubais and the government, on the other, continued in virtually all areas of economic policy making.[57]

From the beginning, the Supreme Soviet provided a forum for opponents of Yeltsin's economic reform to articulate alternative reform proposals. One particularly effective political lobby that united conservative factions in the parliament and called for changes in the government's early privatization proposals was the Russian Union of Industrialists and Entrepreneurs (Rossiiskii Soiuz Promyshlennikov i Predprinimatelei—RSPP), led by Arkadii Volsky. The RSPP, a large umbrella organization, claimed to represent the interests of twenty-five million people, including labor collectives, the directors of large industrial groups, and the military industrial complex, as well as small businessmen and independent entrepreneurs.[58] Volsky's strong personal connections with legislative and ministerial leaders[59] and the RSPP's financial independence[60] made Volsky's group influential in the debates over economic reform.

Volsky met frequently with government leaders, including Gaidar and even Yeltsin, to discuss alternative economic scenarios and to voice his opposition to voucher privatization as stipulated in the 1992 program in particular. In November 1992, prior to the December session of the Congress, Volsky met with Gaidar to work out a new anticrisis plan. In late 1992 and 1993, Volsky spoke out against the government's program to transfer property to the population through vouchers, explaining that he considered a reversal in the fall in production a higher priority than macroeconomic stabilization or the transformation of the ownership regime.[61] He advocated maintaining state control of unprofitable firms until the state could restructure them and privatizing only the profit-making firms. For this latter group of firms, he argued that the government should grant the control of an enterprise to workers and managers since this would be consistent with Russian tradition.[62] Volsky's RSPP lobbied for increasing the transfers to employees in the early privatization cases and for greater subsidies to state enterprises.

Throughout the voucher phase of privatization, Volsky actively engaged in uniting industrialists and conservatives in the Supreme Soviet. He collaborated with Speaker Ruslan Khasbulatov and Yurii Gekht (the leader of the Promyshlennyi Soiuz—Industrial Union, a large conservative faction in the Supreme Soviet) in order to obtain additional concessions from the government for enterprise employees. Volsky also forged a political alliance between the RSPP and Smena, another conservative faction in the parliament, and later joined forces with the Free Russia People's Party (led by Alexandr Rutskoi, the vice president) and the Democratic Party of Russia (led by Nikolai Travkin). Together, Volsky, Travkin, and Rutskoi created a broad-based opposition group, the Civic Union (Grazhdanskii soiuz), which served as a unified front against Yeltsin's promarket team of economists.[63]

As the strength of opposition groups like the Civic Union grew, so did the boldness of their demands for greater transfers to employees. The defense of employee rights—as empty as it was since most benefits went to managers—resonated well with Russian politicians. This boldness of employee ownership demands became especially apparent in the debates over the 1993 privatization program. In spring 1993 a group of deputies led by Vitalii Kliuchnikov, the deputy chairman of the Russian Federal Property Foundation, supported a proposal in the Supreme Soviet to allow employees to obtain 90 percent of their enterprise's shares.[64] The main criticisms from the parliament regarding the draft 1993 state privatization program (as summarized by the Supreme Economic Council) were that (1) the sale of property for vouchers would hinder investment, (2) the role of the GKI would remain paramount, (3) sectoral privatization would occur according to presidential decrees, and (4) the workers' terms had not been improved.[65]

Given that GKI officials had hoped to limit employee ownership from the start, they opposed a program that, by earmarking 90 percent of shares, would essentially transfer Russian industry to enterprise insiders. First of all, it was well understood that enterprise directors and, in some cases, midlevel managers would benefit much more from employee ownership than the rank-and-file workers.[66] Enterprise directors had reason to feel confident that large transfers to employees would be an effective way to maintain control over their enterprises.[67] After all, these directors were practiced at controlling their workers throughout the Soviet period.[68] It would be easy to gain control and even ownership of the shares held by the workers.

For example, to maintain control, directors pressured workers to use their vouchers to invest in the firm's investment fund. The directors would set up a room to collect their employees' vouchers and then hire a representative to use the vouchers to purchase company shares. As a result, the representative would become the legal and sole owner of the block of shares. Individual workers were then told they were owners in the company's investment fund. In order to sell their individual share of the fund, the worker would have to request permission from the director because he held the fund register. The director would often prevent the sale of shares by (mis)informing workers that they were subject to a holding period before they could sell. Even in the rare case that a worker understood his rights and realized that he had been tricked into relinquishing ownership, he had nowhere to turn. He could not afford legal representation and the unions were too underdeveloped at the time of privatization to provide meaningful support. In a similar vein, workers who acquired their enterprise shares through worker packages (rather than through the exchange of personal vouchers) were also robbed by directors. Workers did not individually have proof of ownership, and the management controlled the share register. When the management did not want to distribute ownership certificates, it would keep them in a safe where the workers would not have access without obtaining management's consent, which would be denied.[69]

In the spring of 1993, Chubais expected the Supreme Soviet to reject the 1993 privatization program unless he increased benefits for employees substantially. Thus, in order to preempt this parliamentary rejection, he requested Yeltsin's supporters on the Supreme Soviet's privatization subcommittee to return the proposed 1993 program to the GKI, allegedly in order to renegotiate the conditions of privatization with regional representatives.[70] Through a series of administrative maneuvers, the government withdrew the 1993 privatization program from legislative consideration and advanced future-voucher as well as postvoucher privatization almost entirely through presidential decree.

The withdrawal of the 1993 program initially occurred as a way of circumventing legislative resistance and preventing the deepening of concessions to workers and managers. This was important because privatization to a large extent was already distorted along the lines preferred by Khasbulatov and Volsky, and Chubais hoped to continue privatization without any further concessions to industrialists. In addition, the withdrawal of the 1993 program marks the beginning of a long process of cultivating support in the regions with the goal of offsetting opposition from the central ministries and the national legislature. Nevertheless, winning regional support and compliance also required additional revisions to the privatization program of a different sort. For instance, in the 1993 program Chubais changed the terms such that regional property funds would no longer return a percentage of the proceeds from small-scale property auctions to the Federal Property Fund (a body created by the legislature that ran the share auctions) and instead would keep all of the proceeds in the region.[71] In addition, regional administrative bodies were granted the control rights for up to 20 percent of the shares of privatized enterprises.[72] They also received the full ownership and control of certain public utilities, such as water supply and some transportation.[73]

The 1994 voucher privatization program resembled closely the 1992 and 1993 programs, but in some respects gave more power to regional authorities.[74] Like the 1993 program, the 1994 privatization program never obtained legislative approval, but it was signed into law by President Yeltsin on December 24, 1993. The first two variants of the 1994 program, setting the benefits for labor, remained the same as in the 1993 and 1992 programs, but the eligibility requirements on the third variant, setting the terms for managers, became less restrictive than in the 1992 program. In addition, the 1994 program improved terms for foreigners and clarified the ownership rights for the land located physically under privatized firms.[75] This program also expanded the pool of property facing mandatory privatization but simultaneously increased the number of enterprises requiring government approval for privatization. Since the approval of privatization plans could come from regional property funds, the 1994 program transferred decision-making authority from Moscow to the regions.

Allying with the regions relieved some of the pressure on the center, but it also created new problems for the government to solve. The central government found itself unable to implement privatization throughout Russia's many regions and municipalities according to a universal set of blueprints— or even according to the legislation as it was adopted.[76] Several oblast soviets passed motions to suspend voucher auctions (such as in Chelyabinsk, Novosibirsk, Voronezh, Bryansk, and Barnaul) and demanded to conduct privatization according to their own terms (such as in Tatarstan, Bashkortostan, and the Tula, Arkhangel'sk, and Lipetsk oblasts).[77] According to the estimates of one prominent Russian economist and specialist on privatization, Aleksandr Radygin, there were calls to cancel voucher auctions and concerted efforts to resist central GKI directives in one in every three regions of Russia.[78] Thus,

Chubais had to reconcile the demands for special privileges from regional administrations with those of industrialists in the ministries in Moscow, thereby confounding his ability to implement privatization according to a universal program either by sector or region. The efforts of regional leaders to forge their own way not only in industrial privatization but also in land privatization, such as in Tatarstan, proved to be an ongoing challenge to central privatization authorities seeking to institutionalize a uniform ownership structure.

In many respects, the government's compromise first with industrialists and legislators and then later with the regional administrations was a Faustian deal, since a central ideological goal motivating this phase of privatization was, in the words of Andrei Shleifer and Maxim Boycko, the "depoliticization" of economic relations. As these two economists involved in designing privatization explain, "The goal of privatization was to sever the links between enterprise managers and politicians, including both the Moscow industrial ministers and local officials, so as to force firms to cater to consumers and shareholders rather than politicians."[79] Yet the more the government provided exemptions and privileges to special sectors and groups during the voucher privatization process, the more political the implementation process became.

The material transfers to citizens through vouchers, to rank-and-file employees and managers through special buying privileges and to regional governments through direct transfers, appear to have been motivated by the need to spur economic regime change and ensure the stability and viability of a private property system. Although the concessions were enormous, legislative resistance to new property distribution endured. The Supreme Soviet remained strongly opposed to Yeltsin's team of privatizers and their chosen path of reform until Yeltsin disbanded the late Soviet-era parliament on September 21, 1993. The government's troubles carried over into the new legislative arena as well. The new legislative structure, consisting of the Duma and the Federation Council, often resisted the government's subsequent privatization programs with similar tactics and with equal fervor as the Russian Supreme Soviet.[80]

Opposition to mass privatization was a safe position for legislators to take. Mass privatization, once it began to run its course, was highly unpopular with the general public.[81] Although the government promised tremendous gains from privatization, few ordinary Russians felt they had benefited directly and instead sensed that they had been deceived. One problem was that in the early phase of the voucher program the government led the Russian people to believe that vouchers, and the shares bought with vouchers, would appreciate significantly.[82] For example, Chubais tried to attract public support for voucher privatization by estimating in a press conference that the future value of industrial shares bought with an individual voucher would be equivalent to two or three Russian cars in the future. When a member of the press inquired the following day whether his estimate had been genuine or a figure of speech, Chubais answered: "I think it was a figure of speech backed up by real calculations. . . . Under the circumstances, a privatization voucher could be sufficient to buy 2 or 3, and with luck, even more Volga cars. So, I confirm the point made yesterday."[83] His estimate and other public comments on the future value of shares from privatization reverberated in the media for months. The press also quoted Chubais as stating, "On the real rate of the voucher . . . the figure of 10,000 rubles and 20,000 dollars was mentioned here. I think the real price will be somewhere in between."[84] While few Russians expected to find two Volgas parked outside their home after privatization came to a close, many did expect to gain something from the "people's privatization." They hoped the companies they invested in (and often worked in) would prosper under private ownership, or that they might receive dividends from stock ownership.[85] Indeed, the 96 percent participation rate suggests some degree of hopefulness among Russians.[86] However, those who invested their voucher in the shares of the companies where they worked or lived typically earned nothing, and most of the Russians who invested their vouchers in legitimate mutual funds never collected dividends.[87] Moreover, due to the illiquidity of the Russian securities market, shareholders could not sell their shares easily. As one World Bank publication explains, individual investors were typically "locked in to their holdings or were squeezed out of more profitable assets by aggressive raiders."[88]

The government certainly was not the only one responsible for fueling unrealistically high expectations from privatization; private investment companies and mutual funds also created unreasonable expectations and ultimately caused widespread disillusionment. The most notable example was Sergei Mavrodi's investment company, MMM. Flouting one of the few laws regulating the Russian equity market (which barred companies from offering guaranteed returns when advertising), MMM promised sky-high returns in a year's time. Mavrodi developed a televised advertising campaign in the form of short soap operas to attract investors. These advertisements traced the (not so) gradual enrichment of a fictional Russian couple that had invested in

MMM. Unfortunately for the millions of Russians who invested their vouchers or rubles in MMM shares, the pyramid scheme collapsed and Mavrodi was arrested for tax evasion. The precise number of vouchers exchanged for MMM shares varies according to source, but the estimates are in the millions.[89] MMM announced that it had ten million shareholders, but the government estimated the number of Russians that bought MMM shares (for cash or vouchers) to be less than half that number.[90]

MMM is the most well-known example of Russia's bogus investment companies, due not only to the large number of citizens who lost their vouchers or their personal savings to this scheme, but also to the fate of the pyramid scheme's mastermind, Mavrodi himself. Despite cheating millions of Russians of their savings, Mavrodi was released from prison shortly after his arrest to run for a seat in the Duma—and won! Running in a special election in a town outside of Moscow, Mavrodi announced that he wanted a parliamentary seat to gain immunity from prosecution. That way he would be free to work and earn back the value of the shares.

Other pyramid schemes with less high-profile directors and less dramatic conclusions, like Telemarket and Khopyor, also cheated millions of Russians out of their vouchers or rubles and similarly tarnished public perceptions of mass privatization. A string of collapses among voucher investment funds around the time of MMM's collapse in 1994, such as Russki Dom Selenga, Tibet, the Popular Investment Construction Company, and Chara (the favorite bogus fund of the intelligentsia), created enough ill will within the population to compel the government to take its regulatory role more seriously. In November 1994, President Yeltsin issued a decree to create a federal securities commission. The president assigned Chubais to set up the commission within three months and to draft the legal codes necessary to govern trading. The decree required the operators of investment companies to obtain a license in order to trade shares and called for the official registration of share issues.[91]

Securities regulation came late in the privatization process. After years of managers absconding with the shares of the workers and denying outside voucher holders and investors access to auctions by means of physical obstruction and deliberate misinformation campaigns, it is not surprising that the "people's privatization" did not win more supporters. While often outside the control of privatization officials in Moscow, the collapse of investment funds, enormous pyramid schemes, and the manipulation of voucher auctions did little to support regime change. On the contrary, these calamities during implementation undid much of the goodwill toward market reform that mass privatization was intended to generate.

Russian Monetary Privatization

Voucher privatization came to a close at the end of June 1994, except in Moscow where vouchers remained valid through the end of the year. The free transfer of property to voucher holders, workers, and managers represented the bulk of Russian privatization, accounting for 71 percent of the shares of 16,462 enterprises by mid-1994.[92]

To continue the privatization process, the Yeltsin government proposed a new approach that relied on monetary transactions instead of free transfers. Although the Duma rejected the privatization program in five rounds of voting, Yeltsin ignored the Duma's vote and signed a presidential decree in July 1994 initiating the postvoucher, monetary phase of privatization.[93] During monetary privatization, the government organized share auctions, public tenders, and direct sales to privatize the shares of prime enterprises in leading sectors, such as in the energy, telecommunications, and metals, among others. For analytical purposes, monetary privatization can be divided into two distinct phases: aggressive privatization and gradual privatization.

With the conclusion of voucher privatization, rapid systemic change and depoliticization were no longer the key priorities of the Chubais team. Success would not be measured any longer according to how much property was transferred or the extent to which the process appeared systemically irreversible.[94] By 1994, enough property had been privatized that the reversion of the ownership regime to state ownership seemed improbable. As a result, the new privatization approach had no pretense of widespread property distribution and instead favored large investors. Dmitri Vasiliev, the deputy privatization minister at the time, explained monetary privatization in the following way: "Our aim is to form a layer of effective owners. This is privatization in favor of a very small circle of people."[95]

For a short time, the government's priority was not only to use privatization to locate large investors to raise revenue for the federal budget. It also sought to raise capital for privatizing enterprises. The initial monetary privatization program decreed by Yeltsin on July 22, 1994, allocated 51 percent of privatization income to enterprises and the rest to government bodies at the local, regional, and federal level. In this decree, only 10 percent of the proceeds would be directed to the federal budget. On May 11, 1995, less than one year later, Yeltsin issued a decree overturning the terms of the first decree[96] and instead earmarked 55 percent of the proceeds from privatization for the federal budget.[97] By 1998 the privatization program allocated 71 percent of the proceeds from privatization to the federal budget, 10 percent to local budgets, and 7 percent to the budget of the "component parts" of the Russian Federation, with the rest divided among relevant state privatization administrative bodies.[98]

What accounts for the shift in priorities? On a general level, the government realized that the goal of irreversibility had been achieved and thus the need to ensure popular support (or at least popular acquiescence) was less critical. Furthermore, by 1994 the public had realized that many of the benefits discussed during the early years of privatization, such as cash dividends from share ownership, never materialized.[99] The government would find it hard if not impossible to convince anyone a second time around that privatization would serve the immediate material interests of ordinary Russians. After all, despite the widespread distribution of vouchers, Russians could see with their own eyes the emergence of a narrow group of wealthy property owners. As one deputy in the parliament explains it, no one felt small share ownership was worth fighting for, at least not on an individual level. Thus, the government knew that no one would fight to keep widespread distribution (that is, the voucher mechanism) in place.[100]

In addition, the change in the government's priorities resulted in part from the personnel shift in the Yeltsin administration. Specifically, when Anatoly Chubais became first deputy prime minister in November 1994, his priorities within privatization changed. While retaining his portfolio as the Director of the GKI, he also became responsible for improving macroeconomic stability. Previously, Chubais concentrated his energies on privatizing as much property as possible. Once he was deputy prime minister, though, he sought to use privatization as a noninflationary way to raise revenue for the budget—albeit within the constraints of protecting the transformation of the property regime.[101] He knew better than to repeat the mistakes of past leaders who tolerated inflationary measures to cope with budget shortfalls. During Chubais's stewardship of GKI, Central Bank governor Viktor Gerashchenko relied twice on printing large amounts of rubles to meet state obligations, with near hyperinflation in 1992 and early 1994 as the result. Gerashchenko stepped down only after the collapse of the ruble on Black Tuesday on October 11, 1994.

It was in the context of the recent destabilizing inflation of 1994 that Chubais committed himself to stabilizing the economy. Rather than simply printing money, the government would borrow more aggressively from the population (with GKOs—the high-yield, ruble-denominated treasury bonds) and from the international financial community (with loans from the World Bank, the IMF, and other institutions). Chubais intended privatization to become another instrument of revenue generation. Alfred Kokh, the acting director of the Russian State Property Fund at the time and a former deputy prime minister, describes a fierce pressure to reach annual revenue targets at all costs in order to raise money for the budget.[102]

Moreover, the imperative of closing the budget deficit in a noninflationary manner reflected clear domestic political concerns. In the months preceding the December 1995 Duma elections, the government had to find a way to pay salaries to teachers, health care providers, military personnel, and pensioners without generating inflation. Meeting the government's obligations to state employees would remain a top priority into the first half of 1996, given that the presidential elections would follow only six months after the Duma elections. It was well understood that wage arrears and high inflation would undermine Yeltsin's bid for reelection.

Despite the inclusion of financially attractive enterprises in the privatization process, the State Property Fund could not come close to reaching its revenue targets. For one, there was not much personal savings sitting in Russian banks available for investment in enterprises since high inflation had erased most small-scale personal savings. Deposits were also low because many Russians distrusted the banking sector and preferred to keep their money at home rather than in a bank.[103] Moreover, well-endowed domestic entrepreneurs and other Russian wealth holders did not consider Russian enterprises as attractive an investment as businesses abroad or foreign currency speculation. Capital flight figures in Russia during this period are commonly estimated at $20 billion per year.[104]

Furthermore, those willing to keep their money in Russia preferred to keep their rubles in government treasury bonds rather than shares in Russian enterprises.[105] The State Property Fund could not easily compete with the GKO (short-term state bond) market since this market promised extremely high returns on short-term investment. Why risk investing in a small block of enterprise shares when you could put your money in the bond market and double your rubles in a half-year! These were the terms of investment in the months preceding the ruble crash in August 1998.

Given these challenges, GKI officials scrambled to find new ways to raise capital. Privatization officials argued that it was out of a pressing need to meet their revenue target that led them to agree to the most (in)famous series of auctions during this period, known as the "loans-for-shares" auctions, also known as "collateral auctions" in Russian *(zalogovy auktsiony).*[106] Despite the government's genuine need for revenue, especially prior to the parliamentary and presidential elections, these auctions raised only a fraction of their potential. Why did these notorious auctions fail to raise more revenue for the budget, given the government's desperate need to close budget gaps? To answer this question, it is necessary to explore the evolution of loans-for-shares program.

Vladimir Potanin, the director of Oneximbank, a leading Russian bank, initially proposed a version of collateral auctions in which a consortium of Russian banks would provide the state with a loan and the state would use enterprise shares as collateral for the loan. The idea of a consortium was later abandoned in favor of a program in which individual banks (in partnership with one other bank as the guarantor of the loan) would compete for the right to make a loan.[107] Hence, in this privatization program, instead of buying enterprise shares through public auctions, banks would bid for the right to hold shares in a trusteeship as collateral. In the first round of auctions, the bank that bid the highest loan (at least in principle) would win the right to hold the shares as collateral. If the government failed to repay the loan in one year's time, the bank could auction off the shares. Then in a second round of auctions, the banks could sell the shares and keep 30 percent of the profits from the sale.

While the shares only served as collateral (and thus no transfer of ownership needed to occur), the government never planned to repay the loans in order to regain ownership of the shares. In fact, top privatization officials themselves acknowledged that defaulting on the loans "was something we more-than-half-expected—after all, the point was to inject huge sums into the budget, not pay them out."[108] Certainly it is telling that the government did not budget any money to repay the loans before the term expired. Thus, the benefits of trusteeship were tremendous. In one assessment by the World Bank, the loans-for-shares program, "allow[ed] almost unconditional ownership of shares after the expiration of the loan repayment period," thereby "inefficiently transferr[ing] majority ownership rights over the crown jewels of Russian industry to an exclusive group of state-favored banks."[109]

Given the unorthodoxy of the plan, the responsible privatization officials needed to justify the collateral auctions on several grounds to domestic and international observers. First, as already noted, the government was desperate to raise money for the budget.[110] GKI officials argued that, without this program, the privatization revenue targets would be impossible to meet. Second, collateral auctions provided a way to circumvent restrictions that the Duma had attempted to impose on the privatization of oil companies. Third, the loans-for-shares program would bolster Russian banking by increasing the assets of banks. Following the mid-1995 banking crisis, the government had been exploring ways to strengthen the financial sector.[111] Fourth, this program would promote and facilitate domestic ownership of strategic enterprises. Finally, the loans-for-shares program would continue the speedy transfer of state assets to the private sector, further solidifying the viability and endurance of a private property system.

A final political justification, which government officials did not articulate, was that these auctions offered an especially quick way for the government to transfer extremely valuable, barred assets to domestic actors and, in doing so, reward the loyalty of bankers and industrialists close to the Yeltsin administration. That is, the loans-for-shares program compromised revenue for the sake of advancing the *related* imperatives of ensuring political loyalty to Yeltsin and protecting the new ownership regime.[112] Some observers have taken this argument a step further by contending that the government was seeking to buy the support of a rich group of potential Yeltsin backers (and expected campaign contributors), and thereby thwart the Communist Party from capturing the presidency in 1996.[113]

The loans-for-shares program turned out to be the most controversial and most widely criticized program in the entire Russian privatization process. The nearly unanimous condemnation of the auctions is hardly surprising when one considers the justifications put forth by the government. Certainly "strengthening the banking sector" either by allowing the banks to keep 30 percent of the profits from the immediate sale of the shares or by allowing them to become the new proprietors of the shares seemed inappropriate to many. As Mark Blitzer, the chief economist of the World Bank in Moscow, remarked even before the auctions occurred, "Why should the banks reap so much of the upside if the government manages to stabilize independently?

... The upside gains are too unlimited."[114] After all, strengthening the banks through the transfer of capital euphemistically meant enriching a small group of financial oligarchs.

These transfers to the banks occurred at the expense of ordinary Russians since they deprived a bankrupt state of the means to pay wage arrears and buttress the social safety net. Like "employee privatization," which tended to favor managers over rank-and-file workers, the loans-for-shares program contributed to the perception that privatization was intended to enrich the few.[115] Throughout the entire privatization process, Russian citizens observed ostentatious wealth on display while poverty was increasing dramatically. Indeed, the Gini coefficients for Russia nearly doubled from 1990 (26.9) to 1996 (48.3).[116] Chubais, as a symbol of privatization, had already been blamed for impoverishing the nation and concentrating wealth among a small portion of the population. These auctions only exacerbated economic inequality and fueled suspicion toward Chubais and the privatization process.[117]

Moreover, few actually expected the loans-for-shares program to ensure or protect the domestic ownership of Russian blue-chip companies. The justification was that collateral auctions would prevent better-endowed, foreign buyers from outbidding domestic investors since only domestic banks could participate in most auctions. As it stood, though, the banks could sell the shares after one year and foreigners could then legally provide up to one-quarter of the capital of any consortium bidding on these shares.[118] Therefore, after a one-year delay, wealthier foreigners could still gain access to this property, with the only difference being that the private banks would secure the bulk of the profits rather than the state (and by extension the Russian people who relied on public salaries or services).[119]

Curiously, these beneficial terms for the banking sector and the forgone revenue for the state were not the only or even the primary reasons for the controversy. Rather, much of the controversy stemmed from the conduct of the auctions themselves, which prima facie appeared to favor particular bidders and to have undersold Russia's blue-chip companies.[120] In fact, it was the banks that lost the competitive auctions, such as Inkombank, Rossiisky Kredit, and Alfa Bank, that provided the press with many of the details of collusion, corruption, and favoritism in the auctions.[121] In several instances, the losing banks claimed to have placed significantly higher bids but were disqualified for suspect reasons, such as tardiness (placing the bid twenty-four minutes late). Instead, certain well-positioned banks, such as Oneximbank,

Menatep, Stolichny, and Imperial, won competitions for valuable enterprises in auctions with bids only slightly higher than the starting minimum bid. For instance, in November 1995 Oneximbank acquired a 38 percent stake in Norilsk Nickel by bidding only $100,000 over the starting minimum bid of $170 million. The higher bid from Rossiisky Kredit of $355 million was disqualified for not demonstrating adequate proof of financial guarantees. A year and a half later, Oneximbank's subsidiary, Swift, obtained the title to the controlling stake for $252 million in a second auction. All calculated, the privatization of the world's largest nickel producer and one of Russia's best companies raised only $77 million for the federal budget.[122] The initial bid and the final sale price in August 1997 represented paltry sums when one considers that this firm's revenues in 1995 were estimated to be between $2.5 and $3 billion.[123]

Similarly, the organizers of the auction for a 78 percent stake in Yukos (Russia's second-largest oil company at the time) rejected the $350 million bid for a 45 percent stake from a consortium of Rossiisky Kredit, Inkombank, and Alfa Bank in favor of Menatep bank's $309.1 million bid for the 78 percent stake, allegedly because the consortium used Treasury bills as deposits. This explanation failed to satisfy the losing consortium since participants in other auctions did not face the same limitations and requirements (and may even have failed to present certificates identifying the sources of their capital).[124] In the second round the following year, Menatep sold 33.3 percent of Yukos to its subsidiary, Montblanc, for $160.1 million, just $100,000 over the starting bid.

Clearly, the loans-for-shares auctions were not competitive because the auctions' organizers and the eligible bidders were closely related, if not the same party. In other words, all parties were either the affiliates or the subsidiaries of one financial entity organizing the auction, with other financial entities shut out from participating. As a further example, in the auction for the oil company Sidanko, Oneximbank organized *and* placed the winning bid for a 51 percent share of the oil company, with a bid only $5 million above the $130 million starting bid. Rossiisky Kredit tried to place a bid but was excluded. Likewise, the participants in the Yukos oil company auction were all related to Menatep: Menatep organized the auction and provided the funding to both of the auction's bidders, Laguna Company and Reagent Investment Company. The winner of the second round auction in 1996 for a 33 percent stake in Yukos was Montblanc, a Menatep subsidiary. Once again, in the auction for a 5 percent stake in Lukoil, the organizers and participants were closely related. The winning bid by Imperial bank, which is partially owned by Gazprom and Lukoil, was only $100,000 above the starting price.

For many, the loans-for-shares auctions epitomized the entire post-voucher privatization process and substantiated claims that privatization in general was a scheme intended to cheat the Russian people and to enrich those close to the government. A wide circle of actors criticized the collateral auctions, including the bidders that lost, the general population, many Western observers, President Yeltsin,[125] and the top privatization officials themselves.[126] For instance, Moscow's popular mayor, Yuri Luzhkov, repeatedly called for overturning privatization's results and for nationalizing numerous companies including Yukos, Norilsk Nickel, the North-Western Shipping Company, and the automaker Zil.[127] Most of the major Russian political parties called for nationalizing improperly privatized enterprises in the six months leading up to the 1996 presidential elections. Several candidates featured nationalization in their political platforms, including President Yeltsin's most threatening opponent, Gennadii Ziuganov of the Communist Party.

Like many Russian economists and politicians, Western observers and advisers condemned the loans-for-shares auctions. For example, Jeffrey Sachs, a former American adviser to the Russian government, recommended nationalization of certain properties, explaining, "The second stage of privatization appears to have delivered literally tens of billions of dollars of state assets in the oil, gas, and metals sectors to powerful insiders in the government and the commercial banks."[128] Similarly, economists from the World Bank and the IMF expressed their disapproval, with Ira Lieberman and Rogi Veimetr writing, the "Russian privatization program has moved from the outstanding accomplishments of the Mass Privatization Program to the point where the program is now widely regarded as collusive, corrupt, and failing to meet any of its stated objectives."[129] In sum, critics of the collateral auctions spanned the entire ideological spectrum, from the Communist Party to the World Bank. Strong international criticism did not prevent the Russian government from carrying out the auctions. They proceeded as planned.

Shortly following the auctions, several commissions formed domestically to investigate the legality of Russian privatization. The Duma set up a parliamentary commission and the State Audit Chamber established a group to study specific loans-for-shares auctions. In early 1996, members of the government and even the GKI itself jumped on the bandwagon,[130] creating their own committees to analyze the outcomes of controversial auctions.[131] President Yeltsin criticized Chubais for underselling Russian property, and dismissed him (actually suspended him) from the government until after the elections.[132]

In several instances, the newly established committees investigating privatization corruption drafted harsh reports on the mishandling of numerous privatization auctions, including but not limited to the collateral auctions. The November 1997 report by the State Audit Chamber recommended the return of many of the privatized companies to public ownership, naming prominent enterprises like Norilsk Nickel, Svyazinvest, and Tyumen Oil Company. The report cited violations of legal procedures and asserted that collusion between the government and well-positioned companies robbed the budget of trillions of rubles.[133]

The Duma commission investigating the results of privatization similarly found that property was drastically undersold. The commission reported that although "70 percent of state enterprises" were privatized between 1992 and 1998, "only $20 billion was earned," which "immediately went to West for debt." The committee specifically cited the sale of Norilsk Nickel, writing that Norilsk Nickel, "which has no equal in the world, is worth tens of billions of dollars and until recently earned up to $3 billion [in revenues] a year, was then sold for $170 million" to Oneximbank.[134]

Despite incriminating findings, the consequences of such studies were limited. The institutional and financial resources needed to follow through on these findings were minimal. As one (pro-Yeltsin) member of the Duma commission explained, his commission simply lacked the resources to hire lawyers and trained specialists to prosecute white-collar economic crimes.[135] Despite the registration and publication of corrupt dealings by legislative and independent oversight bodies, the results of the loans-for-shares auctions thus far have been upheld. There have been only scattered instances in which the government overturned the results of smaller auctions or in which the responsible parties faced any real punishment. The acting director of the GKI who oversaw the collateral auctions was forced to resign when shares of Norilsk Nickel were reauctioned in the summer of 1997 and other high-profile GKI officials had to step down several months later following a scandal involving a suspected kickback in the form of an advance on a book contract. Specifically, five top privatization officials (Alexander Kazakov, Maxim Boycko, Anatoly Chubais, Petr Mostovoi, Alfred Kokh) each had received a $90,000 advance for their participation in writing a book on privatization. The payment resembled a bribe more than a simple advance because the publisher providing the payment was Segodnia Press; and the primary owner of this press, Oneximbank, had been one of the most favored banks in privatization. Additionally, Kokh was already under investigation for corruption in a different book deal, which also involved Oneximbank.[136]

Besides these firings, evidence of corruption in privatization did not lead to any criminal convictions and had no impact on the status of privatized property generally. The decision to allow the suspect privatization decisions of the past to stand was confirmed by Yeltsin's successor, Vladimir Putin, and conveyed to leading members of the business community. At a July 28, 2000, meeting in the Kremlin, twenty-one business leaders (popularly referred to as the oligarchs) and political leaders, including Prime Minister Mikhail Kasianov and President Putin, confirmed the existing structure of ownership. Putin himself issued a statement asserting that this meeting was intended to "remove all speculation" about the possibility of a "redistribution of property." The state, he said, was involved in these discussions because it was "vitally interested in the development of the economy." Participants in the meeting also released a joint statement announcing the "common opinion that privatization, with all of its complications and flaws, was a natural and necessary step on the path to creating an effective and competitive economy."[137] For the time being, it appears that the privatization program under the Yeltsin regime will remain irreversible, for all intents and purposes. Russia's leading businessmen have made clear that they will not relinquish property without a fight.[138] Indeed, all of the compromises that the Russian privatizers made in order to get the process moving were not in vain: Russia's property rights regime change is deeply entrenched.

The backlash following the loans-for-shares auctions and unfavorable economic conditions led to the deceleration of privatization after 1996. Privatization officials publicly claimed to redefine their approach to property reform, acknowledging the need for greater integrity in the process and for more careful preparation of privatization auctions.[139] With the reelection of Yeltsin and the entrenchment of his political and financial supporters, the need to use privatization to ensure the support of well-positioned and resource-endowed elites became less critical.[140]

After Yeltsin's victory, GKI officials tried to continue privatizing Russian industry by attracting foreign participants. The international financial institutions also encouraged foreign participation and allocated new resources to encourage the Yeltsin government to advance structural reforms. Once the 1996 presidential elections had passed, the IMF and the World Bank were more willing to require progress in privatization as a condition for lending, as in the case of the World Bank loan to the Russian coal sector.[141]

In 1997 and 1998, the Russian government had hoped to increase the pace of privatization, but privatization receipts again fell far below GKI targets. Attracting buyers remained difficult due to competition with the GKO market for domestic capital. In addition, the Asian financial crisis in late 1997 made international speculators wary of investing in the so-called emerging markets and brought about a "flight to quality" (that is, the movement of capital to seemingly more reliable Western securities). The August 1998 ruble crash only exacerbated the investment climate. Russian officials often had no choice during these difficult years but to cancel some of the scheduled auctions.[142]

In terms of revenue generation, the main successes in privatization in the late nineties included the sale of shares from prominent blue chip companies. For example, in 1997 the government succeeded in raising $1.875 billion for the federal budget by finally selling a 25 percent stake in the telecommunications monopoly Svyazinvest, after having failed in 1995. The tender was won by Mustcom, a consortium of Russian and Western investors, including Oneximbank, Deutsche Morgan Grenfell, and Morgan Stanley.[143] In December 1998, the government sold a 2.5 percent stake in Gazprom to Ruhrgas, a German company, raising $660 million. In 1999 eleven major enterprises were slated for auction, including stakes in notable companies such as Lukoil, Svyazinvest, Gazprom, Rosneft, Slavneft, and Tyuman Oil, among others.[144] With the government failing to achieve its privatization goals in 1999, the shares in these and many other enterprises remained on the auctioning board in subsequent years.[145] Several energy companies mentioned above did ultimately find buyers, such as the $74.7 million stake in Lukoil that sold in 2000 and the $1.86 billion stake in Slavneft that sold in 2002.[146] Other especially lucrative energy and metals privatization auctions completed subsequently included a $1.08 billion stake in Onako in 2000, a $91 million stake in Kuzbassugol, a $21.8 million stake in Norsi Oil in 2001, a $34.1 million stake in Matrosov Mine, and a $830 million stake in Sibneft in 2003.[147]

In sum, during this period of gradual privatization GKI officials moved forward gradually but typically failed to reach their revenue targets. They also failed to redeem themselves or bring greater legitimacy to the idea of privatization. Overall, the so-called careful preparation of projects, said to be the goal of the period following the collateral auctions, certainly did not salvage the reputation of the leading privatization officials, nor did it have much impact on the new ownership regime.

Ultimately, the results of large-scale privatization have disappointed many Russians.[148] Voucher privatization and monetary privatization, as they were carried out, endowed and empowered industrial managers and created a powerful small circle of fabulously wealthy business elites—the so-called oligarchs. Many of the new Russian capitalists amassed their wealth and power through collusion, deception, and political intrigue, rather than through smart investing and successful risk taking. Similarly troubling, newly enriched Russians, having gained access to previously state-owned wealth, initially preferred to send their capital abroad rather than invest in Russia's new economy.

The Russian economy has enjoyed very few of the benefits expected from privatization: it has not created incentives for investment and new entrepreneurial activity. Nor has it led to the widespread restructuring of privatized enterprises or the improvement of general economic welfare. For most of the 1990s, Russia's economy contracted. The long-awaited improvement in the economy's performance after 1999 is most often attributed to the 1998 Russian financial crisis (and the concomitant weakening of the ruble) and the rise of oil prices, rather than to industrial restructuring following the transformation of property rights.

One especially detrimental consequence of privatization is the disillusionment it created among the mass public. Public opinion research demonstrates that most Russians condemn large-scale privatization as a failure. Indeed, one would be hard pressed to locate ordinary Russians who speak favorably of the country's privatization experience. A 2000 poll conducted by the Fund for Public Opinion (FOM) reports that 58 percent of Russians are displeased with privatization's outcome and agreed that privatization's results in Russia should be revised (21 percent disagreed). A 1998 survey conducted by the All-Russian Center for Public Opinion Research (VTsIOM) reports that 70 percent of respondents "support nationalizing major companies that have been privatized since 1992," whereas only 15 percent oppose nationalizing privatized property.[149] Privatization and the larger capitalist transformation have taken on a very negative meaning for ordinary Russians. The narrow distribution of wealth that followed and the perception of widespread corruption fueled public hostility toward the capitalist regime change.[150]

When evaluating the choices in privatization, it is necessary also to keep in mind the context under which privatization programs were first designed. That is, it is important to recall the crisis conditions of the 1990s. While little can be said to justify the abuses and corruption within privatization, it can be acknowledged that the Russian privatizers did overcome substantial political and economic obstacles to institutionalize a capitalist system of ownership. Formally transferring the ownership rights for such a vast amount of property—an amount estimated to be as much as 70 percent of the Russian economy—occurred relatively quickly and peacefully. The free or nearly free transfer of shares in 15,052 large enterprises by mid-1994 was indeed an impressive feat.[151] Moreover, Chubais accomplished his goal of irreversible property regime change seemingly early in the process. In the future, even if the courts overturn the results of individual auctions within monetary privatization as in the case of Yukos, private ownership in Russia appears to be firmly entrenched. In short, regime change has occurred quickly, definitively, and essentially bloodlessly.

The privatization experiences in Russia and the Czech Republic underscore the importance of individual leaders attempting to drive through a radical program of regime change. Leaders like Václav Klaus and Anatoly Chubais were instrumental to the transformation of the property rights system and much of their motivation came from a personal ideological commitment to founding a liberal economic system in their respective countries. The Czech and Russian cases reveal the primary role of local leaders in designing and implementing privatization and the secondary role played by foreign advisers and external actors. After all, in the Russian case, ownership reform began during the late Soviet period. These privatization initiatives occurred without any external pressure from outside lenders, although sometimes in consultation with visiting academics and advisers from the West. Moreover, Russian officials at times implemented privatization programs, like the loans-for-shares program, against the advice and will of international lenders. Some analysts go so far as to characterize the interaction among Russian politicians and technocrats, on the one hand, and Western consultants and advisers, on the other, as a relationship among equals, suggesting that Russian economists contributed as much to the theoretical debates on liberal economic reform as their Western counterparts.[152] One could take this position even further and argue that the Russian privatizers played the Western donors and foreign lenders exceptionally well and were able to extract substantial resources with very few concessions to external actors. Irrespective of whether such a position would stand up well to scrutiny, we can be certain that the Russian leaders themselves, like the Czechs, must be acknowledged for their intellectual contribution to the design of mass privatization and the realization of the capitalist property rights transformation.

Part III. Elaborating the Theoretical Framework

5. The Beliefs of Leaders and the Content of Reform

W hen the post-Communist privatization programs were initially under design, the government officials charged with reformulating the system ownership drew from liberal economic ideology to help them develop their approach to property rights reform. Neoliberalism offered a coherent set of ideas that could guide leaders through the process of identifying the kind of system that should follow in the place of Communism as well as the path to achieve it. Its principles posited specific outcomes to flow from neoliberal institutional arrangements—namely, private ownership would create more effective incentives for the channeling of resources to their most efficient use. One property rights specialist characteristically and succinctly restates the neoliberal position on private ownership: "The use of private assets is in general more clearly allocated, and therefore more efficient, than the use of state assets because the principals designing and executing contracts delegating the use of state-owned property have weaker incentives to specialize in monitoring capabilities than do private principals. . . . A considerable empirical literature supports the assertion that private assets are more efficiently used than state assets."[1]

What does it mean to contend that liberal or neoliberal ideology influenced regime change? It does not mean that ideas have any agency on their own. Rather, this contention means that ideologies and the economic theories they imply give rise to a shift in regime type when influential political actors draw from these theories in designing policies.

The Determinants of Large-Scale Privatization

Standard public choice approaches would not consider the effect of ideologies or economic theory on the choices of policy makers. Hence, it is difficult to draw from public choice theory, including theories of state predation, to comprehend the widespread adoption of post-Communist mass privatization, or even programs like the loans-for-shares auctions. In brief, a theory of state predation would argue that a predatory state adopts a particular privatization approach in order to extract wealth or to satisfy its need for revenue.[2] In mass privatization, however, not only does the state give away industrial property essentially for free, it passes up an opportunity to generate income for itself. In collateral auctions the state similarly relinquishes the opportunity to raise revenue since the gains are primarily enjoyed by the private banks (who could sell the shares at a substantial profit) rather than the state itself. One might argue that the urgency for revenue forced the state in Russia to auction state-owned property for loans. However, the funds that backed the bids of banks were often based substantially on government deposits. That said, some forms of postvoucher privatization programs (that relied exclusively on the sale of strategic enterprises and controlling blocks of shares) often *did* have such extractive intentions, but mass privatization—the main mechanism to distribute the bulk of state property in many economies[3]— clearly did not make revenue generation a priority. In a similar vein, the loans-for-shares program in Russia, which transferred some of the most marketable shares of state-owned industry, generated revenues far below what the state could have otherwise extracted. A different explanation for the choice of these programs is clearly required.

An alternative economic theoretical approach might provide greater insight into this widespread policy choice. For example, an optimal policy approach would rely on *economic efficiency* as an explanatory variable for the mass privatization trend in Eastern Europe. That is, leaders across the region adopted a mass distribution program along with monetary privatization because they were seen as efficient ways to improve material welfare. Indeed, during the early economic reform debates, some proponents of mass privatization emphasized its efficiency advantages. In retrospect, however, simple efficiency arguments are problematic. From the earliest years of reform, the bulk of participants involved in the debates correctly anticipated that mass privatization would create a highly inefficient structure of ownership.[4] More specifically, many feared that the diffusion of enterprise shares would create a weak system of corporate governance because a dispersed body of owners could not exercise any oversight power to ensure that managers acted in ways to protect the viability and long-term profitability of their enterprise.[5] Either the dispersed new shareholders, lacking organization, would have no means of enforcing their preferences over the use of property or firm insiders would gain too much control over a firm and allocate a disproportionate amount of revenues to wages relative to capital investment. Moreover, given the absence of functioning secondary markets, there would be no alternative structure to control managers or to provide them with incentives to govern the corporation's property effectively.

The fear that mass privatization would establish private property but with negative economic consequences led the prominent Hungarian economist Janos Kornai to oppose voucher privatization in his own country, claiming that it replaces "impersonal state ownership with an equally impersonal private ownership."[6] That is, the voucher scheme would simply replace one form of inefficient ownership with another. Hungary stands out in the region as an exceptional country without any form of mass privatization. Instead, Hungary sold enterprises through tenders, auctions, and direct sales, mostly to foreign interests. As common as it was, the critique that mass privatization would lead to a dispersed, and thus inefficient, holding of property did not prevent most governments from implementing mass privatization programs. Moreover, the efficiency advantage, not to mention the revenue benefit, of selling to the highest bidder was not sufficiently powerful enough to convince most governments to rely on monetary privatization (especially at the initial phases of privatization) as the primary means of transfer.

Optimal policy approaches that rely on economic efficiency to account for the choice of privatization approaches are all the more troubling when the outcome of the mass privatization is evaluated in retrospect. Indeed, the expected negative repercussions of the voucher scheme for corporate governance structures were for the most part realized, albeit not always in the manner expected. For instance, in the Czech Republic, property ownership was formally dispersed, but the majority of participants placed their shares in investment privatization funds (IPFs), thereby creating dominant shareholding groups. In principle, the IPFs concentrated sufficient ownership power to exercise external oversight. The large amount of property suddenly under the funds' control, however, meant that the newly created bodies had the rights but typically not the resources to serve the oversight function for most enterprises, with the exception of a few premier enterprises in their portfolios.

Thus, for the majority of enterprises, IPFs could do little to guard against asset stripping in the short-term and against the misuse of corporate property down the line.

In contrast to the Czech case, privatization officials in other countries deliberately attempted to correct for the dispersion of ownership. For example, in Poland the state created fifteen investment funds with a lead fund that would have a controlling stake (33 percent) in each privatized enterprise.[7] Participants in Polish mass privatization received shares in these mutual funds rather than enterprise shares directly. In a less direct manner, the Russian government facilitated the concentration of ownership for the sake of corporate governance by allowing vouchers to be immediately transferable; that is, vouchers could be sold or traded as soon as they were distributed. As a result, participants could not only sell or invest their vouchers in private investment funds and enterprises, they could also sell them to other individuals including foreigners. This would allow domestic investors easily and cheaply to accumulate blocks of enterprise shares.

Similarly, the method by which shares were transferred to Russian workers encouraged immediate redistribution and concentration. Although workers could obtain large numbers of shares, those shares had to be individually rather than collectively owned or controlled by the trade union or the enterprise workers' council. Workers were also formally granted the unrestricted right to sell their shares at their discretion. Thus, although worker collectives as a unit would vote on the terms of the employee ownership plans, the worker shares would not be controlled or owned by the worker collective but by the individual members of that collective, facilitating the sale to investor groups. These deliberate attempts to concentrate property holding reflect leaders' concerns that a weakness of mass privatization was its failure to channel property to efficient users. As Boycko, Shleifer, and Vishny explain, "Because shares were always tradable, and were held by workers as individuals, the possibility for the reallocation of shares from the workers to other investors was built in from the start."[8]

Given that leaders expected a diffusion of ownership to cause economic inefficiencies, why did they choose a mechanism that is distinct for its ability to distribute property broadly? Indeed, the expectation (and the realization) that mass privatization would generate weaknesses in corporate governance structures calls into question the utility of interpreting mass privatization as driven by economic efficiency. Irrespective of the efforts of some policy makers to compensate for dispersed ownership, economists involved in the Russian program made explicit post hoc that maintaining "the goal of a better corporate governance system was clearly subordinate" to other goals in the design of mass privatization.[9]

Offering an alternative explanation, policy makers on the ground commonly characterized the choice to distribute property broadly and the imperative to transfer property quickly as politically motivated. For many, speed dominated all other concerns. Czech privatizers Klaus and Tříska write, "Speed . . . was regarded as absolutely essential and therefore no strategy was regarded as feasible, unless it was capable of producing fast results."[10] The voucher method excelled in this regard since it would avoid the piecemeal transfer of enterprises and a lengthy valuation process.

The importance of the speed criterion for privatization had several related political dimensions. First, the advocates of radical privatization and economic liberalization more generally argued that the government must take advantage of the revolutionary moment, or the "period of extraordinary politics," during which great change was possible. It was thought that the population during this time would be caught up in the historical moment and would therefore more willingly tolerate social dislocation and personal material uncertainty. For this reason, dramatic systemic changes should be pursued as early in the process as possible, lest the "tide of reform" change and radical policies become politically untenable. The East European economist perhaps most associated with this argument was former Polish minister of finance Leszek Balcerowicz.[11] Balcerowicz expressed this perspective primarily as it concerned the pain associated with price deregulation and macroeconomic stabilization, but the logic extended to privatization. In the case of Polish property rights reform, Balcerowicz's insight proved to be correct. As Orenstein explains, only a small amount of privatization occurred during the first years of market reform and a limited version of mass privatization was stalled in Poland until late 1995. In Poland's program, much less property was included than in programs elsewhere.[12] By the time the program was debated in the Sejm (the lower house of the National Assembly), the pain of shock therapy had already produced a backlash against systemic reform. As a result, the well-orchestrated efforts of industrialists and labor groups—that is, the political mobilization that Balcerowicz warned against—had already gained sufficient momentum to delay privatization.[13]

While only feasible in some countries, policy makers often preferred rapid privatization, fearing societal or managerial groups might mobilize to block property rights reform—either during the phase of legislative adoption or during implementation. Hence, a second and closely related dimension to speed concerned the fear that the more time that passed, the more opportunity leaders would have to design the program according to parochial interests rather than according to an overall set of economic principles. The Czech coauthor of mass privatization, Dušan Tříska, reflects on this concern: "I always said that we had to implement it [mass privatization] before the managers woke up because, once they did, they would see all of the opportunities for personal profit in other ways, and then resist. On September 17, 1991, in Lucerna Hall in Prague, there was a meeting of approximately 3000 managers and Václav Klaus and I were there. At this time, the voucher privatization law was already accepted and the scheme in preparation. And at that moment, we could see that if these managers now were given the chance, they could block the whole process."[14]

In this regard, a consensus formed among the East European privatization officials that the effectiveness of privatization would depend on the initial pace at which the process could be advanced. Dmitri Vasiliev wrote, "Without privatization, all efforts to stabilize the economy, to control inflation, will be fruitless, and the sacrifices that have been made will be in vain."[15] Foreign advisers echoed these concerns as well. Jeffrey Sachs, a leading adviser to Poland and Russia, claimed at the time, "The need to accelerate privatization is the paramount economic policy issue. If there is no breakthrough in privatization in large enterprises in the near future, the entire process could be stalled for political and social reasons for years to come, with dire consequences."[16] A report by the World Bank's International Financial Corporation (IFC) wrote, "In Eastern Europe and the former Soviet Union, the need for speed and replicability is often overriding."[17]

The urgency of property reform recommended mass privatization over sales since this program could include the broader population in the process. The sale of property would involve foreign investors in the new ownership regime since they could outbid local investors. By contrast, mass privatization could quickly and proactively build a broad constituency to support the capitalist transformation. Thus, even if the diffusion of ownership suggested future problems for corporate governance, it did offer the political benefit of involving a large portion of the citizens—the electorate—in the program. By creating a broad class of share owners, it could contribute to the creation of not only a propertied middle class but also the defenders of the new capitalist order. Moreover, by requiring the active participation of individual citizens in the short run,[18] voucher privatization would socialize the citizenry, transforming ordinary people into capitalists with vested interests in the success of property rights reform.[19]

Ideology-Driven Change versus Politics as Usual

Like speedy privatization, the founding of a broad base of property owners to bolster systemic transformation is often portrayed as political in nature; and indeed it is, in that the architects of privatization were using this approach to mobilize constituencies to support their policy agenda. Characterizing this process as merely political, however, might suggest that mass privatization was simply a technique to build a power base for its own sake. This would not only be reductionist, but it would also be misleading. Privatization, especially at the early stages of the process when the mass distributional mechanism was adopted, should not be understood as politics as usual. Simply put, voucher privatization was not a policy program merely intended to create a structure of ownership that would ensure the political survival of its advocates or to protect a particular hierarchy of power, as implied by mainstream property rights theory like that of Riker and Weimer.[20] On the contrary, power at this stage of privatization was not an end in and of itself. As in many countries, the Czech leaders (after the Velvet Revolution) and Yeltsin's economic team (following the dissolution of the Soviet Union) were driven by a much larger goal than solidifying their own power through the distribution of property. Rather, immediate and widespread distribution was favored since it would anchor the transformation from public to private ownership and accelerate the transition from a communist to a capitalist economy.

Although the architects of privatization in Eastern Europe certainly looked for politically sensitive strategies to establish capitalist property rights, they first and foremost wanted to secure the transformation of the economic system. Their ideologically driven goals of a new capitalist system of ownership took precedence over other standard political considerations. Especially telling is the fact that many well-positioned, liberal policy makers chose a transformation strategy that jeopardized their own careers. In fact, most of the economists directly involved in post-Communist transition understood that radical economic reforms would be painful and destabilizing in the short run and thus hardly an optimal strategy for maximizing one's own personal political ambitions. Moreover, the free distribution of property, despite its populist appeal, meant that the standing administration would forgo an opportunity to raise the revenue necessary to buffer the population against economic hardship.

The political payoff associated with mass privatization (and an aggressive liberal economic agenda) was unclear. For the Czech leaders—the pioneers of the approach—the strategy was politically risky if not potentially suicidal. After all, in the very beginning, organizations such as the World Bank discouraged such a high-risk strategy. The bank's reversal of its position and its subsequent embrace of mass privatization tend to obscure the early political gamble local leaders took in implementing untried economic reforms. Speaking to this point, Egor Gaidar, after being appointed prime minister in 1991, explained to a Russian journalist that in the "best-case scenario" he hoped to survive one year in office. After one year in office, he fully expected to be widely hated in Russia. Nevertheless, his policies of the past year would by then have "set Russia firmly and irreversibly on the road to building a market economy."[21] Thus, the radical reforms might in the long run yield a political payoff, but in the short run this seemed doubtful. Therefore, it is inappropriate to reduce mass privatization to a strategy to strengthen leaders' hold on power. Instead, the goal of Gaidar, Chubais, and other likeminded neoliberal officials at the initial stage of transition was to organize property reform in a way that rendered its institutionalization certain and its realization irreversible.

The design of mass privatization directly reflects the priority of "irreversibility."[22] In contrast to direct sales of property, mass distribution of property creates a larger circle of actors with vested interests in the new regime. Some scholars, such as Timothy Frye, argue further that mass privatization was deliberately designed to "tie the hands" of future governments, in that any subsequent alteration of privatization's course would entail expropriating small benefits from Russian citizens and workers. To advance this argument, Frye notes that the government denominated vouchers in rubles rather than in points so that Russian participants would experience the distribution of vouchers as an actual distribution of wealth (thereby strengthening their desire to protect their newly gained property). Moreover, the program opted for tradable vouchers rather than individual privatization savings accounts since the former creates the need for investment privatization funds and fund managers. Fund managers, like voucher holders, would have incentives to defend the privatization process and the new capitalist order.[23]

Given the goal of irreversibility, it is not clear why Russian officials would also include elements in the program that encouraged or at least facilitated the future concentration of share ownership (after an initial mass distribution), if they cared about having a broad base of capitalist supporters in the medium and long term. Nevertheless, Frye's argument remains convincing since the mass distribution of property, relative to other distributional approaches, makes a reversion to state ownership more difficult. In fact, the property least vulnerable to nationalization was the property privatized through vouchers. For this reason, the calls for renationalizing property in Russia made reference to the property distributed through monetary privatization, not mass privatization.

The period of mass privatization—which in many countries was the main phase of property distribution—should be interpreted as a time when leaders acted on their ideological commitment to the new capitalist regime, suppressing their rent-seeking tendencies and even potentially jeopardizing their professional security for the sake of durable regime change. As one scholar writes in describing the Russian case, the "grand vision" of privatization "represented something vastly more important than simply seeking to improve corporate governance and attract strategic investors. As presented, it was aimed at fundamentally restructuring Russian society and Russian culture."[24]

Even Russia's loan-for-shares auctions (in which the government transferred blue-chip stocks to well-connected bankers) were importantly shaped by the ideological goal of capitalist regime change. To be clear, the loans-for-shares program conforms to some standard interest-based assumptions. Nevertheless, two considerations must remain foremost in any evaluation. First is the timing of the auctions. The loans-for-shares auctions occurred in the fall of 1995, shortly before the Duma elections in December. There was the widespread fear that the Communists would perform well in the elections, which they did. There was also the fear that Yeltsin would lose the 1996 presidential elections to Gennadii Ziuganov, the leader of the Communist Party. Therefore, speed was an important factor, just as in the early 1990s. First, the collateral auctions provided a way to quickly transfer property, since they did not require a lengthy valuation process and foreigners would not be involved, which might have raised issues of transparency. They also provided a fast way to overcome the restrictions that the Duma had imposed on privatizing enterprises in strategic sectors, such as the energy sector. Thus, given the goal of expanding the private sector, collateral auctions were an innovative way to transfer these blocks of strategic enterprises, before Chubais and his associates lost the reins of power and the ability to accomplish this. In other words, even in the loans-for-shares program—a program harshly criticized for catering to greed and self-interest—there was an ideological dimension informing the process. Once again, the speed of transfer and the deepening of the capitalist system of ownership were important factors driving this phase of privatization.

Reconsidering Economic Efficiency

In emphasizing the ideological factors driving mass privatization in Eastern Europe, a blanket rejection of the leaders' concerns for economic efficiency would be a mistake. After all, the desire to break with a Soviet-style command economy in favor of a capitalist system relates in part to these leaders' understanding of the *economic benefits* associated with capitalism. In this regard, "economic efficiency" is still important for the design of large-scale privatization in that this form of privatization was seen as an effective strategy to ensure the realization of (what was perceived to be) an efficient property rights arrangement. In other words, voucher privatization may not have been an economically efficient means of reform, but it was a reliable way to create an efficient economic system in the long term. As noted earlier, Klaus's team believed that private ownership must replace state ownership as quickly as possible because the economy could not improve until communism was abandoned. Thus, the belief in liberal economic principles generated certain expectations about the economic efficiency gains that flow from a capitalist system of ownership—much as it did decades earlier when Marxist-inspired economic principles recommended public ownership (and "scientifically based," state-led allocation of resources) over private ownership (and "arbitrary" market allocation).

Interestingly, East European leaders themselves have made explicit the distinction between the efficiency of the means and the efficiency of the ends in choosing privatization strategies. Klaus emphasized the importance of systemic transformation over short-term efficiency considerations, claiming, "Privatization is usually initiated with the goal of raising the efficiency and prosperity of individual privatized enterprises. It is a common myth, shared by many, that privatization in a post-communist country could and should have the same objective. The thing that really matters in our case is the effect of privatization on the economy as a whole. Instead of asking 'Is the enterprise restructured?', the legitimate question is different: 'Is the economy restructured?' The individual restructuring will have to follow after privatization."[25] Klaus's comment highlights the limitations of narrow economic definitions of "efficiency" and reminds us of the big picture.

The ideological orientation of leaders informed their conception of the role of the state in the economy. Economic liberalism in a narrower sense also inspired the preference to transfer enterprises immediately rather than waiting for the state to restructure them. In the earliest phase of reform discussions, some economists proposed that enterprises be restructured prior to being privatized. In Hungary and East Germany, enterprises typically went through a phase of restructuring to prepare them for privatization. During the early debates in Czechoslovakia, however, Klaus and the so-called radical camp strongly disagreed with restructuring enterprises before privatization due to the belief that the state was not the appropriate actor to restructure them. In effect, it was impossible to restructure enterprises before finding private owners because, as one top adviser to Klaus explained, "if the state had been able to restructure our enterprises we could have still had socialism." This perspective required that the state leave all restructuring to private owners.[26] According to the rhetoric, "state-led restructuring" was equivalent to preserving the Communist economic system. Exemplifying Klaus's position that the state is the "worst imaginable agent to undertake restructuring tasks," he adds: "We have no doubts that it is the new owner, not the government, who will find ideas, time and resources for the necessary restructuring."[27] Using the state to restructure enterprises prior to privatization—as in post-Communist Hungary—was not a plausible reform option given Klaus's liberal beliefs about the role of the state in the economy.

For many property reformers, private ownership took on a deeper significance within the overall regime change. Mass privatization became a means of diminishing the capacity of the state bureaucracy to manipulate not only the economic decisions of firms but also the private behavior of individuals. Czech privatizer Dušan Tříska, in particular, stressed the importance of privatization for disempowering the state apparatus: "Privatization is the core of the whole transformation. You are not privatizing an economy, you are privatizing society as a whole. . . . I am stressing the target of liberalization and privatization, it is not only to increase the efficiency or shift the ownership, but to privatize and liberalize the society."[28] Tříska adds that state ownership is not merely economically problematic but "anti-democratic and extremely dangerous," because "it is through state ownership and [thus control over] employment that the state controls people; it cracks them."[29] He writes, "Privatization is the process within which the new social order is being established."[30]

Similarly, Klaus linked the necessity to liberalize the economy for the sake of the new society and polity. In stressing why liberal economic reform must be the main task of Civic Forum, Klaus submitted that economic freedoms are necessary for the realization of political freedoms. He asserts: "The conditions we want to create in this way, conditions of economic freedom, are the basic prerequisites for all other freedoms, including political ones."[31] Likewise, Tomáš Ježek, the first Czech privatization minister, saw privatization as a distinctly moral imperative.[32] One colleague describes Ježek's privatization mission as a path to salvation.[33]

In Russia, privatization officials took a similarly strong liberal position, arguing that economic recovery was not possible until the state withdrew from economic decision making. As Boycko, Shleifer, and Vishny explain, the "fundamental idea" that the Russian privatizers "subscribed to" was that "political influence over economic life was the fundamental cause of economic inefficiency, and that the principal objective of reform was therefore to depoliticize economic life."[34]

Like the leading Czech economists, several key Russian privatizers were known for their contempt of the bureaucracy and state ownership, as well as their understanding of privatization as a moral imperative. The rhetorical embrace of private property reform by Czech and Russian officials is strikingly similar, especially the remarks of Ježek and Chubais.[35] Early in the reform process, Chubais developed a reputation among both supporters and opponents as strongly driven by economic liberalism.[36] Victor Nekipilov, an adviser and associate of Gaidar, likens Chubais's pro-market ideology to the Bolshevik's communist ideology: "In his behavior he was led by his ideology . . . Chubais wanted to make the people happy, to enrich them . . . and consider[ed] that his reform would stop state interference in the economy . . . and stop corrupted and criminalized areas . . . and that market mechanisms would work and so on. The idea was good but its implementation was bad, which is similar to Bolshevism. He wanted to improve the welfare of people . . . he thought he could make everyone happy. Like communism before: if we give them this kind of property relations, they will be content. He was like a fanatic."[37] While one need not accept the association between liberalism and Bolshevism, Nekipilov is right to underscore Chubais's vehemence and ideological zeal.

Employee Ownership and Ideologically Charged Rhetoric

It is difficult to determine how much significance should be attributed to the symbolically imbued, sweeping statements of the key officials and their opponents. More telling is how leaders translated liberal economic ideas into specific policy choices within privatization. One area in which this is readily apparent is found in the initial resistance to allowing employee shareownership programs within large-scale privatization.

Throughout much of the region, many if not most of the prominent economic decision makers in the early liberal economic teams stood staunchly opposed to employee shareownership plans. In the Czech case, proposals including privileges for employees were given serious consideration in the media during the first year of reform (1990); and employee share ownership plans (ESOP) were supported by several famous Czech economists (including Ota Šik, the most prominent economist from the 1968 reform period) and political parties (such as the Social Democratic Party and the Czechoslovak Peoples Party).[38] However, the Klaus cohort took a strong position and rejected out of hand any advantage to employee benefits in large-scale privatization. They asserted that the equal distribution of property without special privileges for any groups was the fairest way to distribute property, since it would not favor any domestic group over another and would allow all citizens to take part in the transfer of ownership. They argued that a system with special privileges for employees was unjust since it would penalize individuals working in enterprises that were not being privatized, such as in health care or education.[39]

Many Czechs were skeptical of the government's evocation of justice to reject employee ownership. One prominent Czech economist (and a future finance minister under the Social Democrats), Pavel Mertlík, favored greater employee share ownership in privatization. Mertlík attributes the exclusion of employee benefits from privatization to the "ideologization of the concept and theory of ownership in Czech economic thought."[40] Mertlík wrote at the time of the first wave of privatization:

The private joint stock corporation is presented as the only adequate entrepreneurial form and the private property system as the most effective incentive system for the economy. . . . The arguments are mainly ideological (e.g.,
ESOPs are regularly described in the press as Václav Klaus's "ESOP fables")
and their influence on Czechoslovak public opinion seems to have been significant. . . . We can assume that the government's lack of support for workers' self-managed firms can be explained by the fact that the cooperative
movement is still politically suspect and the cooperative sector in Czechoslovakia . . . is deemed the last remnant of Socialism, and as such, must be de-
stroyed.[41]

In the debates over employee ownership in Russia, Chubais and his team
similarly opposed employee share ownership plans (ESOP).[42] In a speech reviewing the results of voucher privatization, Chubais unequivocally states,
"We were strongly against various attempts to divide the property between
the workers. . . . We particularly were against the establishment of the so-
called closed joint stock companies."[43] Thus, for Chubais and his cohort, employee ownership clashed with their liberal vision for a capitalist economy for
post-Soviet Russia. Similar to Klaus and the Czech economists, the Russian
privatizers lashed out at both foreign and Russian proponents of employee
ownership plans, discrediting their proposals as creating a "new dictatorship
of the proletariat."[44]

In many respects this position is not surprising. After all, Chubais's team
sought to dismantle a system that symbolically exalted the worker, not rein-
vent one. For the Russian privatizers, the referent of collective employee ownership was not Western ESOP exemplars. Rather, employee ownership was associated with the type of collective ownership structures characteristic of
reforming Communist states, such as in former Yugoslavia.[45] In order to
counter arguments that employee ownership programs had been economically successful in the West, government advisers would note the infrequency
of ESOPs in the West and the small percentages of shares that employees
owned in the few ESOP cases that existed. Chubais himself maintained that
ESOPs could only work in rare instances and in a developed market environment. Therefore, since employee ownership programs evoked not the West,
but Yugoslavia and the East, ESOP proposals conflicted with the fundamental
goal of the privatizers—the definitive and final break with economic institutions of a Soviet-style, centralized command economy and the establishment
of Western-style capitalist institutions.[46] Indeed, Chubais's resistance to em-

ployee ownership throughout the process and the inclusion of mechanisms intending to minimize worker ownership were consistent with Chubais's ideological vision of the future Russian economy as a Western market economy.

The Nature and Sincerity of Ideology and Beliefs

The simple contention that the architects of privatization were driven primarily by their sincere desire to ensure the founding of a capitalist economy may seem easily plausible, even to skeptics. Such skeptics, however, might become more suspicious of ideological variables if they perceived these leaders to have become much less concerned over time with advancing an ideal (or idealized) society and more concerned with protecting a particular hierarchy of power, raising revenue for the state, or protecting cronies. In a similar vein, it may be even more troubling that, for several of these leaders, their commitment to liberal ideals appeared to become more compromised over the course of transition. At times it seemed that that democracy was being preserved through undemocratic means and capitalism was being protected through noncompetitive, illiberal practices. Such concerns raise the question of whether all relevant actors, or even key actors, must sincerely or enduringly subscribe to an ideology for beliefs to be determinative.[47]

The issue of sincerity has been central to theoretical debates on the role of ideology. Theorists who study ideology in linguistic terms, such as Joseph Schull, contend that the intensity of belief is not the most important measure of an ideology's power.[48] Rather, the determinative power of an ideology rests upon the constraints it places on political debates and the consideration and articulation of alternatives. In Schull's counterintuitive argument, the power of an ideology should not be measured by the sincerity of its advocates (since methodologically this is impossible), but by the commitment to the ideology as revealed consistently in speech and behavior.[49]

Certainly Schull's approach is convenient since it is nearly impossible to prove that leaders are sincere in their professed beliefs, whereas consistency of words and action are more easily measured. It should be stressed, however, that if the term *ideology* becomes too detached from the concept of *individually and sincerely held beliefs,* then ideology as a concept loses its distinctiveness and another term can and probably should be employed to describe the phenomenon. In fact, Schull himself recommends this tack. In his case he recommends the term *discourse,* arguing that consistency in speech is the key measure for the power of a discourse.[50]

However, just as the public statements of leaders expressing their ideological motivation cannot always be taken at face value, the individual digressions from a professed belief system cannot necessarily serve as evidence of insincerity. Certainly, at times leaders exploit ideologies for hidden purposes, and in a similar vein they compromise the personal beliefs they genuinely hold. Inconsistency in outcome due to the need for tactical compromises logically cannot serve as a sufficient condition for rejecting the sincerity of a leader's ideological conviction. Thus, if consistency is not the key measure of the sincerity of belief or the power of an ideology, then what is?

Throughout this study, the professed liberal economic beliefs of Klaus, Chubais, and others have been accepted as genuine (unless otherwise stated)—and this assumption is crucial. In taking beliefs as sincere, though, nowhere is it implied or logically suggested that these beliefs are static or permanent. Indeed, the contention that a leader's beliefs may *evolve* does not detract from the sincerity of the belief at a given point in time. On the contrary, acknowledging evolution is required for the honest representation of personal conviction. Similarly, if a leader's adherence to an ideology diminishes over time, it does not logically follow that the ideals and principles that permeated their earlier attitudes and reasoning were insignificant before those beliefs began to wane. In sum, the fact that a commitment to an ideology diminishes over time does not demonstrate a lack of sincerity but suggests instead that a sincere commitment at one time existed. For this reason, it is neither illogical nor damning that the privatizers' commitment to economic liberalism was more potent when they were faced with the task of systemic transformation. Quite logically, the strength of conviction may have peaked following the Velvet Revolution in Czechoslovakia, the failed 1991 coup in Russia, the fall of the Berlin Wall and reunification in Germany, or any other revolutionary period at the end of the cold war era. In pointing to the possibilities presented by turning points in history, Bruce Ackerman's work identifies certain periods—which he calls "revolutionary moments"—when ideals are seen to dominate material enrichment and more selfish goals characteristic of property rights definition and politics as usual.[51]

Furthermore, the power of ideology is not undermined by an ideology's adaptation to changing circumstances. Indeed, ideology, in contrast to culture or language, is necessarily much more fluid over short periods of time. Further, ideologies are typically flexible enough to vary over contexts, such that an ideology or a "shared belief system" seldom holds the same meaning among those who share it. For instance, in conceptual (and practical) terms, Soviet Communism differed from Chinese Communism and Cuban Communism during the cold war, yet the relatedness and the coherence of these sets of principles and norms were nevertheless broadly recognized as categorically similar—even if not identical—across contexts.

Measuring the beliefs of leaders in any objective and reproducible fashion is not an option in political science. Rather, in order to draw any conclusions about the ideological sincerity of specific leaders, it is necessary to follow carefully their speech, writing, and actions and understand the environment in which they function. The latter is as important as the former since one can always find inconsistencies in the behavior of all individuals and thus feel justified in dismissing their sincerity. In other words, understanding the context is necessary for interpreting the digression. The example of Václav Klaus illustrates this problem well. Klaus was a self-proclaimed Thatcherite, a champion of liberal ideas, and a proponent of liberal solutions to policy problems. Despite his predilection for assuming the role of the great liberal thinker—or perhaps even because of it—his critics liked to bring attention to examples in which he strayed from orthodox liberal policy solutions. His main political rivals, the Social Democrats, criticized him repeatedly for not sufficiently liberalizing the banking sector. Western academics and journalists enjoyed highlighting the social welfare policies adopted under his first administration.[52] Klaus was even chastised by prominent policy advisers, including Jeffrey Sachs, for not adopting austere welfare policies to match his libertarian rhetoric.

Despite the ease with which one can pinpoint disjunctures between Klaus's rhetoric and a number of his policies, Klaus nevertheless was (and seems to remain) a politician sincerely committed to neoliberal ideology. Certainly, Klaus himself would much more prefer to characterize himself as pragmatic and practical rather than ideological. In the Klaus case, however, accepting his policies as pragmatic rather than liberal would be based on the assumption of a false dichotomy; what Klaus saw as a technical solution, another would see as ideological.

More important, the many instances in which Klaus departs from liberal orthodoxy are not signs of a weakness of ideological conviction. They are consequences of political constraints imposed on him by the political context in which he was functioning. Politics is the art of the possible. Since political behavior is never without constraints, context matters immensely for evaluating a leader's motivations. In speaking to this point directly, Klaus explained:

> There is a qualitative difference between ideology and real policy and real politics. . . . You either have real power to do something or you do not because it depends on the way the Parliament works. You do not [always] have fifty-one percent of the votes and so on. There are many reasons for not immediately realizing your idealistic stances or positions. . . . The question is how to do it, always how to do it. What compromises to find, how to solve it. So I just laugh at the [observers] who innocently, regardless of the real situation, suggest total liberalization [for example] of rents. . . . I simply laugh because they are immature people, nothing else can be said.[53]

Klaus's words convey the necessity of interpreting ideological preferences as they interact with other considerations affecting the realization of policy outcomes. Locating ideology as a driving force behind privatization policy making does not require that tactical political considerations never entered into leaders' calculations. In a similar vein, it does not suggest that ideologically motivated preferences could always be realized given political constraints on both the domestic and the international level. The contention about sincerity of beliefs in this study is that leaders designing the institutions of the new post-Communist state were motivated by long-term visions of the kind of society they wanted to build. This determined their broad approach of privatization and many narrower decisions within their overall framework. These choices were made to advance a vision of a new regime. Sometimes a leader's ideals were compromised due to the existence of other constraints. At critical formative periods, however, this ideological imperative of building a capitalist economy and society often worked in concert with, and even overpowered, other considerations in the development of post-Communist privatization policies.

6. Power, Interests, and the Ideological Context

J ust like political elites, societal actors rely upon ideological beliefs to en-
vision a post-Communist political and economic regime, as well as
their place in that regime. Beliefs shape how individuals determine
their policy preferences and their strategies for advancing those preferences within a set of institutional arrangements. In any political space, the aggregate sum of mass and elite beliefs creates an ideological context. This ideological context, however, not only shapes how certain groups define their
material interests within an environment of political change; it also affects the
legitimacy and hence the strength of potential supporters and opponents of
government programs. In rational choice parlance, the ideological context influences agents' calculations of their ability to compete for resources vis-à-vis
other agents and the state by shaping perceptions of authority, legitimacy, and
power in society.

Ideological versus Cultural Variables

The term *ideological context* refers to the ideologies prevailing among
members of the elite and mass groups that are expressed both in popular political discourse and in formal institutions in a given territorial space and moment in time. Although there is some overlap, this concept differs from *culture* and *political culture* in several ways. First, culture is a much broader
construct and can be defined in terms of patterns of behavior, norms, and
traditions, whereas an ideological context more narrowly refers to prevailing
beliefs among actors in society.

A further difference concerns the static connotation associated with both
culture and political culture. When Gabriel Almond and Sydney Verba first
popularized the term *political culture* in the early 1960s in their study on the
determinants of democratic stability, their conception implied a deep-rooted

persistence of behavioral patterns.[1] In discussing the type of political culture essential for democratic development, Almond and Verba emphasized that a "civic culture" in democratic polities takes centuries to develop.[2] They explained that political culture develops through the fusion of attitudinal and behavioral orientations. New patterns could not replace old patterns; they could merely *fuse* with existing patterns. Thus, any transformation is necessarily gradual and protracted.[3]

Since the 1960s, scholars using various methodologies reaffirmed the durability of cultural traits over time.[4] This has been as true for quantitative studies using longitudinal survey data with a large number of cases[5] as for deep historical research and qualitative studies of individual countries.[6] For example, historian Richard Pipes contends that "political culture, shaped by a nation's historic experience, enters the nation's bloodstream and changes as slowly and reluctantly as does language or customs."[7] Certainly there are exceptions. Some scholars of political culture portray culture as more dynamic and malleable; but often in these cases culture is treated as an artifact of politics rather than a determinant of politics. That is, political culture is conceptualized as the product of political machinations rather than a causal variable that determines political behavior.[8] Despite the efforts of several social scientists to refashion the concept of political culture along new lines,[9] political culture as an independent variable maintains a static connotation.

For many, culture remains historically rooted and resistant to change in a way that need not be true of ideologically based variables. Analyzing a specific context in ideological rather than cultural terms allows a larger role for leadership and implies a much greater dynamism. For instance, while external shocks, systemic crises, or even charismatic leaders could profoundly affect the salience of competing ideologies, they would not lead to the rapid *abandonment* of a nation's political culture. Hence, the choice to focus on the ideological context over political culture in this study is predicated on the understanding that ideas and ideologies are more readily subscribed to and, by extension, more easily abandoned than culture.

Studying the ideological context, nevertheless, does not evade many of the problems associated with studying nonmaterial determinants of political change and certainly the term *ideology* carries enough baggage that many scholars prefer to avoid it altogether. To cope with some of these problems, this chapter employs a narrow conception of an ideological context.[10] An ideological context is the sum of mass and elite beliefs, as expressed in public opinion surveys and popular discourse. The ideological context tends to find formal expression in public debates *and* in tangible institutions. To be clear, these institutional expressions are not constituent elements of the ideological context but rather the products of it. For instance, "anti-Communism" as the dominant feature of an ideological context can be manifested not only in popular opinion and political discourse but also in formal lustration (screening) laws and restitution laws. Likewise, "pro-Europeanism" as a dominant feature of the ideological context is not only represented and repeated in public speech and public opinion data, it is also institutionalized in the formal project to join the European Union.[11]

The Ideological Context and Privatization Outcomes

Most of the privatization literature does not look at the ideological context—or culture, for that matter—to explain the evolution of post-Communist privatization. Rather, the literature on post-Communist privatization explains privatization outcomes by emphasizing the ability of various groups in society to block or distort the privatizing agenda of the liberal economic technocrats in Eastern Europe. For example, Boycko, Shleifer, and Vishny's work consistently stresses the demands by economic groups for greater stakes within property distribution to account for privatization's programmatic design.[12] Specifically, the powerful directors of medium and large industrial enterprises (and later also directors of financial groups) were said to have shaped privatization outcomes by lobbying for substantial privileges within large-scale privatization.

The formal benefits lobbied for and obtained by Russian managers in mass privatization were much greater than the benefits for Czech managers. In fact in the Czech privatization legislation, formal privileges were essentially absent. At most, some Czech managers were able to gain access to blocs of property through asset tunneling and other illicit or corrupt practices, but not through formal legal privileges. Rather, the Czech managerial acquisition of property that did occur resulted from the weak corporate governance structures that ensued following mass privatization rather than from deliberate government transfers within the large-scale privatization program.

The assumption behind materialist explanations is that industrial elites would have lobbied the government for special privileges if they had had the power to do so. This assumption misses that Czech managers did not define their material interests in terms of property ownership and fails to shed any light upon their source of strength or weakness. Indeed, superficial assumptions about self-interest and lobbying power would lead analysts to overlook entirely the reasons for the distinct trajectories of benefits for managers in the Czech lands and Russia.

Low Privileges for Czech Managers

The federal government in Czechoslovakia before the split and in the Czech Republic after independence rejected benefits for societal groups in several areas of property rights reform. In the privatization of residential property, for instance, the government deliberately chose not to transfer apartments to their existing tenants, as was common in much of the region, since this would have extended the benefits distributed in the Communist era into the post-Communist era. In essence, those groups of industrial and political elites rewarded with apartments during the previous regime would not automatically enjoy these benefits in the subsequent political system.[13]

In the area of productive property, the Czechoslovak government's resistance to granting group privileges during small-scale privatization set the precedent for large-scale privatization. The Ministry of Privatization made clear that it would reject any privatization project that reserved sizable blocs of shares for employees. Initially, "sizable" meant more than 10 percent, but this percentage was even lower in practice.[14] Privatization officials asserted that the equal distribution of property without special privileges for any groups was the fairest way to distribute property and also served the purpose of encouraging all citizens to take part in the transfer of ownership.

To anyone familiar with the details of the implementation process, the assertion that privatization did not incorporate any explicit benefits for managers leading to greater share ownership may raise doubts—since the government most often selected the top management's "privatization projects" (that is, the formal proposals for privatizing individual enterprises).[15] While it is true that the government chose the projects of head managers more often than competing projects, the significance of this outcome is easily exaggerated because the former faced strong pressures to design projects that the administration found acceptable—namely, projects allocating enterprise shares to the voucher program. The federal Finance Ministry led managers to believe that, regardless of their preferences, allocating shares to the voucher program was unavoidable.[16]

Moreover, in evaluating this outcome, it must be recalled that *initially* the government program allowed *only* the top management to submit a project outlining how an enterprise would be privatized to facilitate and accelerate the process of implementation. Václav Klaus and members of the federal Finance Ministry had pushed for the single-proposal approach. However, following much controversy, the federal Finance Ministry submitted to the Czech Privatization Ministry's preference to force managers to provide the public with information about their firms in order to allow any interested individual to submit a competing proposal.[17] Although informally managers could distort information in ways that disfavored their competition, the decision to permit competition within the process nevertheless was a blow to high-level management. After all, any domestic or foreign investor could then use the procedures of the mass privatization program to gain control over the most profitable enterprises (with minimal exception).[18]

That said, managers were not so weak that the government could ignore them altogether. In fact, Václav Klaus and his deputy Dušan Tříska, attempted to reassure managers that the voucher privatization program would not undermine their control over their enterprises.[19] Klaus and Tříska emphasized that since the Czech (and early Slovak) concept of large-scale privatization depended upon distributing shares equally to all citizens regardless of their level or place of employment, enterprise shares would be dispersed widely among small shareholders. According to their arguments, the voucher method (in contrast to more conventional and seemingly manager-friendly forms of privatization based on direct sales) would facilitate de facto managerial control over enterprises.[20]

Without second guessing the source of these leaders' predictions about the future concentration of ownership, by 1993 it was clear that the voucher method did not simply produce a dispersed system of ownership but instead a highly concentrated structure of control rights, owing to the emergence of investment privatization funds. Following the first wave of privatization, the top thirteen privatization funds in the Czech Republic gained control of 55 percent of vouchers (thereby controlling an estimated 75 percent of the board seats in Czech firms privatized in the first wave).[21] Similarly, in the Slovak Republic's first wave, the top fifteen Slovak investment companies received 40 percent of the voucher points—indicating significant concentration as well.[22] Thus, even if the large investment funds could not interfere with the operation of the enterprises, since the funds tended to be over-committed and under-staffed,[23] the large-scale privatization program created structures that left enterprise managers potentially vulnerable to the preferences of the new owners. Therefore, given that the program jeopardized managerial operational control, it is significant that Czech managers never attempted to block or reshape the government's privatization program for the second wave.

The Contrasting Case of Russian Privatization

The absence of benefits for Czech managers is all the more striking when compared to the abundance of benefits for managers provided in other contexts, such as Russia, Ukraine, Moldova, and Kazakhstan.[24] In Russia, not only did managers gain control over large blocks of property through illicit means, such as asset stripping and swindling workers out of their formal rights; managers also gained access to property because the government incorporated a direct transfer of shares to managers through the three variants within the mass privatization legislation.[25]

As a consequence of formal transfers incorporated into the program, *both* managers and workers gained access to substantial amounts of shares. However, a large portion of the transfers to workers in the short-term flowed to managers in the medium-term. Since workers' shares were fully transferable and owned by individual workers rather than by labor unions or worker councils, it was relatively easy for managers to gain title to worker shares through pressure and manipulation. Yeltsin's privatization officials were well aware of the probable consequences of increasing the ease of transfer, with labor's weakness noted in their own writing.[26] For example, Shleifer and Boycko write that during the process "the usual strategy of managers is to hide behind the workers and to insist on greater benefits for the worker collective. Typically this means worker manager buy-outs . . . where managers often get large ownership stakes and complete control in exchange for promising high wages to the worker."[27]

As the chairman of the State Property Committee, Chubais lobbied aggressively for the conditions facilitating the movement of shares—that is, individual over collective ownership and full rights of transfer. The intent behind these conditions was to limit worker ownership specifically as well as to facilitate the transfer of shares from firm insiders to outsiders more generally. While no study has been able to identify precisely the extent of employee share ownership that distinguishes managers from rank-and-file workers, most survey research confirms that *both* workers and managers gained access to a high degree of property. Quantitative research consistently reveals that *a clear majority* of enterprises are employee owned (for example, 59 percent in 1995 and 64.7 percent in 1996),[28] even if the extent to which labor dominates "employee ownership" is much less reliably quantified. As one national survey reports, rank-and-file workers were majority owners in less than one-third (26.7 percent in 1995 and 30.5 percent in 1996) of the Russian enterprises designated "employee-owned."[29] In addition, a focused study reports that in twenty-seven of twenty-eight firms designated "majority employee-owned," at least 75 percent of the workers responded that the general director and the top manager were the real owners.[30]

The auctions and tenders conducted during the monetary phase of privatization further augmented formal legal transfers to managers. Firm managers tended to set the location, structure, and timing of the share auctions. Their involvement in the organization of auctions often enabled them to prevent outside investors from gaining access to auctions in order to gain the title themselves. This occurred by disqualifying potential bidders with bogus charges or by physically preventing them from reaching the auction sites.[31]

The Russian experience is hardly unique in the region. Managers and workers in Ukrainian privatization similarly acquired substantial amounts of former state property through informal and formal legal transfers. First of all, Ukrainian employees obtained the right to own shares in their enterprises through both the government's leasing and voucher programs. From 1992 to 1994, prevoucher privatization consisted primarily of transforming former state-owned companies into closed joint-stock companies and reserving the shares of the newly created corporations for worker collectives. The leasing program enabled workers to buy leased firms easily. Given that the sale prices were unadjusted for inflation, worker collectives took advantage of this opportunity in approximately 80 percent of leased enterprises. In addition, after 1994 the Ukrainian government initiated a voucher privatization program allowing citizens to participate in privatization share auctions. Once again, worker collectives had the first option to buy the shares of their enterprise with vouchers or cash. Moreover, managerial employees could buy independently from the worker collectives an additional 10 percent of the enterprise shares using cash and vouchers. Initially, managers were given the right to purchase an additional 5 percent of the shares. However, since managers had been successful in stalling privatization, the Kuchma government increased the amount to 10 percent in 1996.[32]

The Power of Managers

What accounts for managers' bold efforts and the success of those efforts to gain title to property in Russia and Ukraine, especially relative to the Czech Republic? Why were Czech managers so passive, even in the second round, when they saw the consequences of voucher privatization for ownership? Standard analyses of post-Communist privatization would argue that Czech managers were more passive and thus fared worse in mass privatization because they were less powerful than their counterparts abroad. Speaking to this issue, Anders Åslund accounts for the extensive privileges for managerial elites in Russian privatization by arguing that the Russian *nomenklatura* elite was "more powerful . . . and far more prepared to fight" for property than in other country cases.[33]

Without a doubt, managers in Russia had more power than managers in the Czech Republic in that they were better situated in the political arena to lobby for greater share ownership. An easy alliance formed between managers, ministry elites, and members of parliament that served to advance Russian managerial claims to industrial property. However, this observation still begs key questions such as why Russian managers were more powerful. Why were they better able to form alliances with parliamentary blocs? What factors affected Russian managers' calculations that made them willing to fight for greater property ownership? By asking these questions, the importance of power is not challenged. Rather, this series of questions points to the need to examine the source behind the power of groups in society in order to better grasp which variables can explain the varying positions of property claimants across countries.

The Czech Managerial Lobby

From the beginning of reform, Czech management was constrained in its efforts to lobby effectively for privileges in the large-scale privatization program, especially during the debates over the design of voucher privatization. The first and simplest reason that Czech managers did not lobby against voucher privatization was that the government's commitment to rapid privatization did not afford them much time. That is, managers had little time to organize themselves into an effective interest group such that they could amend the specific legislation. This was not accidental, however, since the reform team advocated rapid and radical privatization in part for the very purpose of avoiding managerial resistance—that is, to advance the program of privatization before managers as well as labor could identify and articulate a set of interests. On this issue, Klaus writes, "We know that we have to act rapidly, because gradual reform provides a convenient excuse to the vested interests, to monopolists of all kinds, to all beneficiaries of paternalistic socialism to change nothing at all."[34]

However, the lack of time elucidates only part of the story. The managers' link to the Communist past also constrained their ability to organize and act collectively and left them unwilling to resist government pressure to participate in voucher privatization. Within a context of anti-Communism, this association initially prevented them from advocating an alternative program with more favorable terms.

Many managers were dismissed by employee vote during the short period when employees had the right to approve or reject top management through enterprise committees organized by the revolutionary movements that took power in Czechoslovakia.[35] Furthermore, not only did top level managers lose their positions due to *informal* anti-Communist fervor, but, more formally, the lustration law also led to the exodus of top managers from industry. The lustration law, as an anti-Communist screening law, required the bureaucratic and industrial elite to resign from certain top posts for past acts of political collaboration with the Communist Secret Police (St.B.). Others had to leave their posts due to their rank in the St.B. and the Communist Party. As a result of these developments, those managers who maintained their positions felt their situation to be too precarious to challenge the government's program. Professor Milan Matejka of the Prague School of Economics explains that "managers remained quiet. They thought that if they spoke out they could be replaced . . . many life-time managers were replaced after the revolution because often they were incompetent and had simply been appointed by Communist Party committees . . . So [those who stayed] could not say anything because the standard response would have been, 'yes, you were former communists and now of course you are opposed to privatization.' Managers were afraid to resist."[36]

Matejka's opinion is common among many observers of post-Communist economic reform. As Dušan Tříska, the coauthor of the Czech voucher privatization program, explains, "Managers were taken by every possible group as potential criminals, and everyone took them as representatives of the old regime." Tříska adds that as a result, it was not necessary to cater to them.[37] Klaus led managers to believe the process was unavoidable.[38]

Anti-Communism and the Impotence of Labor

Similar to management, Czechoslovak labor was unable to organize effective resistance or even influence the form of the mass privatization program owing to the ideological context. Initially, the main labor union in Czechoslovakia, the Czech and Slovak Confederation of Trade Unions (ČSKOS), sought to influence post-Communist policy making and even proposed its own legislation on economic reform to the legislature. However, many members of the assembly considered ČSKOS to be a holdover institution from the Communist past and refused to support to its proposals, even though ČSKOS had showed important signs of reforming itself. These attempts to function as a genuine trade union, and not an instrument of a political party, made little difference, though. In the early days following the Velvet Revolution, lending support to labor in general entailed a political risk. Only those members of the parliament who were decisively on the left—such as members of the Communist Party or Obroda (an organization of expelled 1968 Communists) were interested and willing to support labor. Ironically, support from the left was entirely unwelcome since ČSKOS itself was attempting, on the one hand, to distance itself symbolically and substantively from its Communist past and, on the other, to refashion itself as a labor union of the west European social democratic type.

To increase its influence and improve its ties, the ČSKOS tried in vain to shed its reputation as a Communist institution or as the mere continuation of the Communist-era trade union. Technically speaking, its Communist image was without factual basis. Unlike the Soviet/post-Soviet Russian trade union FNPR, the ČSKOS was, in fact, a reformed institution with a new structure and a new leadership. It had severed its link to the Communist past after the revolution: Over 80 percent of former trade union leaders had been dismissed,[39] and 90 percent of the members had given up their Communist Party membership immediately after the Velvet Revolution. Moreover, the ČSKOS prohibited all formal affiliations with political parties in enterprises and workshops. Nevertheless, its reputation as a Communist holdover stuck.

Labor union officials note that any attempt to transform the image of Czech labor was thwarted by unfavorable media coverage. Following the Velvet Revolution, the press focused on the behavior of the federal trade union leadership, which opposed the Velvet Revolution, rather than the local trade unions, which formed strike committees in support of the student demonstrations. During the Jan Palach week of student demonstrations in January 1989, the directing board of the Communist trade union spoke out against the demonstrations, and the central council of the trade union denounced student mobilization during the Velvet Revolution. The behavior during this crucial period of the elite officers of the former federal trade union tarnished the reputation of trade unions in general after the revolution, despite the response of subordinate trade union branches, which in fact rejected the central directives and formed strike committees in support of the demonstrations.[40]

According to those involved in the ČSKOS, the efforts of depoliticization and de-Communization of the trade unions went unacknowledged, with frequent stories in the press suggesting that nothing in the trade unions had changed. One former union leader writes that the media's portrayal of the ČSKOS as essentially Communist and antidemocratic was effective. He explains: "The image of the trade union movement was unavoidably discredited without its fault by the bygone communist époque.... [This influenced] several actions of the trade union ... and had also a negative effect on the attitude of the members towards their own organization."[41]

Regarding large-scale privatization in particular, the ČSKOS lobbied unsuccessfully to augment the ownership share for employees in privatized enterprises. The main trade unions failed to convince mainstream members of the parliament or the government to reserve a significant bloc of shares for employees within the program of voucher privatization, even though the Scenario for Economic Reform included employee transfers as an acceptable means to privatize property. The very weakness of labor is accentuated by the workers' inability to acquire the rights to even the legal amount allotted to them. As already noted, the percentage of shares reserved for employees turned out to be much lower in practice than the 10 percent (and later amended to 5 percent) maximum allowed by law.[42]

In short, labor failed to build alliances with parliamentary factions and change the course of privatization. Given its desire to transform its image, labor rejected opportunities to ally with the Communists or the left in parliament for the very same reasons that mainstream politicians preferred to avoid any association with labor—to avoid the appearance of seeming too far to the left.[43]

Anti-Communism and Resistance from Industrialists

In essence, the ideological climate served the Czech privatization team well in that it preempted opposition to the voucher program from managers and labor and it frustrated their attempts to form alliances within government to push for greater share ownership. Furthermore, it discredited privatization's opponents as soon as they began to speak. In fact, even those members in government who opposed the use of vouchers and who could have served as effective allies for managers were similarly unable to alter the voucher privatization process due to anti-Communist fervor and their backgrounds in the Communist *nomenklatura*. Given the large numbers of elites who had at one time been party members, this problem was broadly relevant. The anti-Communist logic was that government officials opposed voucher privatization either because they were old Communist ideologues or because they were protecting the *nomenklatura* managers. Therefore, even when they opposed voucher privatization on technical grounds, their backgrounds were used to invalidate their position. Strangely enough, this was a concern for the reform Communist economists from 1968 as well as recent members of the *nomenklatura;* the Klaus team could dismiss the substantive criticisms of both rather easily by emphasizing their political affiliations in the past.

Several key industrialists serving in the government at the time, such as Jan Vrba (then minister of industry and trade), Miroslav Grégr (then the Czech minister of engineering), and Václav Valeš (the deputy premier responsible for economic policy) objected to the voucher approach and actively advocated a program of industrial sales that would locate strategic owners. Rather than transfer property to the mass citizenry, they insisted that privatization should serve as a way for companies to gain access to new technologies and capital investment. Minister Vrba in particular felt that the needs of each enterprise should be carefully assessed on a case-by-case basis instead of including all firms in a universal mass distributional program.[44] However, in the years immediately following the Velvet Revolution, the ideological context frustrated their attempts to voice this opposition effectively.

Unlike other pockets of resistance in the government, the preferences of Vrba's ministry could not easily be ignored owing to the ministry's role stipulated by the large-scale privatization law. According to the 1991 law, the Ministry of Industry and Trade was the most important founding ministry in the selection of privatization projects. Therefore, while Klaus could dismiss or ignore the criticism of other ministry officials, the minister of industry and trade had to be reckoned with in order for the process to proceed as planned. By way of compromise, Vrba and Klaus's respective ministries struck an informal agreement that the shares of leading enterprises would be wholly included in voucher privatization only when the government could not find a satisfactory domestic or foreign investor willing to commit resources and new technologies.

As both the agreement and the formal legislation allowed, the Ministry of Industry and Trade worked aggressively to attract foreign investors to the country's strategic sectors and leading enterprises. In June 1991, Vrba traveled to London to launch the sale of fifty major firms and, during the following fall and winter, labored furiously to arrange foreign investments in an impressive list of companies, most notably including Škoda Energo to Siemens; Čokoládovny to Nestlé, Switzerland, and BSN France; Hranice Cement Company to Fabbriche Riuntie Cemento SpA, Italy; Rakona detergent company to Procter and Gamble; Tabak Kutna Hora to Philip Morris; and Škoda carmakers to Volkswagen. Privatization Minister and voucher proponent, Tomáš Ježek, in retrospect, acknowledges that the most important foreign investments were the product of Vrba's efforts from late 1990 to 1992.[45]

To counter Vrba's efforts, Klaus and Tříska applied intense pressure on the Privatization Ministry and on the enterprise managers themselves to dedicate their shares to the voucher privatization program rather than sell them to foreign investors. The Ministry of Finance would appeal to managers by telling them that the widespread distribution of ownership through vouchers would offer them substantial freedom over the direction of their enterprise. In some respects, managers found this attractive because, although managers wanted access to new technology and capital, they also feared that they might lose their positions if a foreign investor became involved with the firm. Vrba bitterly recalls the efforts by the Ministry of Finance to undermine his attempts to arrange joint ventures. He offers the poignant example of Czech automaker Tatra Kopřivnice. Vrba explains, "I started discussions with Fiat and Mercedes about joint ventures [with Tatra Kopřivnice] and these discussions lasted about four or five months. And when the discussions were almost concluded, Tříska went there and told them [the managers] explicitly that they should submit the whole firm to vouchers because then they would have many unorganized owners and they would be uncontrolled. The result was they took Tříska's advice and now they are almost bankrupt."[46]

Differences between the two ministries led to a heated conflict and, like many of Klaus's debates, this conflict was dramatized in the media. Klaus publicly accused Vrba of sabotaging voucher privatization by discouraging enterprises from devoting shares to the program.[47] Vrba, in turn, accused Klaus of politicizing the economic reform process and disregarding the fate of important enterprises. Indeed, the accusations from both sides were accurate. Vrba was in fact doing everything in his power to arrange as many joint ventures as possible, and Klaus was driven by more than mere economic considerations.

The pressure from both Tříska and Klaus on enterprises to allocate shares to the voucher method was motivated by ideological beliefs as well as short-term political considerations. Klaus favored the voucher method because it would transfer property quickly and advance the greater goal of systemic transformation. He often professed his belief that the economy should be owned by private individuals as soon as possible and as much as possible, and that systemic transformation should take precedence over the efficient transfer of particular enterprises.[48] Nevertheless, it is clear that his pressure on companies to reserve large blocks of shares for vouchers was driven by political constraints as well. Once the process began, Klaus feared the political fallout from not having enough property to satisfy the demand of the more than eight million citizens who had bought vouchers. He and Tříska, who had worked out the details of the program, had not anticipated the high level of participation that followed. In fact, they did not order enough voucher booklets, and additional ones had to be printed after the program began.[49]

Klaus had based his reputation on the voucher privatization program, and he was extremely committed to its realization. In fact, he had planned to stake his bid for prime minister on the success of this program. Thus, his anxiety about disappointing the mass electorate made Klaus apply enormous pressure on enterprise managers to assign shares to the voucher scheme and on the founding ministries to select those projects that included high percentages of vouchers.[50] After the election, the pressure was less intense.[51]

While Vrba's ministry did succeed in finalizing several important joint ventures, it was unable to change the general course of Czech privatization. During the first wave, Klaus and Tříska successfully convinced managers to submit vast amounts of shares to voucher privatization. By the second wave, tensions had waned. The privatizers still favored the use of vouchers but were less adamant in cajoling enterprise managers to submit the shares of their entire firm to the voucher program. Furthermore, Vrba no longer posed any threat to the Klaus privatization approach, as he lost his ministerial post following Klaus's election as prime minister.

Before losing his position, however, Vrba was unable to persuade others of the merit of his ideas owing to his symbolic image, an image tainted by his past role in the Communist system. Vrba had been a member of the *nomenklatura* elite before the Velvet Revolution, and although Vrba insists his opposition to vouchers in the early planning stages was technical, his credibility was put into doubt by his professional past. Vrba explains, "I wanted the government to have an industrial policy and I thought the government had to be responsible for restructuring. I thought that certain structures could not be privatized. . . . They said about me: 'Look at him, he is still a Communist and he still wants to govern industry and wants to prolong central control over industry. Vrba just wants to control everything in his hands.' They said I was ruined by living under the Communist system so long and so I could not think in other dimensions. . . . What they said was not true."[52] Vrba claims that his opposition became a form of political resistance to Klaus as the debate over privatization became political: "[When Civic Forum split] I no longer felt comfortable opposing voucher privatization because then the discussions got political and aggressive. 'Those against voucher privatization were in favor of the Communist regime,' according to Klaus. That was his slogan."[53]

Vrba is not unique in attributing his weakened credibility in the privatization debate to anti-Communist politics. Former Education Minister Jan Sokol, a widely respected centrist politician and the former deputy chairman of the Federal Assembly at the time, offered independently a similar interpretation of Vrba's difficulties in advancing his position. When asked why Vrba's ministry did not have more influence, Sokol responded, "Vrba in public is not so convincing. Vrba was formerly communist *nomenklatura* and the director of a factory. This played an enormous role. People just said, 'he is one of them.' There was the belief that his plan would play into the hands of the current management. But of course, this was true for the voucher plan also. The newspapers played it out as capitalism against communism and the public accepted this."[54]

Like several of the 1968 reform Communist economists, the top directors of enterprises and the leaders of labor unions, Vrba was highly constrained by anti-Communism in the post–Velvet Revolutionary ideological context. Vrba exemplifies how the former positions of certain individuals and institutions during the Communist regime directly affected their bargaining position and political power in the post-Communist political environment. While not uniformly true for all political actors and economic groups, it was not uncommon that the more that actors or groups appeared to have benefited from the past regime, the easier it was for others to discredit their opposition to privatization and the more difficult it was for them to oppose radical economic reform in general. Interestingly, the converse was not true: suffering under the past regime translated less reliably into political capital. Several politicians who had been exiled or incarcerated during the Communist period were nevertheless subject to challenges to their character and to accusations of past collaboration, as discussed below.

The Ideological Context in Russia

While the Czech anti-Communist ideological context weakened the power of key economic groups, the same cannot be said for post-Soviet Russia. That is, in Russia there were not equivalent formalized manifestations of anti-Communism as in Czechoslovakia following the Velvet Revolution that broadly disempowered political and economic actors. During the early debates over Russian large-scale privatization, liberals in Russia faced a radically different ideological context than that faced by Václav Klaus and the Czech property reformers. In general, anti-Communist sentiment in Russia was much weaker than in the Czech lands.

The difference in degree of anti-Communist sentiment in these two ideological contexts in the 1990s may be intuitive to most. After all, the Communist Party in Russia had consistently attracted more voters than the Czech Communist Party, with the latter maintaining a weak presence in Czech politics.[55] Moreover, surveys throughout the 1990s capture the difference in popular attitudes toward the Communist past. For example: Speaking to this comparison directly, in the 1993 New Democracies Barometer, 23 percent of Czechs surveyed offered a positive rating of the past Communist regime,[56] in contrast to 62 percent of Russians in 1993, a figure that climbs in Russia to 70 percent by 2000.[57] Also in 1993, only 7 percent of Czechs agreed with the statement "we should return to Communist rule."[58] However, approximately 43 percent of Russians in 1994 agreed with the statement "it would have been better if everything in the country had remained as before 1985." By 1999 almost 60 percent of those Russians surveyed agreed with this statement.[59] The series of New Russia Barometers report similar positive assessments among Russians for the political system before perestroika.[60] Data collected in 1993 by Miller, White, and Heywood reported that in response to the question "Did you ever believe in Communist ideals?" 60 percent of Russians surveyed responded favorably, in contrast to 29 percent of Czechs.[61] And, in response to the question "Did you yourself feel oppressed by the Communist regime?" 11 percent of Russians responded yes, whereas 29 percent of Czechs and 23 percent of Slovaks responded yes.[62]

Public opinion surveys such as these help to underscore the variance in anti-Communist sentiment across countries, and this variance shapes the relative degrees of the legitimacy of actors and institutions in the struggle over property in the post-Communist period. Given this variance in ideological contexts, how did Russian managers and workers benefit from weak anti-Communism and the continued legitimacy of Communist-era institutions and practices? And, more specifically, how did this translate into greater opportunities for increasing share ownership within mass privatization?

Unlike in most other post-Communist states in Eastern Europe, the legislative institutions from the late Soviet period survived into the Yeltsin era and were accepted as legitimate.[63] More important, the members previously elected to the Russian Supreme Soviet maintained their positions. No new elections were called. Thus, when the debates over large-scale privatization began, deputies who had run under a Communist Party platform dominated Russia's legislature.[64] It should be recalled that the deputies serving in 1992 had been elected under conditions that overwhelmingly favored Communist Party candidates. Though some electoral reforms had occurred prior to their election, the effect should not be overstated. For one, the 1990 election for the RSFSR Congress of People Deputies was held within only a few days of the abolition of article 6 in the Soviet Constitution, the article that had previously guaranteed the Communist Party a monopoly on political power.[65] Therefore, practically speaking, article 6 was still in effect for these elections. The registration requirements and the continuation of single-member districts in 1990, moreover, also worked to the advantage of Communist Party–nominated candidates. Thus, elected members of the Russian legislature debating the mass privatization proposals for the most part were ideologically sympathetic, or at least compelled to support employee rights.[66] This stands in contrast to other legislative arenas where privatization was debated among representatives ushered in by the democratic revolutions following the collapse of Communism.

Eventually Yeltsin determined it would be useful to attack the legitimacy of the Russian Supreme Soviet. Following the body's forcible dissolution in October 1993, Yeltsin's administration discredited the Supreme Soviet as Communist holdover in order to justify the government's antidemocratic behavior during this period (behavior including the shelling of the White House, the dismissal of the justices of the Constitutional Court, and the limitations placed on the media). Prior to this time, Yeltsin's economic team had stressed the legislature's frequent attempts to obstruct market reform. In the area of property rights legislation, it is difficult to refute that legislative opposition emerged quickly. Although legislators granted Yeltsin emergency decree powers in October 1991 to carry out his economic program, their support did not last. Indeed the brevity of a honeymoon period in Russia relative to other East European cases is striking. Parliamentary resistance appears as early as January 1992 when Ruslan Khasbulatov, the Speaker of the Supreme Soviet, called for the government's resignation—only two months after the new government had formed.[67]

It was within this environment that Russian managers were able to form alliances with sympathetic members of the federal legislature. Neither the workers nor the managers suffered from Russian anti-Communism. In contrast to the Czech case, Russia never saw the implementation of anti-Communist screening laws that would have left politically appointed enterprise directors anxious about their professional futures. Past power holders had less to fear in an environment in which beliefs about Soviet-era institutions and structures were much more ambivalent. The survival of legislators in the new era and the personnel continuity in managerial circles facilitated alliances among managerial and political elites, allowing a powerful antigovernment block to form and resist Chubais's public-sector reform. Since there were no new legislative institutions or anti-Communist screening laws to dampen managers' expectations and hinder their attempt to seek alliances in parliament, they had much greater power than their Czech counterparts. That is, the *lack* of professional insecurity of parliamentarians elected under the Soviet regime or of managers appointed under the previous system enabled these groups to make bold claims for property. As a result, the Russian privatization team had to cope with formidable political pressures and felt compelled to offer in response numerous exemptions and substantial privi-leges to various groups in order to advance their goal of establishing a Western-style capitalist economy.

Considering Slovakia

While the ability of various groups to gain access to property in Russia certainly highlights the weakness of Czech managers, the issue remains of whether a contrast with Russia serves as the most relevant comparative case here. On the one hand, there are important similarities that should be re-called. Certainly, neither Russian nor Czech managers had held title to indus-trial property under the past regime, and in both cases they worked until the late 1980s with only minimal changes to the command economy. Neither So-viet Russia nor Communist Czechoslovakia underwent substantial reform to the system of state ownership or central party control—unlike Hungary, Poland, and Yugoslavia, which did—such that it might have provided Russian managers with additional material resources. Managers in *both* the Czech and Russian cases gained some autonomy and control in the late 1980s over the daily operations of their enterprises due to industrial organizational reforms. Managers in the late 1980s and early 1990s were for a time subject to the ap-proval of their worker collectives in both country cases.

As suitable as these two cases are for comparative analysis, there are re-gional and size differences between Russia and the Czech Republic that skep-tics could point to as significant. However, even if one were to consider addi-tional cases in which managers were similarly successful in gaining access to privatized property as in Russia, though closer in size and makeup to the Czech Republic, one would still see how the ideological context shapes the ability of groups to alter property reform. For instance, a direct comparison of the ability of Czech and Slovak managers to gain access to property follow-ing the division of the federation illustrates this well. The institutional re-sources and recent historical backgrounds of Czech and Slovak managers are as close as two cases could possibly be, given that they shared a common po-litical and economic space for decades. Yet irrespective of having followed the same path of reform through 1992, Slovak managers were much bolder and much more effective in shaping large-scale privatization after independence than the Czechs were, due to the differing ideological symbolism of each group.

Slovak managers, both as individuals and in groups, successfully lobbied the government to halt and eventually cancel the second wave of voucher privatization after the division of the federation. Rather than privatize through mass distribution, Vladimír Mečiar's government implemented a series of nontransparent direct sales to well-connected industrialists and the directors of large enterprises. Through the direct lobbying of the Slovak Ministry of the Economy by groups such as the Association of Employers Unions (a peak organization aggregating large and medium industrial interests),[68] Slovak managers expanded their realm of influence over property reform and industrial policy.[69] In fact, officials from the Association of Employers Unions consulted directly with the government and parliament on many issues in addition to privatization, such as the budget, foreign trade, and social welfare programs.[70] In the area of property reform in particular, the influence of industrialists was substantial. According to the estimates of a 1997 World Bank study, by the end of 1996, employees and managers acquired nearly two-thirds of the shares of privatized property (if measured in terms of book value) following independence.[71]

Given that institutional structures in the Czech lands and Slovakia were essentially the same, what accounts for the variance in managerial influence? Before considering the influence of ideology, a more immediately intuitive explanation deserves consideration—namely, the difference in material conditions.[72] In particular, did the higher levels of unemployment or sharp economic declines in Slovakia bring greater legitimacy to Slovak managers' demands for a voice in policy discussions? In some respects this did occur and thus could potentially explain some of the variance in privatization outcomes. Quite remarkably, unemployment in Slovakia was nearly four times higher than in the Czech Republic in the months prior to the split.[73] Certainly, Slovak managers could and did exploit public anxiety associated with the capitalist transformation to gain a voice in reform.

Yet, to be precise, although Slovak unemployment was higher, both the Czech Republic and Slovakia reported substantial reductions in industrial jobs during the first three years of transition, with the Czech Republic reporting even slightly greater losses in industrial jobs. Thus, the difference in unemployment levels between the two republics stemmed from the creation of new jobs in the Czech Republic rather than from a more serious decline of existing Slovak industry. As Appel and Gould point out, the higher *total* levels of Slovak unemployment resulted from Slovakia's weaker capacity to create jobs in other sectors (particularly in services and tourism) rather than from a more severely devastated industry.[74] Therefore, in principle there was a strong basis (in terms of public legitimacy) for Czech enterprise directors to make demands on the government's program of privatization, since job losses in the formerly state-owned industrial sector were declining even more quickly than in Slovakia.

One may still argue that overall levels of employment should have been the key indicator of public anxiety, and this public anxiety would have generated support for managerial efforts to reshape privatization and economic reform generally. Surprisingly, however, public fears of becoming unemployed (as measured in survey research) do not accurately reflect the variance in risk of actually becoming unemployed in each republic. According to polls taken in January 1992, 55.5 percent of Slovaks and 53.6 percent of Czechs reported that they were expecting and fearing unemployment in the near future. Similarly, 18.5 percent of Slovaks versus 13.8 percent of Czechs saw unemployment as their biggest problem.[75] Given how similar these measures of Czech and Slovak public sentiment are, there is good reason to assume that both Czech and Slovak managers could have exploited public anxiety about job instability.

Furthermore, it should be noted that both the Slovak and Czech republics experienced a contraction of national production and a loss in real wages. That is, *both* republics suffered declines in industrial output severe enough to produce managerial dissent in *both* countries in 1992 and 1993.[76] Again, it follows logically that if these declines could have legitimated the demands of Slovak managers, the same should have held for Czech managers. After all, why would substantial losses in output fail to serve as a resource for managers in one context and not another? Certainly this undermines an explanation that relies on the difference in material conditions to account for differing outcomes in managerial privileges.

In short, a strictly material explanation would have predicted similar preferences for managers and would have anticipated equivalent degrees of political pressure from managers. Yet this was not the case. As argued elsewhere, the reliance on unemployment to account for alternative preferences or the variance in political pressure can be accused of selectively choosing which "objective economic condition" determines the variance in outcomes.[77] Instead, the differing ideological contexts provide a more powerful explanation.

Important distinctions between the Czech and Slovak ideological contexts in the early 1990s account for differing distributions of power in society, and thus for the varying ability (and preference) of key groups to stake their claims to property during economic reforms. As noted, anti-Communism and pro-Europeanism dominated the post–Velvet Revolution Czech ideological context. While anti-Communism and pro-Europeanism had some resonance in Slovakia, the Slovak ideological context in the early and mid-1990s was dominated instead by questions of Slovak national identity, especially as defined vis-à-vis the Czechs.

Traditionally, Slovaks have been ambivalent toward their Czech partnership, with some Slovaks supporting the union with the Czech lands and others favoring greater autonomy or independence. Throughout the Communist period, those Slovaks favoring the union with the Czech Republic recognized the advantages of the federation for the sake of accelerating economic development and maintaining the predominance of the Slovak identity in a land with large Hungarian and German minorities.[78] Those Slovaks favoring a union at times were criticized for holding patronizing views about the level of their own political maturity and questioning the Slovak nation's capacity for self-administration. In addition, those Slovaks calling for greater autonomy during the Communist period typically argued that the union with the Czech Republic jeopardized the existence of a distinct Slovak identity and emphasized Slovakia's subordinate position within the union.

Hoping to increase Slovakia's influence, Slovak leaders successfully lobbied to transform Czechoslovakia into a federal republic following the Warsaw Pact invasion of August 1968. Nevertheless, federalizing the Czechoslovak state to many seemed insufficient since it did not directly address the desire for real Slovak autonomy. Moreover, as Gould and Szomolanyi argue, the de facto administration of the new state remained in Prague, and the real center of power—the Communist Party—did not change in its organizational structure.[79]

After the Velvet Revolution, Slovaks quickly divided along old familiar lines of unionists and autonomists—a division that was exacerbated by the conflicting interpretations of the Communist experience within Slovakia.[80] As one Slovak specialist explains, despite widespread disdain for the old regime, the system of Communism had transformed an agrarian economy into an industrialized urban economy.[81] In contrast to the Czechs, who had witnessed a relative economic decline under Communism, most Slovaks enjoyed an increase in material consumption.[82] The greater disdain for the Communist past among Czechs relative to Slovaks appears in polling data.

For instance, in the 1993 New Democracies Barometer, 23 percent of Czechs surveyed offered a positive rating of the past Communist regime, in contrast to 50 percent of Slovaks.[83]

Returning to the effect of ideology on interest group power, the Slovak case exemplifies how an ideological context empowers or weakens groups to advance their claims during reform. Initially Slovak managers during the first two years of privatization confronted the same challenges and limitations as their Czech counterparts. For example, they, too, were vulnerable to dismissal due to the lustration law or employee vote and therefore initially remained cautious. Yet as Slovak politicians brought issues of national identity to the fore, Slovak managers found ways to link their demands for a stronger voice in reform to the public debates over national autonomy.

While Slovak managers were timid in the early debates over economic reform, in 1992 they began to openly criticize the direction of economic reform on nationalist terms. For example, Slovak managers argued that Finance Minister Klaus's surprise currency devaluation in the fall of 1991 disproportionately hurt Slovak industry. Specifically, they argued that the devaluation improved Czech exporters' competitiveness abroad but raised the cost of imports for Slovakia's primary and intermediate producers.[84] It was further claimed that the government's international diplomacy intentionally directed foreign investment to the Czech lands.[85] In addition, Slovak industrialists claimed that President Havel's position on eliminating foreign weapons sales would be a burden to Slovakia's industrial base with very little consequence for the Czech economy.

During the debates over economic and political reform, former Premier Vladimír Mečiar masterfully exploited differences in opinions over the appropriate level of Slovak political autonomy within the two republics and effectively misconstrued comments by Czech politicians to bolster his political position.[86] Given Mečiar 's practice of provoking Slovak nationalist sentiment, and given the decades-long controversy over the appropriate political fate of Slovakia, it was relatively simple for Slovak managers to cloak their criticisms of economic reform in the language of national victimization and for this to be accepted as valid. With Slovak economic conditions deteriorating, Ivan Miklos, the first Slovak minister of privatization, writes that Slovak politicians competed among themselves to portray the federal program as an inflexible "Czech invention, created in the Czech environment for Czech conditions, and most importantly, inappropriate for Slovakia."[87] Mečiar openly courted the support of industrial elites and repeatedly accused the governing coalition (KDH-VPN) of not being faithful to "true Slovak interests."[88] In addition to the Movement for a Democratic Slovakia (HZDS), the Christian Democratic Movement (KDH) formally called for a revamping of the country's Czech-driven approach to economic reform.[89] Even the former Communist Party (SDL) and a newly formed association, NEZES (led by Slovak economists-turned-politicians closely associated with Mečiar) voiced similar sentiments.[90] This barrage of criticism from elites across the ideological spectrum successfully linked the governing coalition parties (KDH and VPN) to Prague-centrism in the voters' minds, and Mečiar seldom passed up the opportunity to express his sympathy for the plight of Slovak industry.[91] His strategy of allying with industrialists and questioning the Slovak loyalty of the government proved effective. In the 1992 elections, Mečiar's HZDS emerged from the election as the strongest Slovak political movement in the parliament, having benefited tremendously from the support from managers.[92]

The changing ideological climate—in which issues of national identity and political autonomy were increasingly salient—encouraged and facilitated attempts by industrial elites to place demands on the government to have a greater voice in economic reform. Demands typically included continued price regulation, increased credits for industry, propping up the national currency to facilitate imports of primary goods, and, most important here, the slowdown of industrial privatization. In these demands, managers easily found sympathetic allies to champion these causes. As a result, during and following the negotiations for the division of the country, the managers succeeded in lobbying the government to alter the form of privatization dramatically. Not only was the process delayed, the voucher program ultimately was abandoned in favor of direct transfers in a nontransparent administrative process. Additionally, Mečiar substantially weakened the ownership rights of investment privatization funds and presided over the intensification of clientalization of the Slovak political economy.[93]

Testing the Polish Case

The Slovak case is a powerful example of how the ideological climate can color perceptions and legitimate the claims of particular actors. Other country cases, if studied in detail, illustrate this as well. Consider Poland, a country where anti-Communism played a key role in shaping the distribution of power, but in a counterintuitive way. As in the previous empirical cases, the ideological context in Poland shaped the distribution of power and interests of various actors in a way that strongly influenced the privatization process. Like the Czechs, Polish elites and mass groups were equally oriented toward the West and strongly anti-Communist.[94] However, the ideological context was such that this could not be translated into being antilabor, despite the presence of anti-Communist and anti-Soviet sentiment. The reasons for this are clear: unlike in the Czech Republic, Polish labor was not perceived as a remnant of the past system, but a combatant of the old Communist regime. The decade-long struggle by the trade unions to bring down the Communist regime put labor in a powerful position and rendered them legitimate stakeholders in the new economy. Polish labor had a strong voice in privatization; any attempts to limit the stakes of labor by Polish government officials resulted in diminished and delayed privatization in Poland.

During the famous round-table negotiations in Poland between Solidarity and the Communist government, negotiators on both sides reached an agreement on property rights reforms, promising to transfer large state-owned enterprises to workers. However, following Solidarity's success in the first semifree elections in 1989 and the appointment of Tadeusz Mazowiecki as prime minister and Leszek Balcerowicz as finance minister, neoliberal policy makers attempted to ignore prior agreements to transfer shares to workers and instead championed a more economically liberal course of property rights reform. The first post-Communist finance minister, Leszek Balcerowicz, announced his unequivocal opposition to privatization through transfers to workers. In 1989 Balcerowicz stated during his confirmation hearing before the Sejm, Poland's lower house of parliament: "Our plan is to introduce a western-style market economy. All research and analysis indicates that in such a system there is no place for worker self-management in enterprises, that self-management solutions cannot be effective. In a western-style market economy there simply is no place for self-management."[95]

Krzysztof Lis, the first director of the Polish State Property Committee and an ally of Balcerowicz, expressed similar views on employee ownership. Lis's initial privatization proposal in December 1989 opposed transfers to workers or citizens in general and instead favored traditional case-by-case privatization through direct sales, tenders, or auctions. His proposals were politically untenable, however, generating potent resistance to Polish property reform. Calls for greater employee share ownership came from nearly all sides: leaders in Solidarity, OPZZ, PZPR, the Employers Association, and, of course, the Worker Self-Management Coalition.[96]

Given the broad political support for workers' claims to property, Lis's monetary privatization strategy failed to attract parliamentary support. Instead, the government reached a temporary compromise with the Sejm with the passage in July 1990 of the Act of the Privatization of State-Owned Enterprises, a measure that allowed for 20 percent employee ownership in certain medium-size enterprises with fewer than five hundred workers.[97]

One of the most important indications of labor's power was its right to veto proposals for privatization. As Eric Hanley explains, this power was enormous since it meant the councils could block the process by which they would be dissolved—namely, the first stage of privatization. When a worker council approved the privatization of the firm, it subsequently lost its place to a newly formed supervisory board (consisting of two workers and four appointees of the Ministry of Privatization). Not surprisingly, labor exercised its veto right regularly.[98]

When the Mazowiecki government fell, Balcerowicz continued to serve as the finance minister, but Janusz Lewandowski replaced Lis at the Ministry of Ownership Transformation. Under Lewandowski, the ministry advocated a mass privatization program in which the government would transfer to the population free shares in national investment funds. These funds functioned as mutual funds that would oversee and control shares in Polish industry. In this program, 60 percent of the shares of the funds were reserved for Polish citizens, 30 percent for the Treasury, and 10 percent for employees. A further important component in Lewandowski's program was that the national investment funds would be run by both national and foreign banks and consulting agencies.

Legislative approval of the main mass privatization program in April 1993 (known as the National Investment Funds Privatization Law) did not translate into immediate transfers of ownership rights.[99] In fact, vouchers were only available for trading in November 1995. Thus Polish mass privatization did not begin in earnest until 1996, and even then transfers under the National Investment Funds Privatization Law were limited. This program involved just over five hundred enterprises, or about 5 percent of GDP. By comparison, the Czech mass privatization program involved 1,850 enterprises, despite the fact the Czech Republic's economy is about one-third the size of Poland's economy.[100]

The relatively slow pace of Polish mass privatization is striking. By mid-1994 both the Russian and Czech large-scale mass privatization programs had fully run their courses, but the Polish privatization had transferred only about a half dozen large enterprises. The number of enterprises remained small mainly because a firm's privatization required the approval of the worker council. Given the limited concessions to workers, it is not surprising that many worker councils avoided privatization according to the early privatization legislation.

Throughout most of the process, the major Polish parties and political groupings (from both the left and the right) voiced their strong opposition to privatization, with only a few known liberals, such as Balcerowicz and Mazowiecki, consistently pushing for extensive privatization of medium- and large-scale industry. When the center-right regained control of the parliament in 1997, both coalition partners, AWS (an umbrella party that was a successor of Solidarity) and UW (a party led by Balcerowicz), called for increased privatization in their platforms. Nevertheless, conflicts once again arose over who the new owners should be. While AWS supported privatization through "enfranchisement" (namely, distributing shares to citizens and especially workers), UW favored monetary privatization, arguing that free distribution would deny the government much-needed revenues to fund pension reform and other social welfare programs. During the center-right's second stay in office, new privatization legislation failed to win parliamentary approval. Thus there have been few large-scale enterprises privatized after 1996, although bank privatization has been carried out successfully.

Despite the slow pace of privatization, the Polish private sector as a share of GDP has shown a marked increase. From 1990 to 1999 the percentage of the Polish GDP produced in the private sector grew from 30 percent to 65 percent by some estimates.[101] This increase, however, stems primarily from the small-scale privatization of shops and services, from the liquidation and sale of assets of state to private firms, and from new industrial start-ups.[102] Moreover, further transfers through mass privatization are not expected because the existing Polish national investment fund structure cannot effectively manage many more firms. These funds are already overextended in terms of personnel.

One student of Polish labor and privatization, Agnieszka Paczynska, attributes the delay in privatization to the power and the institutional resources of the trade unions. She explains that even later government attempts to amend the legal framework governing privatization confronted sharp opposition from labor, given the expected decrease in the number of shares distributed to workers in privatized enterprises.[103] To characterize the power of labor, Paczynska offers the following quote from a Polish weekly: "There is no other country in Europe in which union activists are the core of executive and legislative power. . . . The unions have [even] demanded the right to give opinion on the state budget, which would be a clear interference in the prerogatives of the Sejm. Authorities, and not only the current Solidarity group, seem to be intimidated by the power of the unions."[104]

Tracing the position of labor from the early reform debates, Paczynska explains that workers had not opposed privatization initially but wanted to maintain some control over their enterprises. Rather than resisting privatization as a general strategy, worker groups instead focused attention on protecting wages and ensuring the best social package possible.[105] Resistance to industrial privatization grew over time, in particular after the early years of recession. In 1991 support for state ownership was 44.7 percent, but by 1993 support had increased to 59.6 percent.[106]

Ideology and the Political Power of Labor

Even scholars who interpret the implementation of shock therapy as a sign of labor's weakness, nevertheless recognize the central role that labor played in decelerating the pace of privatization.[107] For instance Mark Kramer writes, "The Polish government deliberately accorded a central role to workers in the large-scale privatisation programme. This concession greatly slowed down the rate of large-scale privatisation, but the government was willing to accept that cost in order to maintain social tranquility. . . . Polish leaders recognised the importance of giving workers a voice in key decisions. . . . Each of the [early] governments, especially Suchocka's, did its best to provide workers with a sense that they could have a meaningful voice in decision making without having to resort to work stoppages or other protests."[108]

Indeed, in more than any other context, labor in Poland directly influenced the pace, extent, and nature of industrial privatization. Polish worker councils were better positioned to advance their demands.[109] Not only could

Polish labor representatives easily form alliances with members of the parliament and government, they could discredit actors who failed to appear sufficiently pro-union. In some respects, emphasizing the ability of labor to form alliances to stall privatization misses the true influence of Polish labor. In other words, the question was not whether organized labor could find allies in the Polish legislature or the government. Labor permeated both! As Levitsky and Way correctly point out, the government was never forced to convince the labor unions or the general public "that it was working in the interests of labor, for it was labor."[110] Recall that at the founding moment of the transition, Solidarity served as both a political party and a trade union. Furthermore, the intellectuals who became members of the post-Communist government for the most part won their positions and gained their legitimacy through their contributions to the labor movement in Communist Poland. After the first elections following the roundtable negotiations, nearly all contested parliamentary seats had been won either by Solidarity or the PZPR, the United Polish Workers' Party (the formerly dominant, Communist-era party), both of which relied on the language and symbols of workers. In short, throughout the first decade of reform, the dominant parties in government typically depended on labor's support for legitimacy.

Thus, in contrast to other anti-Communist environments, the key political actors and parties in Poland were not afraid of appearing too supportive of labor. If anything, they recognized the costs of appearing insensitive to the plight of labor in economic transition. Shock therapy proved to be extremely painful for rank-and-file workers, and the initial support of this reform by Solidarity's elite left it politically vulnerable. The series of collapses of the first three Solidarity governments and the eventual fracturing of the alliance occurred because many perceived Solidarity's leaders to have abandoned the cause of labor.

In sum, although anti-Communism was prevalent in both the Czech Republic and Poland, it weakened labor's credibility only in the Czech Republic and hindered its ability to influence the course of economic reform. By contrast, anti-Communism did not weaken Polish labor since Polish labor was not associated with Communism. Rather, Poland's labor movement led the strikes and advanced the Solidarity movement that brought down Communism. Therefore, when Polish labor tried to resist the government's form of privatization, it was effective: it succeeded in delaying and altering large-scale privatization.[111]

Considering the similar starting points of Slovak and Czech managers immediately following the Velvet Revolution, it is striking to observe the clear contrast in the ability of managers to form alliances with key government actors and open a space for themselves in the policy-making process after the country's dissolution. Understanding the greater influence of labor in Poland or managers in Slovakia and Russia, relative to those same actors in the Czech Republic, reveals much about the ideological bases of power and legitimacy that allow groups to advance claims to ownership.

The ideological context as a variable deserves careful consideration when studying power, interests, and regime change. Like material resources, the ideological context leaves some groups better endowed than others. Social actors, like political elites, can tap the ideas and beliefs circulating in society to promote their own vision of economic reform over that of others.

In the Czech ideological context, anti-Communism served to discredit labor's demands in property rights reform. In Poland, labor remained powerful and could influence privatization, despite the presence of anti-Communism, given the different symbolic relationship between labor and Communism. In a similar vein, the prevalence of Czech anti-Communism made Czech managers reticent and shaped their preferences within privatization. In contrast to Russian and Slovak managers, Czech managers were passive in privatization, preferring to minimize the risk of losing their jobs to becoming proprietors of their firms. In Russia, anti-Communism was less prevalent in the political discourse and did not find expression in formal institutions to anywhere near the same extent. Similarly, Slovak attitudes toward the past Communist regime were more benign than in the Czech Republic and after the split of the country, anti-Communism mattered less for privatization than Slovak national sentiment. In post-Soviet Russia and post-independence Slovakia, the legitimacy and hence the power of managers were not in jeopardy. This directly affected their ability to advance their claims to property during the reformulation of the ownership regime.

Carefully analyzing the effects of the ideological contexts in multiple countries shows the theoretical dangers of simplistically assuming that power, legitimacy, or material interests can be easily attributed to others or that self-interests can be easily surmised.

7. The Ideological Foundations of Building Compliance

I n the early theorizing about the process of post-Communist transformation, many scholars in Western academia focused upon the challenges leaders would face in implementing simultaneous political and economic transformation.[1] How would the newly elected leaders carry out difficult capitalist reforms within a structure of electoral politics? Could the new promarket governments rely on a window of opportunity during which the population would tolerate destabilizing economic policies?[2] Or would neoliberal policy makers be blocked by an electorate wanting to punish them for promoting painful systemic reforms? Implicit in this debate was the concern that newly elected democratic leaders would lack the material resources or the political skill to carry out the type of reforms necessary to institutionalize a market economy.

Other theorists warned for the need to tie the hands of future politicians by making the future nationalization of property more difficult.[3] According to this argument, early privatization officials had to design a privatization program to distribute property broadly in the initial phase so that future leaders would find private ownership politically costly to overturn. Making new property institutions appear immutable would signal a credible commitment to the institution of private property.[4] Furthermore, the economic benefits associated with private property rights were more likely to be realized if the rights were seen to be enforceable. Thus, some scholars looked explicitly at the efforts by state actors to signal their commitment. However, even those theorists who considered the *perception* of credibility as crucial ignored the potential ideological resources that the state has at its disposal to shape perceptions or to signal its commitment to the new regime—namely, the instrumental use of ideological symbols and rhetoric.[5]

Not all property rights theory ignores the ideological resources available to leaders in building public confidence in new institutions. Ideology in this most limited sense—that is, ideology as an instrument of legitimization—does feature in some theoretical approaches to property rights change. In his macrohistorical theory of property rights, Douglass North describes ideology primarily as an instrument of the state to justify programs and as a tool of the opposition to attack existing ownership arrangements. Thus, in North's early work, ideas do not drive the evolution of property rights systems, but nevertheless play a role in the maintenance of and challenge to existing property rights.[6] North's later work on institutional change acknowledges that ideology and beliefs can be forces for change, but he does not develop this line of analysis in his work on property rights.[7] Despite North's interest in ideology, the broader body of theoretical literature on property rights change at best mentions ideology as an instrument of state legitimization as an aside. However, it does not incorporate ideology centrally into a theoretical framework.[8]

Other bodies of theoretical literature in the social sciences have focused more explicitly on the instrumental use of ideology, although not in the study of property rights. For example, the literature on social movements attributes various roles to ideas and beliefs and is especially useful in analyzing how politicians frame particular problems.[9] Framing can reshape the public's interpretation of a given situation and can motivate and legitimate a course of action.[10] Social movement theorists Snow and Bedford describe "framing processes" as the processes by which cultural entrepreneurs consciously engage in the production of meaning and provide interpretations to events in order to attract potential adherents to a larger cause.[11] By assigning new interpretations of events or occurrences, framing processes provide a motivation for a given policy agenda.[12] In related work, cognitive political psychologists Tversky and Kahneman demonstrate how framing can lead individuals to make choices that contradict the rational calculation of preferences.[13]

Framing by social movement organizations tends to become more instrumental over time—that is, more consciously strategic and deliberate.[14] As social movements mature, a self-conscious struggle intensifies within the movement over the most effective way to convey the movement's message and over the selection of the most powerful images and symbols to promote a particular interpretation of material reality.[15] Although the primary goal of framing, as it is used in this literature, is to gain new adherents to a movement's cause, it can be more broadly applied. Indeed, the framing process can be directed toward a number of target groups—that is, not only social movement adherents but also movement constituents, "bystander publics, media, potential allies, antagonists and countermovements, and elite decision makers or arbiters."[16] Moreover, many types of cultural entrepreneurs in addition to social movement activists engage in strategic framing—including journalists, clergy, community and interest group leaders, writers, and politicians.[17]

Ideological Compliance Mechanisms

Strategic framing thus can refer to the efforts of leaders to gain compliance to a new institutional arrangement. In organizational theory, "strategic framing" and "framing processes" can be understood as types of normative compliance mechanisms—that is, mechanisms in which leaders tap popular ideologies to highlight the legitimacy of, and win support for, a new arrangement.

Organizational theorist Amitai Etzioni developed the concept of normative compliance mechanisms as part of his three-tiered analytical framework. The framework addresses the types of compliance mechanisms available to any organization to gain the acceptance of its subjects. In addition to normative compliance mechanisms, organizational leaders may employ coercive or remunerative reinforcing mechanisms.[18] Leaders who use coercive mechanisms threaten subjects with incarceration, taxation, or physical violence to gain acceptance to the new regime. If remunerative reinforcing mechanisms are employed, then leaders offer material incentives to gain compliance.[19]

Etzioni's analytical framework and behavioral insights are useful not simply because they reinforce the notion that political leaders, like social activists, rely on strategic framing in order to build support for, or at least compliance to, a political agenda. After all, even those property rights theorists who do not attribute a role to ideology would acknowledge that governments make ideological assertions, even if only to justify or mask a particular agenda. Rather, Etzioni's framework is useful in highlighting that leaders have a choice as to how they build mass compliance. To make this choice, they draw from belief systems to determine which among the three sets of reinforcing mechanisms is most appropriate to reach a given end. It should be stressed that this choice does not merely represent an intellectual exercise by political strategists. On the contrary, this choice can affect the strength of political resistance as well as the content of a policy program—especially when remunerative mechanisms are chosen that require material incentives to be incorporated into a program.

In the founding of a new property rights paradigm in post-Communist Europe, coercive reinforcing mechanisms have (thus far) not been employed to gain general compliance to the new regime. Nevertheless, coercion historically has been an important mechanism for introducing and maintaining a new property rights paradigm, with the case in point being the Soviet experience of collectivization and dekulakization, where violent coercion against the peasantry facilitated the transformation of the ownership regime.[20] Thus, even if coercion does not seem relevant to privatization, given that distributing property should be much less difficult than appropriating property, coercion as a compliance mechanism bears mentioning since the change of any property rights regime can cause social conflict and may require a coercive state to carry out the transformation.

More commonly, privatization officials have relied upon remunerative compliance mechanisms to build support for the new regime. Remunerative reinforcement has taken the form of monetary transfers or property distribution among targeted sectors of the population. For instance, this occurred with restitution programs in several countries in which the heirs of former property owners received houses and land previously appropriated by the Communist government. Taking a different form, the compliance of elite groups was at times won through fixed auctions in which well-connected investors benefited from sweetheart deals. As a further example, broad social compliance was initially achieved through the distribution of enterprise shares. The free transfer of the shares of formerly state-owned enterprises to the population through vouchers could be characterized as employing a type of remunerative compliance mechanism because it was used to ensure participation and support from the population at large.

Contrasting Czech and Russian Ideological Compliance

In the Russian and Czech cases, government officials offered substantial remuneration to win support for privatization. However, in addition to using material reinforcement, Czech leaders in particular *also* strongly relied upon legitimating ideological reinforcement and the framing of debates to win public support. Specifically, Klaus promoted anti-Communist and pro-

European ideas to develop highly effective ideological reinforcing mechanisms. Klaus repeatedly acknowledged the importance of building a base of support by ensuring the legitimacy of the transformation process.[21] His assessment of his own political approach highlights his deliberate campaigning style and stands in stark contrast to how Russian politicians understood their role as technocrats in the early transition period. Indeed, Klaus's words reveal his early comprehension of the importance of developing effective reinforcing mechanisms:

> It is absolutely essential for reformers to have faith in the success of the reforms to be able to inspire all their fellow citizens and be able to establish broad pro-reform coalitions. The reform is not an academic problem: it is a political affair and it is of immense importance to enlist sufficient political support for it. We realized at the very beginning that establishing a political platform was an indispensable part of reform activities. . . . This required immense political and human efforts, hundreds of political tours, and endless meetings with thousands of people—in other words, it required, and still does, a permanent campaign.[22]

Although Klaus openly acknowledged his political campaigning style, he was less candid when characterizing the content of his campaigns. While Klaus claimed to have taken a pragmatic, nonideological, nonpopulist approach,[23] he in fact developed a highly populist program of mass distribution and legitimated his economic approach with an ideologically charged campaign. Specifically, when addressing the greater population Klaus framed his program as the most liberal approach, an approach that would restructure the former Soviet-style planned economy according to "European" or "Western" economic principles. The beginnings of this approach are seen as early as 1989 when Klaus drafted the "Programmatic Principles" and stressed the goal of creating a "normal country" in the center of Europe. One prominent Czech sociologist attributes Klaus's very success to his ability to portray himself and his program as essentially Western, liberal, and European.[24] Thus, while the popularity of the voucher program rested in part upon its populist material incentives—again, it offered free transfers of property—it also was deliberately strengthened by framing processes, or ideological reinforcing mechanisms, that relied on existing territorial referents and historical memory.

As was common at the time, Klaus pursued a pro-European emphasis, which he combined beautifully with a pro-Czech emphasis; in fact, in many instances he made the two seem equivalent. An effective technique that Klaus employed to gain support for his radical program of economic reform was to insist upon its historical appropriateness. His program would "return" the country to its rightful place as a member of the Western community; that is, he would frame the construction of European capitalist property structures in language suggesting a return to a former self, rather than an adoption of a foreign system. In other words, his pro-Europeanism was coupled with a form of pro-Czech nationalism. This pro-Europe/pro-Czech campaign was not unique to Klaus, even if he attempted to appropriate it as his own.[25] "Return to Europe!" was Civic Forum's successful slogan in the June 1990 elections. Interestingly, this slogan manifests the already prominent popular notion of Czechoslovakia as part of Europe and implicitly reaffirms prevailing conceptions of geopolitical divisions by including the word *return*. (After all, the slogan could have also been "To Europe!") Indeed pro-Europeanism resonated with current popular notions of history. It also resonated with perceptions of geographical spheres and with cultural and religious divides, all of which were commonly used to justify the nation's place in a Western rather than Eastern or Slavic civilization. Yet despite the existing pro-European sentiment, the fact that Klaus chose to stress a more European and more integrative approach, rather than fueling a strictly nationalist identity, was in no way preordained; Premier Vladimír Mečiar's ability to give rise to more nationalist identity in Slovakia during the same time period rules out such a presumption. However, given the Czech tradition of asserting its place in Europe, and the popularity of existing slogans, it was not difficult for Klaus to present the property structures of a Western liberal system as essentially Czech and thereby bring legitimacy to his economic approach.[26]

At the same time, Klaus placed himself in stark opposition to anything that smacked of a compromise between Western capitalist and Communist structures. He sought to link the privatization program to a widespread desire to break with the past, which meant disassembling the Communist system and differentiating the country from the Eastern bloc. In the process of defining himself as the leader who would return the Czechs to Europe, he also implied that those less committed to the free market would hold the country back, keeping it in the Communist era. In order to differentiate his own approach as a Western liberal approach, Klaus would frame the alternative programs in a way that suggested they were "third ways," "reform communist," or just plain "socialist." By contrast, Klaus asserted that he "want[ed] a market economy without any adjectives," insinuating that the society must choose between market capitalism or another version of Communism.[27] In an address to Civic Forum, Klaus's view is summarized: "No path of socialism with a human face, no left alternatives or Obroda [communists expelled from the party after the 1968 Soviet-led invasion of Czechoslovakia] can lead to a modern European State. We are not returning to the year 1968, the key year is 1948 . . . we are following the tradition of the First Republic [1918–1938], Christianity, European Civilization."[28]

Essentially, Klaus implied that the alternatives proposed in 1968 by the economists active in the Prague Spring reforms were equivalent to those they proposed in 1990. For example, Klaus described those economists who proposed alternative paths to reform as a "coherent group of originally Marxist intellectuals" who "dream" of "third ways." He writes, "in the sixties this approach was based explicitly, in the eighties only implicitly, on Marxism."[29]

Certainly, Klaus's characterizations were inaccurate, as both he and his opponents advocated the establishment of a private property system. However, given that only a small technocratic elite was adequately trained in the economic theory needed to follow the details of the proposals, Klaus's gross generalizations were effective in shaping public perceptions of the issues dividing the debate. Framing a debate in ideological terms and then relegating the meat of the discussion to groups of recognized technical experts is a deliberate tactic discussed in the literature on social movements. Namely, the choice of a discursive frame can render the public debate of a problem superfluous and in effect confine the discussion to a smaller circle.[30]

The Nature of Czech Anti-Communist Politics

While pro-Europeanism and anti-Communism served the purposes of the reform team to narrow the debate and even to bring legitimacy to Klaus, the degree to which politicians deliberately used anti-Communism to ostracize or defame individuals who lobbied against privatization from within the government is not easy to assess. Klaus's more virulent sources of opposition claim, for instance, that anyone who opposed his rapid privatization would be accurately or inaccurately associated with the Communist period or identified as a Communist holdover.

The best-known example is that of Jan Kavan, who was strongly opposed to Klaus's program of liberal reform. Kavan was a left-leaning dissident who spent twenty years in exile in England and later became the minister of foreign affairs after the Social Democrats took power in 1998. In 1991 he opposed

Klaus's self-professed embrace of Thatcherism. Kavan insisted that he himself, as the only elected member of the Federal Assembly who had lived in Thatcher's England, should know the perils of Thatcherism.[31] People in Klaus's camp labeled Kavan a Communist and a collaborator with the St.B. (Czechoslovak secret police) and Kavan had to make the choice of whether to resign or face a lustration trial. He chose to fight the lustration case brought against him and won in January 1996. In retrospect, Kavan argues that it was his opposition to Klaus's liberalism that led to his lustration case, and his point of view has sympathizers among the left and the center.[32] It is unclear why anyone in the government would have considered Kavan a great enough threat to want to resort to such tactics. Furthermore, it certainly would be false to reduce the lustration policy to a political vehicle to eliminate the government's more vociferous opponents.

That said, Kavan was not the only prominent opposition politician to face questionable accusations of collaboration. Another notable example is Deputy Premier Václav Valeš, who openly opposed Klaus's approach to reform and also confronted accusations of past Communist collaboration by members of parliament. Valeš ultimately resigned as the Czechoslovak deputy prime minister responsible for the economy in September 1991. When submitting his resignation, he formally cited health reasons. However, according to public statements by President Havel, Valeš's resignation was prompted by "unscrupulous" and "unsubstantiated" attacks on him in the Federal Assembly and in the press that insinuated Valeš had collaborated with the St.B.[33]

It is indeed difficult to judge the extent to which Czech anti-Communism was a technique to win public support rather than a tool deliberately used to discredit individuals who could disrupt the privatization program and the reform process in general. Although it is commonly alleged that there was collusion between the media and Klaus's party to defame individuals, no evidence has ever been brought against Klaus for improprieties. Most likely, a deliberate campaign of anti-Communism in the form of a witch hunt, as Kavan suggests, did not occur explicitly. Klaus, who is one of the politicians most associated with this kind of anti-Communist politics, would have had much to lose by adopting this strategy; after all, many of his closest associates could also be identified as former members of the Communist Party.[34] Certainly, Klaus was too clever to use the label "Communist" carelessly, and he tended to be more precise, calling them "reform communists of the 1960s" or just "1968ers."[35] However, the effect was not much different from calling them

Občanská demokratická strana

Figure 7.1. The cartoon, which reads "To the Left—Or with Klaus? It Is Up to You" was distributed by Civic Democratic Party (ODS) in the 1998 parliamentary elections. It represents Klaus's common practice of labeling his opposition as leftist.

Communists. In the early years of the transition, Czechs responded strongly to any label derived from (or containing) the word *Communism*. Klaus understood this and clearly exploited it for as long as it was useful.

The efficacy of anti-Communist tactics began to wane after the 1992 elections, a point at which the Czech voucher program was well under way. Thus, while anti-Communism was an important force that facilitated the liberal design and the early implementation of the privatization program, it became less salient during the later implementation of the program, and in particular during the second wave of voucher privatization—that is, once Klaus's power was consolidated. However, the anti-Communist rhetoric, even if less potent, never entirely left Klaus's vocabulary. His party continued to frame policy debates in this manner and he embraced the language of a crusader against the left. In fact, he vilified the left and employed the rhetoric of anti-Communism even as late as 1998 in his bid for the parliament—as his parliamentary campaign literature shows.

Russia and Ideological Reinforcement

In Russia, President Yeltsin's reformers adopted a different approach to social compliance than the Czech reformers. Although the Russian leaders did seek to build mass support for economic reforms and were concerned with the appearance of fairness, for the most part they relied upon material incentives to promote the mass privatization process. In fact, their own writing and public statements reveal their tendency to eschew ideological campaigns and political slogans, favoring instead tangible material incentives. Anatoly Chubais, the architect of Russia's mass privatization program, explained the future viability of the program, submitting that, "as it has been planned . . . each citizen of Russia will in reality become a proprietor, not at the level of slogans and appeals, but at the level of a monetary document in his pocket. The implementation of this program will itself become an irrevocable guarantee for [a] more comprehensive process of reforms."[36] As Russian privatization officials themselves acknowledge, they sought to advance the process by buying popular support with a voucher mechanism and employee benefits and by co-opting powerful groups through granting numerous concessions, privileges, and exemptions. In a speech to the Congress of People's Deputies, Chubais stated: "A legal framework has been laid down to get privatization really moving. It is essential to this end to achieve a correct balance of interests of all social groups involved. . . . The privileges and exemptions provided under our privatization program are the largest in the entire history of privatization throughout the world. At the same we are convinced that it is equally impossible to get privatization moving without providing effective incentives."[37]

Yeltsin's property reformers simply refused to frame the transformation using nationalist rhetoric. They rejected the idea that there was anything distinctly Russian within the program. Their twin refusals stemmed from their unfaltering belief in the idea that all people are economic beings. Therefore, if the economic incentives were substantial, they saw no need for an ideological framework to build support. Their approach resulted from their belief that all people are rational, self-interested actors who respond automatically and predictably to material incentives.

Their public statements and scholarly publications confirm this attitude directly. For instance, Maxim Boycko in collaboration with others wrote in the paper "Hunting for Homo Sovieticus" that there was nothing unique to the Russian nation to preclude the implementation of a liberal capitalist regime.[38] The paper used survey research to demonstrate that Russian and American attitudes resembled each other and that individuals in both groups would respond well to capitalist incentives.

According to his logic, any legitimating campaigns linking privatization to specifically Russian cultural or historical symbols, or any revision of the program to make it appear particularly suited to the Russian context, would imply that Russians do not respond rationally to material incentives. In turn, this would suggest that the Russian nation somehow fit outside the liberal economic paradigm—thereby rejecting the universal premise of their liberal belief system. In a similar vein, Piotr Aven, minister of economic relations and an economist working with Gaidar, speaks to this point directly: "There are no special countries. All countries from the point of view of an economist are the same in what concerns the stabilization of their economies."[39] Peter Rutland explains that this idea found strong support "in the West, where the consensus seemed to be that the logic of supply and demand knew no national boundaries."[40]

Moreover, the Russian privatizers did not see it as their place to launch a cultural campaign, since they thought of themselves as economic technocrats and not politicians—a distinction they themselves make clear.[41] Undertaking an explicitly ideological campaign was distasteful to the reformers, as such a campaign would have smacked of the Communist era. In Boris Yeltsin's memoirs, the former president criticizes his team of liberal economic reformers for not wanting to "dirty their hands with politics."[42] Even Yeltsin himself was uncomfortable using ideology to build political support during his early years of power. George Breslauer and Catherine Dale note Yeltsin's early public rejection of a national ideology. In charting Russia's course of systemic transformation, Yeltsin told the Supreme Soviet in 1992 that "we do not need a new –ism to solve Russia's problems"; in the new Russia, populations will be "liberated from arbitrariness and ideological chains."[43]

Thus, in contrast to the Czech officials, Yeltsin and his reformers initially attempted to establish an entirely new system of property relations without developing ideological reinforcing mechanisms. Although both the Czechs and the Russians certainly sought to present their privatization programs as distributionally just, only the Czech reformers attempted to link the creation of the new property regime to the founding of a post-Communist national identity. In Russia, the exclusive emphasis on material incentives and the blatant lack of ideological justification for mass privatization greatly hindered the Russian property reformers' attempts to implement and sustain the privatization program as they designed it. Ultimately, it led them to concede certain privileges to factoral, sectoral, and regional groups against their preferences, and even against some of the liberal ideals that inspired the construction of a new property regime.

Not surprisingly, Yeltsin's political opposition exploited the government's inattention to symbolic politics and its failure to link the reform program to cultural or historical legitimating symbols.[44] During the implementation of voucher privatization, Yeltsin's opponents discredited the program by portraying it as a challenge to the Russian identity.[45] The perceived "foreignness" of privatization undermined the efforts of the privatization team because many Russian politicians began to portray private property, and liberal reforms more generally, as a Western imposition and alien to Russians. For example, prior to the 1996 presidential elections, Communist Party candidate Gennadii Ziuganov wrote, "Russia is an autonomous economic organism with laws of operation that make it fundamentally different from the Western model of a "free" market. Today, this unique organism is gravely ill. . . . The main cause of illness has been the attempt at capitalist restoration, undermining the material and spiritual foundations of society and government and increasingly exposing the inherent incompatibility of Western bourgeois civilization and Russian civilization. Capitalism organically does not fit with the flesh and blood, the way of life, the habits and psychology of our society . . . today it is not taking root—and will not take root—in Russian soil."[46] Numerous industrial and parliamentary leaders similarly exploited the symbolic implications of a capitalist regime for Russia's geopolitical and cultural identity. For instance, influential industrialist organizer Arkadii Volsky asserted very early in the process, "A real transformation of the market is not possible without considering national traditions and specific features of our country."[47] Volsky claimed that radical, swift privatization would fail since it ignored "the mentality of the Russian people, who have been told for decades that private property is awful."[48] As was common among opponents at the time, Volsky stated, "The only possible model for Russia is Russia. . . . We must build our model in our own way."[49] Other political opponents in the legislature would attack the government's reform path more strongly than Volsky, claiming that "the current leadership is going to deliver the country into bondage to the West."[50] And while many of the strongest diatribes against Western economic models came from actors and groups whom the foreign press portrayed as opponents of democracy and freedom, some moderates writing for centrist newspapers expressed similar sentiments as well. As one mainstream journalist characteristically writes, "The past five years have proved that the Western 'liberal idea' is alien to Russian society and may even be fatal if the 150-million strong Russian people turn into a community of self-centered individuals putting their personal rights and freedoms above anything else."[51]

The Campaign for the Russian Idea

The government's appreciation of the value of linking capitalist economic reform to a legitimating Russian ideology (especially one relating to the formation of a new national identity) would follow only several years later. After Yeltsin's difficult reelection in 1996, the president appointed Georgy Satarov to head a commission to be responsible for articulating a "Russian idea." Largely in response to the public backlash against economic reforms, the government was determined to bring legitimacy to the years of post-Communist transformation. The earliest parliamentary hearings to discuss the formulation of the Russian idea focused primarily on defining the Russian nation. The concept of a national identity based on an economic ideology proved to be especially sensitive, as one deputy minister pointed out during the hearings, since under the new Russian constitution no ideology could be considered as compulsory or state sanctioned.[52] Thus, while a national ideology per se was not under discussion, the government nevertheless recognized the need for ideological legitimization of the social transformation. Satarov wrote at the time that the government had become convinced that "people experience extreme discomfort for the lack of such unifying axis (national idea)."[53] As part of this campaign, *Rossiiskaia gazeta*, a semiofficial newspaper, ran a competition for readers to submit the "best idea for Russia," offering a cash prize as an incentive.[54]

After one year Satarov had accomplished so little that he was replaced by a more prominent and seemingly more effective administrator, Boris Nemtsov, the former liberal governor from Nizhny Novgorod, then serving as first deputy prime minister. It was not until 1997 that the Russian government chose to promote an ideology of the "people's capitalism" with the goal of emphasizing both patriotism and economic liberalism. As one Russian journalist remarks, this was the first time during the post-Soviet period that the government adopted patriotic slogans as part of a campaign promoting economic reforms.[55] However, in 1997 the attention to the popular legitimacy of privatization and capitalist reform, broadly speaking, was late in coming. By this time the legitimacy of large-scale privatization had already been tainted by favoritism, collusion, and other forms of corruption.[56]

To anyone familiar with the Russian economic reform team, a contrast between Chubais's and Klaus's use of pro-Western symbolic legitimization may seem suspect. Were not Yeltsin's economists as pro-Western as the Czechs and similarly pursuing a pro-Western agenda? Indeed, they were. To be clear, there is no reason to contest that both the Russian and Czech architects of privatization were liberal and essentially pro-Western. Moreover, in both country cases, ideas about the nation's post-Communist identity and beliefs about the country's place in the international community were important for the reformers' approach to designing regime change. In Russian mass privatization, particularly during the early stages of reform, beliefs about Russia's global identity held by both the architects of, and the participants in, privatization shaped the development of the polity and the economy. However, the key difference between the Klaus team and the Chubais team is that the latter's pro-Western sentiment was not the basis for selling liberal economic reform at home. At best, any Russian rhetorical embrace of a pro-Western economic reform agenda was intended for international and not domestic consumption.

The distinction is important since it relates to the differing popular attitudes toward Europe, the West, and a country's historical experience with Communism. The Czech leadership's pursuit of greater integration with the Western community and further alienation from the Soviet sphere were goals widely shared by political opponents and mass groups. In the post-Soviet context, however, support for a Russian rapprochement with the West has been much more ambivalent. Certainly, Yeltsin's top privatization officials appeared to strongly favor a Western economic orientation: they invited Western economists to advise them and often modeled new market structures on existing Western institutions. They even commissioned Westerners, especially Americans associated with Harvard University's Institute for International Development, to help draft much of the property rights legislation, using Western economic aid to finance this assistance.

However, unlike in the Czech case, the government's early pro-Western, pro-liberal economic attitudes were not explicitly used to reinforce the process of reform in Russia. Not only did the Russian economists not take it upon themselves to do so, their orientation toward a Western, capitalist system had a more limited appeal (especially relative to the Czech case).[57] Since the inception of market reforms, the rejection of the communist past in favor of a Western liberal regime has often been interpreted in post-Soviet Russia as a repudiation of Russia's past and national character. Aleksandr Tsipko, a prominent Russian intellectual, writes "Anti-Communism [is seen] . . . by ordinary people as an attempt to destroy their dignity and the life they have lived. . . . This is all part of the importance of identifying with the new system as a system that is essentially their own, not imposed, but Russian. The new system rejects the past, a distinctly Russian past and gives the people something foreign instead."[58]

The perceived "foreignness" of Russian privatization undermined the efforts of the economic reform team because many Russians began to see industrial privatization, and economic reforms more generally, as alien to them and as challenges to their identity.[59] Given the existing ideological climate in which the West was perceived by the general populace and elites with ambivalence, the Western or foreign connotation of the large-scale privatization program became problematic in Russia. This was not foreordained, since certainly there were some sectors of the population that were pro-Western and idealized the Western economic system. However, by ignoring entirely the Western association of the capitalist reform agenda and remaining essentially passive, Yeltsin's economic team allowed the opposition to make the case for them, with an entirely different set of intentions.

8. The Ideological Fit and the Cost of Compliance

T he previous discussion of the Russian ideological climate—and its relevance to the implementation of a liberal economic reform agenda—leads us to the final means through which ideas shape privatization outcomes. This final path relates to the relationship between the ideological bases of reforms and a given ideological context. In analyzing the role of ideology on several dimensions, this book concludes with the following contention: the implementation of a program of transformation is least costly and most effective when the ideas underlying those programs are easily compatible with the existing ideological context—that is, when they resonate with the dominant beliefs of elite power holders, economic groups, and mass society, and are not perceived to conflict with existing norms.

The notion of an ideological compatibility between an economic paradigm and a particular social context has its roots in Max Weber's *The Protestant Ethic and the Spirit of Capitalism.* In Weber's argument that beliefs (i.e., Protestantism or Calvinism) shaped the evolution of capitalist economic structures, he notes that capitalist ideas could not have taken hold in any given context. According to Weber, there must be a resonance or an "elective affinity" between ideas and context.[1] In a similar vein, John Stewart Mill wrote, "Ideas, unless outward circumstances conspire with them, have in general no very rapid or immediate efficacy in human affairs; and the most favorable outward circumstances may pass by, or remain inoperative, for want of ideas suitable to the conjuncture. But when the right circumstances and the right ideas meet, the effect is seldom slow in manifesting itself."[2]

The "elective affinity" or the "compatibility" between a particular ideological context and an economic paradigm has also been studied by contemporary political economists who focus on the role of ideas in the introduction of new economic regimes. Peter Hall, Kathryn Sikkink, and others theorizing on the role of ideas explore the importance of the "fit" between the ideas of specific groups in society and the ideas underpinning new economic paradigms for how those paradigms are received and supported.[3] This work emphasizes that a new economic program takes on certain meanings and connotations as it enters an existing constellation of prevailing ideas.[4]

The importance of ideological compatibility becomes clear when we compare the political resistance that privatization officials faced and the costs of social compliance in the Czech and Russian cases. In the Czech Republic, political officials facilitated the implementation of privatization by portraying it as anti-Communist (such as with the restitution laws), pro-European (with the institutionalization of a private system of ownership), and thus essentially Czech. It was relatively easy for the Czech reformers to argue this logic by contending that the Communist system was imposed and reinforced from without and needed to be replaced by a system more appropriate to the Czech context—that is, a European system. Given existing territorial and cultural referents, it was straightforward for Václav Klaus to make the creation of a new property system part and parcel of the development of a European-Czech identity.

Given the differences in ideological contexts, a similar strategy would have been substantially more complicated in Russia. Since the inception of market reforms, the rejection of the Communist past in favor of a new Western liberal orientation has often been interpreted in post-Soviet Russia as a rejection of oneself and demeaning to one's past. And while history is certainly subject to reinterpretation and distortion, it would have required a substantial effort to portray persuasively the adoption of capitalism (and private property) as a return to a former self. Russian politicians could not with the same ease as Czech politicians reject Communism as alien. Nor could they overlook the foreign connotation of a liberal property rights system. It would have required not only charisma and skill to promote such a campaign but also *willingness* on the part of reformers. Thus, while a liberal property reform that adapted structures from Western capitalist economies to the Russian context could have been portrayed in more amenable light to the Russian population, this would have required the development of an aggressive ideological framing campaign by privatization officials.

Without suggesting that the ideological beliefs of dominant groups are fixed or that the cultural significance or symbolism of a new economic project is immutable, it is necessary to emphasize here that certain contexts are simply more amenable to particular types of reform. Reorienting the ideological context is possible, but it requires exceptional leadership and carries a high cost.

The malleability of social norms or ideological contexts may undermine a power-of-ideas argument in the eyes of some. If widely held ideas and beliefs are subject to manipulation, how do ideas matter during implementation? That is, if distributive issues can be reframed or programs can be repackaged to fit a given context, how does the ideological context constrain the development of property rights structures?

To put it in Gramscian terms, particular ideologies take root organically in some contexts more naturally than others. Antonio Gramsci made clear that political reeducation and the reorientation of society must start with the beliefs that already dominate society. In this vein, Gramscian theorists note that the reception of a new ideology depends upon the extent to which it builds upon an existing stock of beliefs, identities, and myths. As Snow and Bedford write, "There is no such thing as a *tabula rasa* or empty glass into which new and perhaps alien ideas can be poured."[5] There is a cost to introducing a new paradigm, and that cost depends upon the ideas already prevalent in society. As the Czech and Russian cases show, ideology constrains and distorts the implementation of property reform when the ideas behind the design of a program do not fit (relatively) effortlessly with the ideological context *and* when political entrepreneurs lack the skill or the will to develop ideological reinforcing mechanisms that avoid changes within the structure of the program.

Consider the Russian experience. The liberal economic beliefs of the Russian privatizers prevented them from developing effective reinforcing mechanisms. Anatoly Chubais rejected, as a matter of principle, the necessity of developing an ideological legitimating campaign. He refused to associate the privatization program with positive Russian symbols and neglected to find those elements in the program, as Klaus did, which showed how the transformation of the economic regime would reinforce existing political norms or a post-Communist identity. Thus, given the lack of an immediate resonance between the liberal ideas behind privatization and the ideas of elite and nonelite groups, and given the indifference (if not refusal) on the part of the

Russian privatizers to creating ideological reinforcing mechanisms, the incompatibility between the ideas supporting the program and the ideological context had a generative effect on policy content. Namely, in the Russian case, it required the privatizers to employ and constantly escalate materialist appeals to various groups. These material concessions changed the nature of Russian mass privatization such that the final program in certain respects resembled more the preferences of industrialists like Volsky and Khasbulatov than it did the preferences of Chubais and Gaidar.

By altering the program to include, at least formally, greater privileges for labor and managers, Russian officials in essence made the program more compatible with the ideological convictions of key political groups in the legislature and the economy. However, this alteration within the program was not part of a liberal ideological campaign that they initiated (in which existing aspects in the program received a special emphasis), but rather a compromise grudgingly conceded in order for property reform to be realized quickly.[6] This marked programmatic revision demonstrates how a lack of compatibility can lead to tangible changes in the new ownership arrangement.

In short, through the development of an ideological legitimating campaign, the Czech reformers were able to equate the institutionalization of a European or Western-style property regime with a return to a former self and to bolster the privatization process. Klaus played on the notion that a European property system was organic to the Czech soil, and its (re)establishment could be understood as part of the process of rebuilding what had been repressed. In contrast, in post-Soviet Russian society, European or Western symbols and policy programs lacked an existing equivalent nationalist connotation,[7] thereby increasing the costs of political reinforcement. Ultimately, these costs were determinative since they were higher than reformers could or were willing to pay.

In sum, the loss of an empire and an ideology left the Russian identity in tatters. The construction of Western structures—without employing an alternative ideological legitimating mechanism—served as one more blow against the Russian purpose and position in the world. While an ideological campaign in Russia based largely on liberalism or on the West would not likely have allowed the government to overcome pressures to transfer large amounts of shares to employees, and may have proved excessively costly in terms of human effort and skill, there is no reason to reject the possibility that a differently designed, ideological reinforcing mechanism could have strengthened the process of property reform. The liberal ideas underpinning the privatization program could have been repackaged to appeal to the dominant culture. That is, the privatizers could have avoided any Western connotation, appealing instead to the Russian desire to be seen as part of the "normal" or "civilized" world—words that reverberate throughout Russian popular discourse. The Russian privatizers' rejection of ideological reinforcing mechanisms exacerbated the need to offer vast privileges and concessions to different economic groups against their policy preferences, and even against some of the ideals that inspired the construction of a new ownership system.

Ideology is important not only for the way in which leaders "sell" a path of reform to the larger public; leaders also draw upon particular sets of ideological beliefs when deciding how to build support for a new economic paradigm. One curious element of the Russian-Czech comparison is that the leaders of the Czech privatization process seem ideologically quite similar to those leading the Russian process. Nevertheless, these two teams of promarket, liberal economists held very different beliefs about their roles as technocrats and their roles as politicians. Furthermore, the Russian leaders, most notably Anatoly Chubais, subscribed to the belief that material incentives were sufficient to generate a desired popular response, whereas the Czech team, and especially Václav Klaus, recognized the political advantages of ideological legitimization for shaping popular attitudes and behavior.

Does this imply that Chubais was more liberal than Klaus? I doubt that such a case could be made. More important, the exercise would represent a misunderstanding of both the nature and the power of ideology. Asserting that the leaders of both the Russian and Czech privatization movements were economic liberals does not require rank-ordering them. Moreover, in order to argue that ideology determines the choices of actors, it is not necessary to show that these actors subscribe to an ideology with equal fervor or with identical interpretations. As Joseph Schull argues, the subscribers to a shared ideology need not, and typically do not, share identical beliefs. An ideology— even if interpreted differently by various actors—wields power nevertheless since it constrains choices and delimits the realm of possible options.[8] Stating the case more strongly, Peter Hall asserts that the ambiguity of an idea or the multiple interpretations of an ideology enhances its power rather than detracts from it.[9] Multiple meanings allow diverse groups to unite on common ground. In post-Communist Europe, economic liberalism indeed was understood somewhat differently and thus applied differently depending upon the context. Nevertheless, leaders who understood themselves to be undertaking a liberal economic agenda enjoyed certain advantages (advantages that often served to reinforce the liberal orientation of their agenda). First, it provided a means to forge relationships or alliances with similarly minded leaders domestically and regionally. Second, in some contexts (but not all) this stance lent professional credibility by virtue of one's association with a community of internationally recognized experts. Third, a liberal orientation that provided policy direction in one issue area could provide guidance or suggest policy options in other realms.

Lessons from Post-Communist Privatization

Many of the findings in this study on privatization and ideology are relevant to officials seeking to carry out structural reforms in a variety of areas. For example, this study shows that ideological appeals can be as effective as material incentives in building a base of support, if not more so. In fact, the findings suggest that leaders who are more sensitive to the symbolic implications of their programs and the perceptions of affected actors are more likely to achieve success during implementation. Second, this analysis demonstrates that leaders who are ideologically rigid in the way they pursue their goals may fall short of achieving their ultimate policy agenda. Hence, ideology can strongly drive the ends of reform, but it should not overly restrict the means. Third, material incentives may work to win support for a program of reform. Usually, however, they are more expensive than ideological appeals. Moreover, the costs of incorporating material incentives may be so great that they distort the outcome and even the initial objectives of a reform agenda.

Fourth, the observations of post-Communist privatization in this book discredit the previously recommended strategy of insulating the technocrats responsible for carrying out structural reforms.[10] Instead, it supports a strategy where both political leaders and technocrats actively engage in building popular support for structural reforms, especially with ideological reinforcing mechanisms. Some East European politicians, most strikingly Václav Klaus, understood and exploited the symbolic significance of capitalist reform from the very beginning, whereas others in Poland and Russia, like Leszek Balcerowicz and Anatoly Chubais, appreciated much more slowly the value of selling their programs on an ideational level to the public at large.

On a related point, this study shows that leaders can benefit from highlighting the elements of their programs that resonate with dominant ideological and theoretical trends in the international lending and advising community. Such efforts may attract resources that tip the political balance in their favor within the domestic political arena. Thus, leaders can enjoy substantial advantages in their domestic political battles when they are "cosmopolitan" enough to know how to appeal to, and negotiate with, lending officials.[11] However, pleasing the international community in this respect is still second to winning the support of domestic constituents. This cannot be stressed enough. Ultimately, leaders like Brazil's President Lula da Silva might accomplish more of their policy agenda by actively selling their program to trade unions and managerial groups and by taking their programs to the far reaches of the countryside than by hobnobbing with IMF and World Bank officials.

Analyzing the role of ideology in structural reform not only suggests certain avenues for accomplishing policy goals and institutionalizing new political and economic arrangements, it also exposes important gaps in the academic literature on post-Communist privatization. Most directly it compensates for the blind spots within standard materialist explanations, such as the failure to account for the variation in the perception of interests and power among similar groups across countries. In addition, a careful study of ideological factors helps to avoid the mistaken assumption of a unidirectional diffusion of policy ideas from the West to the East, or from foreign advisers to national officials. In other words, acknowledging how local leaders' innovative ideas and normative convictions shaped privatization serves to disabuse Westerners of the notion that external actors coercively imposed a particular model of property reform on passive local actors. Moreover, the excessive focus on the IMF and the World Bank's influence on capitalist reform in transition countries misses the ideological and political appeal that fast and extensive privatization had for national leaders.[12] Thus it not only denies domestic leaders the credit for the development of techniques to institutionalize new private property systems, it is condescending to national leaders because it attempts to shield them from the responsibility for the poor economic performance in much of the region in the early years of transition.

Without question, the pain of systemic reform brought about great material uncertainty and caused acute suffering for millions of people. When evaluating the architects of privatization and judging the outcomes of their efforts, however, we should not lose sight of the context in which the region's privatizers found themselves in the early 1990s. That is, before extolling the virtues or condemning the missteps of privatization's technocrats—or even the foreign advisers, for that matter—it is necessary to return to the situation on the ground during the early 1990s. As disappointing as privatization has been for many living in the region, one must remember the sense of urgency of reform and, in Russia, the economic crisis (and even the fear of famine) at the time of Communism's collapse. Throughout the region, leaders faced real uncertainties about the strength of former Communist elites at home and the possibility of a resurgence of hardliners in Moscow. Moreover, the newly appointed or elected leaders who designed privatization had mainly academic, not policy-making, backgrounds. Finally, recall that policy design had to move forward despite weak empirical information and unreliable statistical data and despite the lack of precedent for transforming a planned economy into a market economy. Only with these realities and constraints in mind can we evaluate the choices and the motivations of privatization officials.

East European leaders faced the daunting task of fundamentally changing their country's systems of governance and exchange. The motives of new leaders like Chubais, Vasiliev, Klaus, Ježek, Balcerowicz, and others examined in this book were grander than can normally be said of career politicians working under ordinary circumstances—even if the motives and the behavior of some of these key actors appeared to change significantly over time.[13] Considering the scope of their project, it becomes even clearer that public sector reform in the initial years of transition was both ideologically driven and largely idealistic. Revolutionary change of the kind that occurred in post-Communist Europe rests upon and even relies upon leaders activating ideas and following their vision of the kind of society they hope to create.

Notes

Chapter 1. The Ideological Determinants of Post-Communist Economic Reform

1. Harvey Feigenbaum and Jeffrey Henig, "The Political Underpinnings of Privatization: A Typology," *World Politics* 46, no. 2 (1994): 185–208.

2. For a formal study demonstrating the tendency to link personal material conditions and ideas about private property, see Joan Debardeleben, "Attitudes Towards Privatization in Russia," *Europe-Asia Studies* 51, no. 3 (1999): 447–65.

3. The terms *voucher privatization* and *mass privatization* are used interchangeably in this book. They refer to the large-scale privatization programs in post-Communist countries in which the state distributed vouchers or coupons to the country's citizens (or residents) for free or for a small administrative fee. These vouchers were then tradable for shares in public enterprises.

4. See Oleh Havrylyshyn and Donal McGettigan, "Privatization in Transition Countries," *Post-Soviet Affairs* 16, no. 3 (2000): 257–86, and Debardeleben, "Attitudes Towards Privatization in Russia." Especially critical assessments are Black, Bernard, Reinier Kraakman, and Anna Tarassova, "Russian Privatization and Corporate Governance: What Went Wrong?" *Stanford Law Review* 52 (July 2000): 1731–90; Marshall Goldman, *The Piratization of Russia: Russian Reform Goes Awry* (New York: Routledge, 2003); Ira Lieberman and Robi Veimetra, "The Rush for State Shares in the 'Klondyke' of Wild East Capitalism: Loans-for-Shares Transactions in Russia," *George Washington Journal of International Law and Economics* 29, no. 3 (1996): 737–68; Andrew Weiss and Georgiy Nikitin, "Effects of Ownership by Investment Funds on the Performance of Czech Firms," in *Designing Financial Systems in Transition Economies: Strategies for Reform in Central and Eastern Europe,* edited by Anna Meyendorff and Anjan Thakor (Cambridge, Mass.: MIT Press, 2002); Gerhard Schusselbauer, "Privatization and Restructuring in Economies in Transition: Theory and Evidence Revisited," *Europe-Asia Studies* 51 (January 1999): 65–83; Philippe Aghion, Olivier Blanchard, and Wendy Carlin, "The Economics of Enterprise Restructuring in Central and Eastern Europe," *CEPR Discussion Paper no. 1058* (London: Centre for Economic Policy Research, 1994); Ralph Heinrich in *Privatization, Corporate Governance and the Emergence of Markets,* edited by Eckehard Rosenbaum, Frank Bonker, and Hans-Jurgen Wagener (New York: St. Martin's Press, 2000).

5. Countries implementing mass distribution programs include Armenia, Bulgaria,

Czech Republic, Georgia, Kazakhstan, Kyrgyz Republic, Lithuania, Moldova, Poland, Romania, Russia, Slovakia, Ukraine, and Uzbekistan.

6. Harry Broadman, "Ownership and Control of Russian Industry" (paper prepared for OECD Conference on Corporate Governance in Russia, Moscow, 31 May–2 June 1999), 2.

7. John Nellis, "Time to Rethink Privatization in Transition Economies?" *International Finance Corporation Discussion Paper 38* (Washington, DC: World Bank, 1999), 16.

8. David Ellerman, "Lessons from Eastern Europe's Voucher Privatization," *Challenge* 44, no. 4 (2001): 14–37.

9. David Ellerman, "Voucher Privatization with Investment Funds: An Institutional Analysis," World Bank Policy Research Paper No. 1924 (1998); Joseph Stiglitz, "Whither Reform" (paper prepared for the Annual Bank Conference on Development Economics, Washington, DC, 28–30 April 1999), 21–22; Bernard Black, Reinier Kraakman, and Anna Tarassova, "Russian Privatization and Corporate Governance: What Went Wrong," Stanford Law School John Olin Program in Law and Economics, Working Paper No. 178, September 1999.

10. Nellis is quoting William Megginson and Jeff Netter, "From State to Market: A Survey of Empirical Studies on Privatization" (paper presented to the Global Equity Markets Conference, Paris, December 1998). Nellis, "Time to Rethink Privatization," 3.

11. Joseph Stiglitz made this unambiguously clear in a recorded public lecture in Claremont, California, 6 April 2002.

12. Stiglitz, "Whither Reform?" 21–22.

13. Some of the discussion on the determinative force of ideology in this and subsequent chapters draws from Hilary Appel, "The Ideological Determinants of Liberal Economic Reform: The Case of Privatization," *World Politics* 52, no. 2 (2000): 520–49.

14. Public address at the National Convention of the American Political Science Association, Washington, DC, 28 August 1997.

15. See Mark Blyth, *Great Transformations: Economic Ideas and Institutional Change in the Twentieth Century* (New York: Cambridge University Press, 2002); Kathleen McNamara, *The Currency of Ideas: Monetary Politics and the European Union* (Ithaca: Cornell University Press, 1998); Kathryn Sikkink, *Ideas and Institutions: Developmentalism in Brazil and Argentina* (Ithaca: Cornell University Press, 1991); Judith Goldstein and Robert Keohane, eds., *Ideas and Foreign Policy: Beliefs, Institutions and Political Change* (Ithaca: Cornell University Press, 1993).

16. Malcolm Hamilton, "The Elements of the Concept of Ideology," *Political Studies* 35, no. 1 (1987): 38.

17. This aspect (the moral imperative, the ought and not just the is) of ideology is developed in Clifford Geertz, "Ideology as a Cultural System," in *The Interpretation of Cultures* (New York: Basic Books, 1973).

18. Hamilton, "The Elements of the Concept of Ideology," 36.

19. Sven Steinmo's work on ideas recommends that scholars limit their discussion of "ideas" to problem solutions and that they not use the term *idea* to refer to other mental constructs like norms, beliefs, culture, and so on. Thus Steinmo's specification of the term *ideas* captures this one component or aspect of an ideology. Sven Steinmo, "A Political Economy of Policy Ideas: Tax Policy in the 20th Century," MS, November 2001.

20. Some Marxist scholars of ideology when emphasizing the manipulative aspect of

ideology argue an ideology "naturalizes" the political order by masking ideological propositions as truth claims. See Jorge Larrain, *The Concept of Ideology* (London: Hutchinson, 1979), and the discussion of Larrain and other neo-Marxists in Rhys Williams, "Religion as Political Resource: Culture or Ideology?" *Journal for the Scientific Study of Religion* 35 (December 1996): 368–78.

21. See reviews by Albert Yee, "The Causal Effects of Ideas on Policies," *International Organization* 50, no. 1 (1996): 69–108, and Sheri Berman, *The Social Democratic Moment: Ideas and Politics in the Making of Interwar Europe* (Cambridge, Mass: Harvard University Press, 1998), especially chap. 2.

22. Political arguments, especially those emphasizing stakeholders, are plentiful. Maxim Boycko, Andrei Shleifer, and Robert Vishny, *Privatizing Russia* (Cambridge, Mass: MIT Press, 1995); Lynn Nelson, and Irina Kuzes, "Evaluating the Russian Voucher Privatization Program," *Comparative Economic Studies* 36 (Spring 1994): 55–67; Cheryl Gray, "In Search of Owners: Privatization and Corporate Governance in Transition Economies," *World Bank Research Observer* 11, no. 2 (1996): 179–98; Lynn Nelson and Irina Kuzes, *Property to the People, The Struggle for Radical Reform in Russia* (London: M. E. Sharpe, 1994); Anders Åslund, *How Russia Became a Market Economy* (Washington, DC: Brookings Institution, 1995); Joseph Blasi, M. Kroumova, and D. Kruse, *Kremlin Capitalism: Privatizing the Russian Economy* (Ithaca: Cornell University Press, 1997); Debardeleben, "Attitudes Towards Privatization in Russia."

23. Andrei Shleifer and Robert Vishny, *The Grabbing Hand: Government Pathologies and Their Cures* (Cambridge, Mass.: Harvard University Press, 1999), 10.

24. Oliver Blanchard et al., *Post-Communist Reform: Pain and Progress* (Cambridge, Mass.: MIT Press, 1993), 39.

25. Åslund, *How Russia Became a Market Economy,* 158. He also underscores the strength of managers in Anders Åslund, *Building Capitalism: The Transformation of the Former Soviet Bloc* (New York: Cambridge University Press, 2002), p. 274–75.

26. Roman Frydman, Andrzej Rapaczynski, and John Earle, *The Privatization Process in Central Europe* (London: Central European Press, 1993); Roman Frydman and Andrzej Rapaczynski, *Privatization in Eastern Europe: Is the State Withering Away?* (London: Central European Press, 1993), especially chap. 5; Mitchell Orenstein, *Out of the Red: Building Capitalism and Democracy in Post-communist Europe* (Ann Arbor: University of Michigan Press, 2001).

27. In Feigenbaum and Henig's typology of privatization, the three approaches within privatization research are differentiated according to the interests of the primary actors. That is, Feigenbaum and Henig identify material interests at the core of different strands of privatization theorizing: an administrative perspective is built upon a politically defined public interest, the economic perspective upon privately defined individual interests, and the political perspective upon malleable, divided interests in conflict. Feigenbaum and Henig, "The Political Underpinnings of Privatization," 203.

28. Harold Demsetz, "Toward a Theory of Property Rights," *American Economic Review* 57 (May 1967): 347–59; Terry Anderson and P. Hill, "The Evolution of Property Rights: A Study of the American West," *Journal of Law and Economics* 18, no. 1 (1975): 163–79; Douglass North, *Structure and Change in Economic History* (New York: W. W. Norton, 1981); William Riker and Itai Sened, "A Political Theory of the Origins of Property Rights: Airport Slots," *American Journal of Political Science* 35 (November 1991): 951–69; William Riker and David Wiemer, "The Economic and Political Liberalization of

Socialism: The Fundamental Problem of Property Rights," *Social Philosophy and Policy* 10, no. 2 (1993): 10; Gary Libecap, *Contracting for Property Rights* (Cambridge: Cambridge University Press, 1989); Thrainn Eggertsson, *Economic Behavior and Institutions* (Cambridge: Cambridge University Press, 1990).

29. In his more recent works, Libecap looks at the role of politics in determining the property rights for natural resources, such as oil, minerals, and fisheries, in twentieth-century America. Typically, Libecap's objects of study are limited to those rights governing common pool resources rather than to rights governing resources more generally or in regime change, as in Eastern Europe. Libecap, *Contracting for Property Rights;* idem, "Property Rights in Economic History: Implications for Research," *Explorations in Economic History* 23, no. 3 (1986): 227–52; idem, "The Political Allocation of Mineral Rights: A Reevaluation of Teapot Dome," *Journal of Economic History* 44 (1984): 381–91; Gary Libecap and S. Wiggins, "Contractual Responses to the Common Pool, Prorationing of Crude Oil Production," *American Economic Review* 74, no. 1 (1984): 87–98.

30. The tendency in interest group or pluralist theory to neglect state interests and to ignore the state as an actor as well as an arbiter, spurred the movement in political science and political sociology to "bring the state back in"—namely, to reintroduce the state as an actor in political analysis. See Theda Skocpol's "Bringing the State Back In: Strategies and Analysis of Current Research," in *Bringing the State Back In*, edited by Peter Evans, Dietrich Rueschemeyer, and Theda Skocpol (Cambridge: Cambridge University Press, 1985), 3–37. Also see Stephen Krasner's review of the statist literature, "Approaches to the State," *Comparative Politics* 16, no. 2 (1984): 223–46, and Gabriel Almond's critique in "The Return to the State," *A Discipline Divided: Schools and Sects in Political Science* (Newbury Park, Calif.: Sage, 1990).

31. Levi writes that rulers seek to maximize state revenue "subject to the constraints of their relative bargaining power, transaction costs, and discount rates" (Margaret Levi, *Of Rule and Revenue* [Berkeley: University of California Press, 1988], 2).

32. The Demsetz approach has been replicated by numerous economists and economic historians, such as in John McManus, "An Economic Analysis of Indian Behavior in the North American Fur Trade," *Journal of Economic History* 32, no. 1 (1972): 36–53; Terry Anderson and P. Hill, "The Evolution of Property Rights: A Study of the American West," *Journal of Law and Economics* 18, no. 1 (1975): 163–79; Douglass North and Robert Thomas, *The Rise of the Western World: A New Economic History* (Cambridge: Cambridge University Press, 1973); Douglass North and Robert Thomas, "The First Economic Revolution," *Economic History Review* 30 no. 2 (1977): 229–41; R. Palmer, "The Origins of Property in England," *Law and History Review* 3 (1985): 1–50.

33. Harold Demstez, "Toward a Theory of Property Rights," *American Economic Review* 57, no. 2 (1967): 347–59. Demstez's study identifies the introduction of fur traders from Europe and the subsequent decline of available meat and clothing for indigenous populations as the impetus behind the definition of exclusive land rights in the American Northwest and border regions of Canada. Demsetz argues that the emergence of the transnational fur trade rendered the gains from internalizing externalities (that is, creating exclusive property rights) greater than the costs.

34. North, *Structure and Change.*

35. Neo-institutionalist economist Thrainn Eggertsson calls attention to the "economistic" tendencies in the property rights literature and urgently calls for the inclusion of political interests alongside economic interests as well as a greater appreciation of politi-

cal institutions and the need for a theory of the state. In his influential book, *Economic Behavior and Institutions* (Cambridge: Cambridge University Press, 1990), Eggertsson labels the theories of virtually all property rights scholars as "naive theories of property rights" precisely because they "seek to explain the development of exclusive property rights without explicitly modeling social and political institutions" (250).

36. William Riker and David Weimer, "The Economic and Political Liberalization of Socialism: The Fundamental Problem of Property Rights," *Social Philosophy and Policy* 10, no. 2 (1993): 79–102.

37. Building upon rational choice assumptions of utility-maximizing actors, an earlier article by Riker and Sened also considers the political calculations of state actors in setting ownership arrangements. Specifically, Riker and Sened argue that the state actors will establish a set of property rights if (1) groups in society are vying for control over a resource, (2) that resource is scarce, and (3) the government expects the material or *political* benefits from new property rights to exceed the costs of enforcing them. William Riker and Itai Sened, "A Political Theory of the Origins of Property Rights: Airport Slots," *American Journal of Political Science* 35, no. 4 (1991): 951–69.

38. Speaking most directly to this lacuna, see Levi, *Of Rule and Revenue*, 4, 17, 22.

39. On inferring interests from outcomes, see Robert Wade, "East Asia's Economic Success: Conflicting Perspectives, Partial Insights, Shaky Evidence," *World Politics* 44, no. 2 (1992): 309.

40. For critiques of the rational choice paradigm, see Donald Green and Ian Shapiro, *Pathologies of Rational Choice Theory: A Critique of Applications in Political Science* (New Haven: Yale University Press, 1994); Stanley Kelley, "Rational Choice: Its Promises and Limitations," *Critical Review* (Winter 1995): 9; Sven Steinmo, Kathleen Thelen, and Frank Longstreth, eds., *Structuring Politics: Historical Institutionalism in Comparative Analysis* (New York: Cambridge University Press, 1992); Karen Schweers Cook and Margaret Levi, eds., *The Limits of Rationality* (Chicago: University of Chicago Press, 1990); Jane Mansbridge, ed., *Beyond Self-Interest* (Chicago: University of Chicago Press, 1990); and Peter Hall and Rosemary Taylor, "Political Science and the Three New Institutionalisms," *Political Studies* 4, no. 5 (1996): 44.

41. See Blanchard et al., *Post-Communist Reform,* especially chap. 3; and Boycko, Shleifer, and Vishny, *Privatizing Russia.*

42. For a discussion of individual strategies for coping with uncertainty in transition, see Michael Burawoy and Kathryn Verdery, eds., *Uncertain Transition: Ethnographies of Change in the Post-Socialist World* (Lanham, Md.: Rowman and Littlefield, 1999), especially the introductory chapter.

43. For World Bank/OECD figures, see Ira Lieberman et al., eds., *Between State and Market: Mass Privatization in Transition Economies* (Washington, DC: World Bank, 1997), 5.

44. For an explicit discussion of the influence of the Czech mass privatization program on the design of the Russian program, see Boycko, Shleifer, and Vishny, *Privatizing Russia,* chap. 4.

45. In this book, *neoliberalism* and *economic liberalism* are used interchangeably. In general, both terms seek to emphasize a limited role for the state in the economy. For some, though, the term *neoliberalism* implies a greater acknowledgment of the role of institutions. This is not a distinction directly relevant to this study. A more important distinction is the temporal association of the term *neoliberal.* It is associated with body

of theory or an economic paradigm popularized in the late twentieth century, whereas economic liberalism sits more broadly within the history of ideas. A quintessential neoliberal (or economic liberal) perspective on private property rights—that is, the liberal perspective on private property rights associated with this late-twentieth-century trend—will be specified in chapter 5.

46. The question of why so many neoliberals gained positions of policy-making authority is analyzed within the context of the international influences on East European property development in chapter 2.

47. In the Czech Republic, the lustration law was an anti-Communist screening measure that required the bureaucratic and industrial elite to resign from certain top posts for past acts of political collaboration, in particular with the Communist Secret Police. Vojtech Čepl, "Lustration in the ČSFR," *East European Constitutional Review* (Spring 1992): 24–26; Jirina Siklova, "Lustration or the Czech Way of Screening," *East European Constitutional Review* (Winter 1996): 57–62.

48. See Hilary Appel and John Gould, "Identity Politics and Economic Reform: Examining Industry-State Relations in the Czech and Slovak Republics," *Europe-Asia Studies* 52, no. 1 (2000): 111–32.

49. See chapter 6, note 64.

50. On the early tensions between the legislature and the government, see Ivan Elistratov and Sergei Chubaev, "Pravitel'stvo vozvrashchaetsia . . ." [The government returns . . .], *Izvestiia,* 15 April 1992, p. 1.

51. Amitai Etzioni, *A Comparative Analysis of Complex Organizations: On Power, Involvement and Their Correlates* (New York: Free Press, 1961), 4–22.

52. For a discussion of the dependence of normative compliance mechanisms on material incentives and coercion potential, see Levi, *Of Rule and Revenue,* 68.

53. For instance, North considers ideology primarily as an instrument of the state to justify programs and as a tool of the opposition when attacking existing arrangements. Ideas do not drive the formation of property rights systems, but they have played an important role in the maintenance of and challenge to existing property rights. North, *Structure and Change,* 50–52.

Chapter 2. The International Dimension of Post-Communist Privatization

1. See John Ikenberry, "The International Spread of Privatization Policies: Inducements, Learning, and 'Policy Bandwagoning,'" in *The Political Economy of Public Sector Reform and Privatization,* edited by Ezra Suleiman and John Waterbury (Boulder: Westview Press, 1990), 88–110.

2. Ognian Hishow, "Makroökonomische politik und reformfortschritte im ostlichen Europa: Differenzierung durch unterschiedliche transformations-konzepte" [Macroeconomic policies and reform progress in Eastern Europe: Distinguishing between the different transformation paths], *Bundesinstituts für Ostwissenschaftliche und Internationale Studien* 25 (1997).

3. On donor aid to Poland and Russia, see Janine Wedel, *Collision and Collusion: The Strange Case of Western Aid to Eastern Europe, 1989–1998* (New York: St. Martin's Press, 1998). Again, see Stiglitz's diatribe against the Western advisers in "Whither Reform."

4. For an overview of IMF conditionality, see Benjamin Cohen, "Balance of Pay-

ments Financing: Evolution of a Regime," in *International Regimes,* edited by Stephen Krasner (Ithaca: Cornell University Press, 1982), 315–36.

5. IMF Survey, 5 February 1996, pp. 48–49, quoted in Stone, "Russia and the IMF," 1.

6. "World Bank/ IMF Agenda." *Transition Newsletter,* June 1997, http://www. worldbank.org/html/prddr/trans/mayjun97/art12.htm (accessed 10 November 2003).

7. The seven identified firms were (1) OJSC Design Bureau of Automated Lines "Rotor" (Vologda), (2) Svyazinvest, (3) Gazprom, (4) Lukoil (Moscow), (5) Bor (Primorskiy Krai), (6) Moselectrofolga (Moscow), and (7) Balashovo Bakery Combinat (Saratov). The government also committed to privatize shares in an additional eight enterprises by 31 March 2000. In this pledge, there were several qualifications, however, leaving the government with the option of not privatizing shares if market conditions were not desirable as "determined on advice of independent financial advisors." Quoted from "Russian Federation, Letter of Development Policy for the Third Structural Adjustment Loan," mimeo, 1999.

8. Ibid.

9. Commission of the European Communities, RAPID, 22 March 1993.

10. "Eastern Europe Report," *American Banker Bond Buyer* 1, no. 22 (1991): 7.

11. Randall Stone, *Lending Credibility: The International Monetary Fund and the Post-Communist Transition* (Princeton: Princeton University Press, 2002).

12. See U.S. Congress, Senate, Committee on Banking, Housing and Urban Affairs, *Impact of IMF/World Bank Policies toward Russia and the Russian Economy,* 103d Cong., 2d sess., 8 February 1994, 1–3.

13. For more on these loans, see Kirill Koriukin, "World Bank Warns of Delay in Loans," *Moscow Times,* 16 January 1999, and Kirill Koriukin, "Lebed Steps in on Mine Privatization," *Moscow Times,* 12 August 1999.

14. *AP Worldstream,* 8 September 1999.

15. Comment from author's interview with an anonymous World Bank official, Washington, DC, October 1999.

16. The EBRD was founded to provide "needed support to nurture a new private sector." See http://www.ebrd.org/about/index.htm (accessed 10 November 2003).

17. European Commission, *Enlargement: PHARE Publications* (Brussels, Belgium: European Communities, 2003), http://europa.edu.int/comm/enlargement/pas/phare/publist.htm (accessed 28 October 2003).

18. Agence France Presse, 25 June 1991.

19. "Eastern Europe Report," *American Banker-Bond Buyer* 1, no. 22 (1991): 7.

20. PAP Newswire, 22 July 1993.

21. "East European Energy Report," *Pearson Professional Ltd.,* no. 59 (27 August 1996): 25.

22. Agence France Presse, 22 July 1999.

23. Japan Economic Newswire, 24 April 2000.

24. Xinhua General Overseas News Service, 4 July 1996.

25. Deutsche Presse-Agentur, 16 September 1998.

26. United Press International, 8 May 1996 and AP Worldstream, 8 September 1999.

27. Xinhua General Overseas News Service, 6 August 1992 and 17 December 1992.

28. The State Department official, Deirdre Clifford, is quoted by Wedel. According to Wedel, the figure of $58 million is confirmed by two U.S. AID officials. Wedel, *Collision and Collusion,* 252 nn 44–47.

29. These figures are quoted in Wedel *Collision and Collusion,* 254 n. 96. She attributes the figures to interviews with Ira Lieberman at the World Bank (July 1996) and Renae Ng at the EBRD (September 1996).

30. Wedel, *Collision and Collusion,* 142.

31. "World Bank/ IMF Agenda." *Transition Newsletter,* June 1997, http://www.worldbank.org/html/prddr/trans/mayjun97/art12.htm (accessed 10 November 2003).

32. Wedel, *Collision and Collusion,* 137.

33. Boycko, Shleifer, and Vishny, *Privatizing Russia,* 142.

34. Based on several discussions with representatives of the Eurasia Foundation and the Pew Charitable Trusts (May 1995). The author wrote the 1995 white paper on economics education in transition states for the Pew Charitable Trusts.

35. The European University in Budapest taught Western-style economics among other social science disciplines. For information on these institutions and programs, see the following Web sites: http://www.users.nevalink.ru/eusp/; http://www.sgh.waw.pl/; http://www.eerc.ru; and http://www.eerc.kiev.ua.

36. Brochure provided by Christine Evans, EERC project coordinator at the Eurasia Foundation. For more information on the EERC, read Gregory Ingram, "Origins of the EERC," http://www.eerc.ru/wieerc/Ingram.html.

37. Eurasia Foundation's EERC project coordinator Christine Evans provided the author with the figure of $9,271,830 spent thus far, based on the amount of funding received and receivable through fiscal year 2001 (e-mail correspondence 30 November 2000). It should be noted that there is some risk of double counting when looking at the sums allocated by the international financial institutions and private and semipublic foundations.

38. "World Bank/ IMF Agenda," *Transition Newsletter,* June 1997, http://www.worldbank.org/html/prddr/trans/mayjun97/art12.htm (accessed 10 November 2003).

39. The literature on policy learning and policy transfer is extensive. See Colin Bennett and Michael Howlett, "The Lessons of Learning: Reconciling Theories of Policy Learning and Policy Change," *Policy Sciences* 25 (1992); David Dolowitz and David Marsh, "Who Learns What from Whom: A Review of the Policy Transfer Literature," *Political Studies* 44 (1996): 343–57; Mark Evans and Jonathan Davies, "Understanding Policy Transfer: A Multi-level, Multi-disciplinary Perspective," *Public Administration* 77 (1999): 361–86.

40. John Ikenberry, "Creating Yesterday's New World Order: Keynesian 'New Thinking' and the Anglo-American Postwar Settlement," in *Ideas and Foreign Policy: Beliefs, Institutions and Political Change,* edited by Judith Goldstein and Robert Keohane (Ithaca: Cornell University Press, 1993).

41. Boycko, Shleifer, and Vishny, *Privatizing Russia.*

42. Jeffrey Henig, C. Hammett, and Harvey Feigenbaum, "The Politics of Privatization: A Comparative Perspective," *Governance* 1, no. 4 (1988): 442–68. Ikenberry, "The International Spread of Privatization Policies."

43. Author's interview with John Nellis, a senior manager in the World Bank's Enterprise Reform and Privatization Unit, 11 November 1999.

44. In 1995 the author participated in one of these meetings funded by the Soros Foundation's International Renaissance Foundation held in the Crimea, Ukraine. Although substantive meetings were held, full days of tourist activities in Yalta were organized for participants and evenings were filled with banquets and dancing. International

Renaissance Foundation's 1995 Conference on the Problems of Privatization, Simferopol, Ukraine, 13–17 October 1995.

45. On the influence of ideas on policy through epistemic communities, see Peter Haas ed., *International Organization: Knowledge, Power and International Policy Coordination* (Special issue of *International Organization*) 46, no. 1 (1992).

46. Ibid.

47. On ideas as roadmaps, see Goldstein and Keohane, "Ideas and Foreign Policy," introduction.

Chapter 3: The Origins and Design of Czech Large-Scale Privatization

1. The intellectual freedom of economists was not without certain limits, however. The Communist Party would not tolerate any fundamental critiques of Communist economic ideology and punished prominent economists for direct attacks on the party. For instance, the government expelled Miloš Zeman from the Forecasting Institute for publishing an article in *Technický časopis* in August 1989 that directly criticized the current regime. *ČTK Czech National News Wire* (hereafter cited as *ČTK*), 27 June 1996.

2. *Reuter Library Report,* 10 April 1988.

3. For a comprehensive discussion of economic reforms in Czechoslovakia during the Communist and post-Communist period, see Zdislav Šulc, "Stručné dějiny ekonomických reforem v Československu (České republice), 1945–1995" [A brief history of economic reforms in Czechoslovakia (Czech Republic), 1945–1995], *Studie Národohospodářského ústavu* 3 (December 1996): 62–70. For a more general discussion of the reform period in Czechoslovakia in relation to other Communist bloc countries, see Jan Adam, *Economic Reforms in the Soviet Union and East European Countries since the 1960s* (New York: St. Martin's Press, 1989).

4. For specific details on political developments in the final years of Communist Czechoslovakia, see Patricia Koza, "Czechoslovakia's Leader Replaced," United Press International, 17 December 1987; "Czech Party Leader, Echoing Moscow, Backs Economic Reform," *Reuter Library Report,* 10 April 1988; Leslie Colitt, "Reformist Premier Steps Down in Prague," *Financial Times,* 11 October 1988, 2.

5. See Martin Kupka, "Transformation of Ownership in Czechoslovakia," *Soviet Studies* 44, no. 2 (1992): 298.

6. Ibid., 297–311.

7. Ibid.

8. Jan Sokol, the vice chairman of the federal assembly from 1990 to 1992 explains that Klaus and Havel knew each other for many years before their collaboration in Civic Forum. For instance, Sokol recalled the meeting he attended with both Klaus and Havel in 1967 when all three were discussing and working on an official, non-Marxist, literary magazine to which Klaus was contributing articles. Author's interview, Jan Sokol, Prague, 30 January 1996. Klaus confirmed this in author's interview, 16 January 2001, Los Angeles.

9. Havel appointed Klaus as minister of finance and Dlouhý as chairman (equivalent to minister) of the State Planning Commission, and then in June as minister of economics. Dyba first served as an adviser to Czechoslovak deputy premier, and in June as minister of economic policies and development. Komárek was appointed deputy prime

minister in charge of all economic ministries. All four economists had been working in the Forecasting Institute.

10. Ian Traynor, "Prince of Prague," *Guardian*, 3 November 1994, p. T4.

11. Timothy Garton Ash, "Prague: Inside the Magic Lantern," in *We the People: The Revolution of 1989 Witnessed in Warsaw, Budapest, Berlin and Prague* (Cambridge: Granta Books, 1990), 104.

12. Ibid.

13. On the Czechoslovak economy before the Velvet Revolution, see Jan Adam, "Transformation to a Market Economy in the Former Czechoslovakia," *Europe-Asia Studies* 45, no. 4 (1993): 627–45.

14. See Karel Dyba and Jan Švejnar, "Czechoslovakia: Recent Economic Developments and Prospects," *American Economic Review Papers and Proceedings* (May 1991): 185–90. Cited in Adam, "Transformation to a Market Economy," 628.

15. For example, see *Slovenský denik*, 6 September 1990, 1; *Mladá fronta DNES*, 6 September 1990, 1–2; *ČTK*, 12 September 1990.

16. In the political science literature on the role of ideas, crises are often considered consequential because they can lead to greater uncertainty, and this uncertainty opens up a space for intellectual entrepreneurs. In the Czech case, it was heightened uncertainty (without an economic crisis) that facilitated the introduction of new ideas. On crisis, see Goldstein and Keohane, "Ideas and Foreign Policy," 15–19; Ikenberry, "Creating Yesterday's New World Order," 59, 83; and Halpern, "Creating Socialist Economies," 110.

17. Garton Ash notes that when Civic Forum was discussing who would fill which posts in the interim government, there was resistance to putting certain people in key positions since they were still Communists, such as Valtr Komárek. Garton Ash notes a similar concern for the appointment of 1968 reformer and expelled leader Alexandr Dubček. Interestingly, although Dubček was an important national and international figure, ideologically he essentially was a reform Communist, which made him less appealing to those wanting to create a Western-oriented government. Timothy Garton Ash, "The Prague Advertisement," *The Uses of Adversity* (Cambridge: Granta Books, 1989), 124–25.

18. Policy declaration of the federal government on 3 July 1990 by Prime Minister Marian Čalfa. Cited in Zdenka Mansfeldová's insightful paper "Professional and Political Strategies in Economic Discourses" (prepared for the Symbolic Politics and the Process of Democratization in Eastern Europe Conference, Berlin, 21–28 August 1994), 8, mimeo.

19. Garton Ash, "Prague: Inside the Magic Lantern," 105.

20. Ibid.

21. Jan Švejnar, "A Framework for the Economic Transformation of Czechoslovakia," *PlanEcon Report* 5, no. 52 (1989): 1–18. For the sections on privatization, see pp. 7–8.

22. In addition, Švejnar's paper served as a basis, albeit with significant amendments, to the proposal known as the Scenario for Economic Reform, brought forth by Klaus and others later that spring. Švejnar notes that entire paragraphs from his paper were translated and transferred from his published paper and included in the Scenario for Economic Reform. Author's interview, Prague, 14 December 1995. For extensive excerpts of the Scenario, see "Document: Ze scénáře ekonomické reformy" [Document: From the scenario of economic reform], *Lidové noviny*, 4 September 1990, p. 2.

23. My characterization of this debate is greatly influenced by a series of discussions with Zdenka Mansfeldová, a Czech sociologist at the Academy of Sciences in Prague, and

her paper "Professional and Political Strategies in Economic Discourses."

24. The Klaus concept is outlined in Klaus's book *Czechoslovakia at the Crossroads* (Prague: Lidové noviny, 1990); cited in Mansfeldová, "Professional and Political Strategies in Economic Discourses," or see position taken in the Scenario of Economic Reform (note 22).

25. Komárek's views on economic reform can be found in his coauthored text *Prógnoza a Program* (Prague: Academia Publishers, 1990), as well as in published newspaper articles, such as Valtr Komárek, "Otazníky nejen u cen" [Questions concern not only the prices], *Hospodářské noviny*, no. 25, 20 June 1990, pp. 1, 3; Valtr Komárek, "Jak bych to řešil já" [How I would solve it], *Rudé právo*, 15 July 1991, pp. 1, 2. For explanation of Komárek's position, see Jiří Sekera, "Alternativní scénáře reformy" [Alternative scenarios of reform], *Hospodářské noviny*, no. 5 (1990): 1, 5.

26. Mansfeldová, "Professional and Political Strategies in Economic Discourses."

27. Ibid., 6. Also see Zdenka Mansfeldová, "Justice as an Ethic Legitimacy of Economic Reform" (paper presented at the conference on Normative Foundations of the Polity: Conceptual Approaches in East and Central Europe, Bremen, 20–22 January 1995).

28. On the Komárek-Klaus debate, see "Klaus versus Komárek," *Svobodné slovo*, 7 April 1990, p. 1; Zdeněk Hoffman, Pavel Páral, "Rychle, nebo postupně" [Quickly or gradually], *Rudé právo*, 9 June 1990, p. 1; Eva Procházková and Vladimír Matějovský, "Nejde o vítězství, ale o prohru" [It is not about winning but losing], *Mladá fronta DNES*, 9 June 1990; Vladimír Diviš, "Klaus versus Komárek," *Rudé právo*, 18 July 1991, pp. 1, 2, 32.

29. Author's interview with Jan Sokol, Prague, 8 February 1996.

30. The group of economists with which Václav Klaus surrounded himself when designing a liberal program of economic transformation consisted of Tomáš Ježek, later the Czech Minister of Privatization and chairman of the Fund of National Property; Dušan Tříska, deputy minister of finance and adviser to Klaus; Ivan Kočárnik, deputy minister of finance and then finance minister; Karel Dyba, later minister of the economy; and Vladimír Dlouhý.

31. Quoted from Klaus's address to the fourth annual meeting of the CEEPN-Central and Eastern Europe Privatization Network. The proceedings of the meeting were published in Andrea Bohm and Marko Simoneti, eds., *Privatization in Central and Eastern Europe 1993* (Ljubljana: CEEPN Annual Conference Series, 1993).

32. *Lidové noviny*, 17 October 1990, p. 4.

33. Author's interview with Otakar Turek, Prague, 25 January 1996.

34. Author's interviews with Jan Vrba, 15 January 1996; Josef Kotrba, 25 January 1996; and Jan Matějka, 16 January 1996, Prague.

35. For more on Svaz Průmyslu see Raj Desai and Mitchell Orenstein, "Business Associations and the State in the Czech Republic," *Emergo* (Spring 1996): 29–43.

36. The role of the FNM is delineated by articles 27–40 in Act 92/1991 Coll., the large-scale privatization law.

37. Author's interview with Jan Sokol, Prague, 30 January 1996.

38. Ibid.

39. The formal name of the Ministry of Privatization was the Czech Ministry for the Administration of State Property and Its Privatization. Like the FNM, the name of this institution was a concession to the gradualists. The first minister of privatization op-

posed the cumbersome name, as it offended his liberal sensibilities. Despite Ježek's claims that he never got acclimated to the name, the ministry constituted a compromise in name only and was intended only to privatize property rather than contribute to the administration of property. Author's interview, Tomáš Ježek, Prague, 1 March 1996.

40. *ČTK*, 15 October 1990.

41. In addition to press accounts cited below, this section relies heavily upon two interviews with Jan Sokol, the former chairman of the Civic Forum parliamentary group and the deputy speaker of the Federal Assembly (the federal parliament). Sokol later served as minister of education under the Social Democrats and was a candidate for president in the third round of the 2003 elections. Author's interviews with Jan Sokol, Prague, 30 January 1996 and 8 February 1996.

42. Author's interview with Jan Sokol, Prague, 30 January 1996.

43. On Klaus's positioning himself against "praguocentrist tendencies" at a Civic Forum meeting in 1990, and on the resonance of his antidissident rhetoric, see Magdalena Hadjiisky, "The Failure of Participatory Democracy in the Czech Republic," *West European Politics* 24, no. 3 (2001): 55–56.

44. *ČTK*, 14 October 1990.

45. See interview with Klaus in which he explicitly states that in voting for him, the delegates of Civic Forum expressed their support for his program of economic reform. *Lidové noviny*, 15 October 1990, p. 1.

46. See *Mladá fronta DNES*, 15 October 1990, pp. 1, 2; *Lidové noviny*, 15 October 1990, p. 1.

47. *ČTK*, 21 November 1990.

48. *Lidové noviny*, 2 November 1990, p. 1.

49. *ČTK*, 14 October 1990.

50. Restitution was a program transferring to former owners the property rights for housing and small businesses that had been confiscated during the Communist regime. The initial legislation, later referred to as the Small Federal Restitution Law, was extended the following year by the Large Federal Restitution Law (Act. 87/1991 Coll.), changing the starting date for which claims to confiscated property were valid.

51. Ježek had been involved in the design but, at this time, served in the Czech government as privatization minister and thus was not formally a sponsor of the bill.

52. For a detailed outline of the voucher method and the process by which citizens could participate, see the official document published by the Czech Ministry of Finance: Kupónová privatizace: Informační příručka, 1991; Federální ministerstvo financí, *Hospodářské noviny*, 10 September 1991, p. 8, or, more briefly, see Eva Marikova Leeds, "Voucher Privatization in Czechoslovakia," *Comparative Economic Studies* 35, no. 3 (1993): 19–37.

53. On the widespread belief that those with capital are suspect, see comments by Slovak prime minister, *ČTK*, 1 October 1990.

54. *Lidové noviny*, 27 September 1990, p. 1; On strikes, see *Mladá fronta DNES*, 27 September 1990; *ČTK*, 2 October 1990.

55. See interview with Šik: "Záporů bude víc než kladů: Ota Šik kritizuje kupónovou privatizaci" [There will be more disadvantages than advantages: Ota Šik criticizes voucher privatization], *Rudé právo*, 23 January 1992. On the resistance by Šik and others, see Josef Kotrba, "Privatization Process in Czech Republic: An Overview," *World Bank*, December 1993, mimeo. Also see Josef Kotrba, "Privatization Process in the Czech Re-

public: Players and Winners," in *The Czech Republic and Economic Transition in Eastern Europe,* edited by Jan Švejnar (San Diego: Academic Press, 1995).

56. Václav Klaus, "Jde vlna za vlnou: Proč právě kupónová privatizace" [One wave comes after another: Why voucher privatization], *Hospodářské noviny,* 2 September 1991.

57. Goals enumerated in author's interviews with Tomáš Ježek, Prague, 1 March 1996.

58. See interview with Tříska in "Osvobodit se od státu" [To free oneself from the state], *Respekt,* no. 45 (19 November 1991): 9, in which he responds to Ježek's criticism and labeling of 97 + 3 as *"akciový socialismus,"* or socialism by corporate stocks.

59. Author's interview with Tomáš Ježek, Prague, 1 March 1996 and Dušan Tříska, Prague, 13 February 1996.

60. Rudolf Baránek as the outspoken leader of the Association of Entrepreneurs has left his mark on the privatization process and in particular on small-scale privatization. Already in the summer of 1990, Baránek claimed 130,000 members, a surprising figure when one considers the limited degree of private commercial initiatives. Although many doubt the figures he quotes as his membership base, he has clearly wielded influence through his aggressive behavior and transparent political ambition. On this organization during the summer of 1990, see "Podnikatelé nejsou spokojení," *Lidová demokracie,* 26 July 1990. For an analysis of this association and a discussion of Baránek's lobbying efforts see Raj Desai and Mitchell Orenstein, "Business Associations and the State in the Czech Republic," *Emergo* (Spring 1996): 29–43.

61. Author's interview, Tomáš Ježek, Prague, 1 March 1996.

62. See "Náprava křivd byla kompromisem" [The rectification of wrongdoings was a compromise], *Mladá fronta DNES,* 22 June 1994, p. 6.

63. *ČTK,* 7 November 1991.

64. Ibid.

65. For Ježek's comments on his conflict with Klaus over the extension of time to review projects, and the reply by Klaus, see "Další kolo konfliktů Klaus-Ježek" [The next round of conflict Klaus-Ježek], *Rudé právo,* 16 November 1991, pp. 1, 2. In this article, Ježek explicitly states that Klaus's position is based upon electoral politics rather than economic reality. Also see interview with Ježek in "Pochod Údolím Smrti" [March through the Valley of Death], *Mladý svět,* no. 47 (28 October 1991): 10, 11. Further, Ježek told the Czech newspaper *Práce* regarding the need to extend the period to review privatization projects, "Everyone agrees with me in the corridors or at the toilet, but they are afraid to say so publicly." Quoted in "Row over Pace of Privatization," *Financial Times,* 6 November 1991.

66. *ČTK,* 7 November 1991.

67. See Kotrba, "The Privatization Process in the Czech Republic: Players and Winners," 189.

68. Author's interviews with employees of the Privatization Ministry, Alena Zemplinerová, 1 February 1996 and Eva Klvačová, 2 November 1995, Prague. Joshua Charap and Alena Zemplinerová, "Management Buy-outs in the Privatisation Programme of the Czech Republic," *Management and Employee Buy-outs in the Context of Privatization,* OECD Special Report 1, no. 3 (1994).

69. Author's interview with John Nellis, senior manager at the World Bank in the Enterprise Reform and Privatization Division, Washington, DC, 11 November 1999.

70. Author's interview with Václav Klaus, Prague, 31 May 2000.

71. Data from 1994 STEM Polling Survey, *ČTK,* 23 February 1999.

72. "The Czech Republic," *World Bank Report 1997*, 91, Table 1.

73. Although this was repeated many times by the government—for example, see United Press International, 21 December 1995—at this time the EBRD (European Bank for Reconstruction and Development) estimated that private-sector share of the Czech GNP was 70 percent at the end of 1995, reaching 80 percent only in 1999. *EBRD Transition Report 2002: Economic Transition in Central and Eastern Europe and the CIS* (London: EBRD, 2002).

74. Raj Desai and Vladena Plockova, "The Czech Republic," *Between State and Market: Mass Privatization in Transition Economies*, edited by Ira Lieberman et al. (Washington, DC: World Bank, 1997), 91, Table 2.

75. Author's interview with Dušan Tříska, 13 February 1996, Prague.

76. *ČTK*, 23 January 1998.

77. Andrew Schwartz, "The Czech Approach to Residual Share Management," *Between State and Market: Mass Privatization in Transition Economies*, edited by Ira Lieberman et al. (Washington, DC: World Bank, 1997).

78. Author's interview with analyst at Patria Finance, 9 November 1995. Name omitted due to analyst's preference for anonymity.

79. Only Credit Anstalt ultimately lost control of its investment fund, Kvanto. Komerční and Československá obchodní banka bought back Motoinvest's shares, and Živnostenská banka bought its stock from other shareholders in order to prevent ceding control to Motoinvest. For an excellent summary of events, see Ákos Róna-Tas, "The Czech Third Wave: Privatization and the New Role of the State in the Czech Republic," *Problems of Post-Communism* (November/December 1997): 53–62.

80. Ibid., 60–61.

81. Ibid.

82. See *ČTK*, 9–12 November 1994 and 29 February 1996.

83. Crystalex was controversial because it was sold to a domestic company, Porcela Plus, for $10 million instead of to a British company offering $27 million. It was alleged that the decision was influenced by past donations made by Porcela Plus to ODS. See *ČTK*, 8 December 1998 and 20 June 1997. The government's sale of Becherovka to Value Bill, a consortium of Czech and French investors, was controversial in part due to a higher bid from Stock Plzen and in part due to the personal relationship of one member of the winning consortium, Karel Schwarzenberg, who enjoyed close ties to ODA, which controlled both the National Property Fund and the Privatization Ministry. Alex Friedrich, "Becher Privatization Goes Sour for Local Bidders," *Prague Post*, 10 September 1997. On Telecom, see Jana Havlingerová et al., "Na privatizaci Telecomu padl stín" [A shadow fell over the privatization of Telecom], *Mladá fronta DNES*, 14 May 1998, pp. 1–2.

84. *Právo*, 13 January 1999; *ČTK*, 4 January 1999.

85. *ČTK*, 7 October 1998 and 23 February 1999.

86. Data from *ČTK*, 4 May 1998.

87. Ibid., 13 May 1998.

88. Ibid.

89. Ibid.

90. *ČTK*, 27 November 1998 and 11 March 1999. On the intention to increase the pace of bank privatization, see the statements of Ivo Svoboda (former finance minister in May 1999) in *ČTK*, 10 May 1999.

91. Some bank privatization had occurred in March 1998 under Tošóvský's caretaker

government, with the sale of a 36 percent stake in IPB Bank to Japanese Nomura.

92. For criticism of this privatization, see *Lidové noviny,* 31 May 1999.

93. ČEZ, a dominant power producer, and Transgas were slated to have some shares auctioned off. In 2000 privatization of Transgas shares did occur, but ČEZ's privatization was postponed. Other enterprises, like Ceptro and MERO ČR were less certain. *ČTK,* 5 March 1999, and *Hospodářské noviny,* 5 March 1999.

94. *ČTK,* 4 October 1999. For other surveys on privatization by IVVM, see *ČTK,* 4 May 1998. Another polling agency STEM reports that 80 percent of Czechs are not satisfied with how privatization was carried out (and 18 percent approve). *ČTK,* 7 October 1998. Also see a later STEM survey with similar negative results, *ČTK,* 27 July 1999.

95. Lieberman et al., *Between State and Market.*

Chapter 4: The Origins and Design of Russian Large-Scale Privatization

1. Much has been written on the economic and political reforms during perestroika and glasnost, and hence only a brief summary of developments is provided in order to set the context for the introduction of privatization reforms during the transition from the Soviet to post-Soviet period of Russian politics. For more on perestroika and the debates surrounding economic reform, see Anders Åslund, *Gorbachev's Struggle for Economic Reform* (Ithaca: Cornell University Press, 1991); Padma Desai, *Perestroika in Perspective: The Design and Dilemmas of Soviet Reform* (Princeton: Princeton University Press, 1989); Lee Cooper, *Soviet Reform and Beyond* (New York: St. Martin's Press, 1991); Jan Adam, *Economic Reforms in the Soviet Union and Eastern Europe since the 1960s* (New York: St. Martin's Press, 1991); Peter Boettke, *Why Perestroika Failed: The Politics of Socialist Transformation* (New York: Routledge, 1993); Bundesinstituts für Ostwissenschaftliche und Internationale Studien, ed., *The Soviet Union, 1988–1989: Perestroika in Crisis?* (Boulder: Westview Press, 1990).

2. For a detailed analysis of the factors inducing Gorbachev and other Communist elites to encourage academic researchers to undertake new studies in domestic and especially foreign policy options free from the constraints of official Communist dogma is found in chapter 5 of Jeffrey Checkell's *Ideas and International Political Change: Soviet/Russia Behavior and the End of the Cold War* (New Haven, Conn.: Yale University Press, 1997). Also see Åslund, *Gorbachev's Struggle,* 15–24.

3. For further discussion on economic reforms during 1987–1990, see Åslund's *Gorbachev's Struggle.* Also see Peter Rutland's "The Economy: The Rocky Road from Plan to Market" and Simon Clarke's "Privatisation: The Politics of Capital and Labour," in *Developments in Russian and Post-Soviet Politics,* edited by Stephen White (Durham, NC: Duke University Press, 1994).

4. Gorbachev's program is outlined in his book *Perestroika: New Thinking for Our Country and the World* (New York: Harper and Row, 1987).

5. Estimate from Clarke, "Privatisation," 167.

6. For the text of the Law on Property, see *Ekonomika i zhizn',* no. 11 (1987): 142–58.

7. In *Gorbachev's Struggle,* Åslund outlines the scholarly debate on economic reform in great detail. See especially chapter 5.

8. These proposals appeared in widely read newspapers, such as Bogomolov's article in *Literaturnaia gazeta* (16 September 1987) and Krashvili's article in *Moskovsky novosti,*

no. 23, (1988), cited in Åslund, *Gorbachev's Struggle*, 137. For a discussion of the contribution of several other liberal economists submitting articles to the popular press on privatization, such as Larisa Piiasheva, Vasili Seliunin, Vladimir Tikhonov, Pavel Bunich, and Iurii Chernichenko from 1987 to 1989, see Vladimir Shlapentokh, "Privatization Debates in Russia: 1989–1992," *Comparative Economic Studies* 35, no. 2 (1993): 19–32.

9. For the full text of the program in translation, see: G. Yavlinsky, B. Fedorov, S. Shatalin, et al., *500 Days Transition to the Market*, translated by David Kushner (New York: St. Martin's Press, 1991).

10. A. Davydov and V. Kurasov, "Russian Deputies Vote Yes," *Izvestiia*, 12 September 1990, p. 1; *Current Digest of the Post-Soviet Press* 42, no. 37 (1990): 8 (hereafter cited as *CDPSP*).

11. Gorbachev's rejection of the five-hundred-day plan is summed up in the report entitled "Transition to the Market," cited in Åslund, *How Russia Became a Market Economy*, 38.

12. G. Allison and G. Yavlinsky, *Window of Opportunity: The Grand Bargain for Democracy in the Soviet Union* (New York: Pantheon Books, 1991). See Mikhail Berger, "Resignation Submitted," *Izvestiia*, 18 October 1990, 2; *CDPSP* 42, no. 42 (1990): 4.

13. "Ideas and People: 'I had no right to deprive people of hope,'" interview conducted by Mikhail Leontyev, *Nezavisimaia gazeta*, 13 April 1991; *CDPSP* 43, no. 18 (1991): 1.

14. Gorbachev confirmed often his commitment to a Communist structure of ownership and opposition to private ownership of industry. He is quoted in April 1990, in commenting on Abalkin's reform proposal: "They want to take a gamble. . . . Let market conditions be put into place everywhere. Let's have free enterprise and give the green light to all forms of ownership, private ownership. . . . I cannot support such ideas." Speech quoted in the *New York Times*, 14 May 1990, p. 1. On Gorbachev and private property, see Shlapentokh, "Privatization Debates in Russia."

15. "Ob osnovnykh nachalakh razgosudarstvleniia i privatizatsii prepriiatii" [About the basic origins of deregulation and privatization of enterprises], *Izvestiia*, 8 August 1991, p. 3.

16. Lynn Nelson and Irina Kuzes, *Property to the People: The Struggle for Radical Reform in Russia* (London: M. E. Sharpe, 1994), 27.

17. Full text published in "O predpriiatiiakh i predprinimatel'skoi deitel'nosti" [About enterprises and business activities], *Ekonomika i zhizn'*, no. 4 (January 1991): 16. For a more detailed discussion of the Law on Enterprises and Entrepreneurial Activity, see Roman Frydman and Andrzej Rapaczynski, *The Privatization Process in Russia, Ukraine and the Baltic States* (London: Central European University Press, 1993), 18–20. Supreme Soviet RSFSR Law No. 27/927 (1991).

18. For full text of the law, see *Zakony RSFSR o privatizatsii gosudarstvennykh i munitsipal'nykh predpriiatii, zhil'lia* [Law on privatization of state and municipal enterprises in the Russian Federation] (Moscow: Sovetskaia Rossiia, 1991), 3–36. For analysis of this law, see Frydman and Rapaczynski, *The Privatization Process in Russia*, 50–51.

19. The use of privatization savings accounts was outlined in the Law on Inscribed Privatization Accounts and Deposits, 3 July 1991, Supreme Soviet RSFSR Law No. 27/925 (1991).

20. For a detailed discussion of Democratic Russia and its relationship with Yeltsin, see Yitzhak Brudny, "The Dynamics of 'Democratic Russia,' 1990–1993," *Post-Soviet Affairs* 9, no. 2 (1993): 141–70.

21. On Gaidar before his days in politics, see Egor Gaidar, *Dni porazhenii i pobed* [Days of defeat and victory] (Moscow: Vargrius, 1997).

22. Ibid.

23. Chubais had met Gaidar when they both worked briefly on a state commission for economists in 1983 and they both participated in informal meetings between young mathematical economists; *Independent* (London), 5 April 1992, p. 12. For more on the relationship between Gaidar and Chubais, see Chrystia Freeland, *Sale of the Century: Russia's Wild Ride from Communism to Capitalism* (New York: Random House, 2000).

24. *Independent* (London), 5 April 1992, p. 12.

25. See the plan for Soviet economic reform: G. Allison and G. Yavlinsky, *Window of Opportunity: The Grand Bargain for Democracy in the Soviet Union* (New York: Random House, 1991), especially pp. 17–22.

26. Boris Yeltsin, *The View from the Kremlin* (London: HarperCollins, 1994), 126.

27. Ibid., 125.

28. Gavriil Popov, "August 1991," *Izvestiia*, 21 August 1992, p. 3; *CDPSP* 44, no. 34 (1992): 1.

29. Within the first year of the liberals in office, Yeltsin added to his cabinet economists such as Yuri Skokov and Vladimir Lobov, and later Georgy Khizha and Vladimir Shumeiko, and finally, in the place of Gaidar, Viktor Chernomyrdin. Five days before suspending the Congress of Peoples deputies, Yeltsin chose Gaidar to replace Lobov, who had been the economics minister and first deputy prime minister. It was due to Lobov's opposition to privatization and support for central planning that Yeltsin moved Lobov to a different position, appointing him the secretary of Russia's Security Council. For more details about the cabinet reshuffle in September 1993, see "The Reformer Who Came Back," *Economist*, 25 September 1993, 59.

30. It is widely assumed Gaidar was forced out due to pressures on Yeltsin from political conservatives with ties to industry (in particular, Arkadii Volsky, Alexander Rutskoi, and Nikolai Travkin) to appoint a representative of industry at the helm of the government. Rutskoi at the time was Yeltsin's vice president, Travkin was the leader of the Democratic Party of Russia, and Volsky was the leader of the Russian Union of Industrialists and Entrepreneurs. Together, the three founded Civic Union, a parliamentary-industrialists group opposing Yeltsin's reform.

31. John Lloyd, "Gaidar Passes the Poisoned Chalice . . . ," *Financial Times*, 17 January 1994, 3.

32. For full text of the 1991 law, see *Zakony RSFSR o privatizatsii gosudarstvennykh i munitsipal'nykh predpriiatii, zhil'lia* [Law on privatization of state and municipal enterprises in the Russian Federation] (Moscow: Sovetskaia Rossiia, 1991), 3–36.

33. For full text of Accelerating Privatization Decree, see *Rossiiskaia gazeta*, 13 February 1992; for basic provisions, see *Ekonomika i zhizn'*, no. 31 (1991), no. 2 (1992).

34. On nomenklatura privatization, see A. D. Radygin, *Reforma sobstvennosti v Rossii: Na puti iz proshlogo v budeshchee* [Property reform in Russia: On the way from the past to the future] (Moscow: Respublika, 1994), 1–159, especially chap. 4; and Egor Gaidar, "Kak nomenklatura 'privatizirovala' svoiu vlast" [How the Nomenklatura 'privatized' its power], *Literaturnaia gazeta*, 9 November 1994, p. 10.

35. On Chubais's preference for cash auctions, see Martin Vulf, "Chem ekonomicheskaia reform otlichaetsia ot revoliutsii" [How economic reform is different from revo-

lution], *Izvestiia* (*Financial Times-Izvestiia* supplement), no. 140 (1992): iv; or see Åslund, *How Russia Became a Market Economy*, 233.

36. See Nelson and Kuzes, *Property to the People*, 47–50.

37. For Larisa Piiasheva's position, see "Dvoinoi standart" [Double standard], *Nezavisimaia gazeta*, 17 March 1992, p. 5. Also see Piiasheva's comments in *Nezavisimaia gazeta*, 25 November 1993, p. 1.

38. L. Piiasheva, A. Isaiev, V. Seliunin, G. Lisichkin, et al., "Otdat' besplatno: Dokladnaia rossiskomu presidentu o naibolee razumnom sposobe privatizatsii" [Giveaway for free: Report to the Russian president on the most judicious means of privatization], *Izvestiia*, 14 February 1992.

39. S. Menshikov, "Poiski panazei vsegda vedut v tupik" [The search for a panacea], *Rossiiskaia gazeta*, 22 May 1992.

40. For example, see liberal alternative proposal in A. Sidorov, "Privatizatsiia mozhet idti po-drugomu" [Privatization can be carried out differently], *Izvestiia*, 22 July 1992, p. 2.

41. Ruslan Khasbulatov, "Ne tam by diktatorov ichshete" [Don't search for dictators there], *Komsomol'skaia pravda*, 9 October 1992.

42. Freeland, *Sale of the Century*, 54.

43. Irina Demchenko, "Russian Economy: Crisis Enters New Stage," *Izvestiia*, 18 September 1992, pp. 1–2. [Reproduced and translated in *Russian Press Digest*, 21 September 1992].

44. In a speech to the Congress of People's Deputies, Speaker Khasbulatov cited the findings of a survey conducted by the Institute of Social and Economic Problems of the Population. It found that 50 percent of Russians identify themselves as "deprived," 30 percent as "really hurting," 10 percent were barely managing to survive physically, and 10 percent of those surveyed considered themselves well off. See *Rossiiskaia gazeta*, 2 December 1992; *CDPSP* 44, no. 48 (1992): 7.

45. An ally of Chubais, the chairman of the subcommittee on privatization in the Supreme Soviet, explains that revisions to the 1992 program were absolutely necessary "because the alternative was to give up on privatization entirely." He explains that increased employee ownership was purely a concession to the Supreme Soviet and did not reflect the preferences of the privatizers. See Petr Filippov, "Kuda poshel protsess?" [Where has the process gone?], *Delovoi mir*, no. 26, 6–13 February 1994, p. 19, cited in Nelson and Kuzes, *Property to the People*, 137.

46. Specifically, by choosing the second variant, worker collectives could buy 51 percent of their enterprises for 1.7 times the book value of those shares, not adjusted for inflation. One journalist calculates that owing to inflation, enterprises purchased in the first quarter of 1993 sold for 4 percent of the real price of January 1992. See Geoff Winestock, "Privatization Endangered by Political Rift," *Moscow Times*, 10 March 1993, p. 1.

47. For further detail on and analysis of the three variants, see Frydman and Rapaczynski, *Privatization in Eastern Europe*, 53–58.

48. For the full text of the speech, see *Official Kremlin News Broadcast*, 1 July 1994. Also, see Chubais's diatribe against employee ownership in "Darovaia sobstvennost' ne sdelaet cheloveka khoziainom" [Property given away will not make a man an owner], *Izvestiia*, 26 February 1992, p. 2. For further discussion of the privatization officials and their view of employee ownership, see Mikhail Berger, "Privatizatsii ugrozhaet diktatura proletariata" [Privatization threatens the dictatorship of the proletariat], *Izvestiia*, 3 June 1992, p. 2.

49. For comments by Chubais on the use of public support for advancing privatization in 1992, see *Argumenty i Fakty*, 28 November 1992, p. 3.

50. Yelena Kotelnikova, "State Property Committee Gains Time," *Kommersant-daily*, 23 February 1993, translated by *BBC Summary of World Broadcasts*, SU/1623 Special Supplement, 26 February 1993, p. C1.

51. For full text of the law, see "Dokumenty: Gosudarstvennaia programma privatizatsii gosudarstvennykh i munitsipal'nykh predpriiatii v Rossiiskoi Federatsii na 1992 god" [Document: State program for the privatization of state and municipal enterprises for the year 1992], *Biznes Moskovskie novosti*, no. 28 (1992): 13–14.

52. While estimates vary between 70–77 percent depending on the source, 72.5 percent was cited by the former chairman of the State Property Committee in Alfred Kokh, *The Selling of the Soviet Empire* (New York: Liberty Publishing House, 1998), 146.

53. For full text of the decree, see "O gosudarstvennych garantiiach prav grazhdan Rossii na uchastie v privatizatsii" [About state guarantee of rights to Russian citizens on participation in privatization], *Rossiiskie vesti*, no. 93, 18 May 1993, p. 3. For commentary on decree, see *Kommersant'*, no. 24, 5 July 1994.

54. On parliamentary opposition, see Al'bert Plutnik, "Atakuia pravitel'stvo, oppozitsiia boitsia uspekha reform" [Attacking the government, the opposition is afraid of the success of reform], *Izvestiia*, 9 April 1992, pp. 1–2.

55. On transfer of powers to the ministries, see *Trud*, 21 April 1993, p. 1. On annulling presidential decrees, see United Press International Press Release, 21 July 1993.

56. *Izvestiia*, 22 July 1993, pp. 1–2.

57. On tensions between the ministries and the State Property Committee, see Aleksandr Privalov and Natal'ia Kalinchenko, "Privatizatsionnye caprichos" [Privatization caprices], *Kommersant'*, no. 1, 18 January 1994, pp. 43–45.

58. Eric Lohr, "Arkadii Volsky's Political Base," *Europe-Asia Studies* 45, no. 5 (1993): 818. Also see Sergei Parkhomenko, "Vol'skii sozdaet partiiu pragmatikov" [Volsky forms a party of pragmatists], *Nezavisimaia gazeta*, 13 May 1992, p. 2.

59. Volsky had worked in the military industrial complex during the Brezhnev period and eventually rose to the position of chief of industry for the Communist Party under Mikhail Gorbachev.

60. Lohr, "Arkadii Volsky's Political Base," 817.

61. See interview with Arkadii Volsky in "Volskiy on Privatization, Other Issues," FBIS-SOV-92-196, 8 October 1992, from *La Republica*, 3 October 1992, p. 19.

62. *Guardian*, 17 April 1993, p. 34; *Financial Times*, 18 November 1992, p. 3.

63. For further discussion of Volsky's alliances with conservative parliamentary factions, see Lohr, "Arkadii Volsky's Political Base," 824–26, and Michael Ellman, "Russia: The Economic Program of the Civic Union," *RFE/FL Research Report* 2, no. 11 (1993): 34–45. Also see Evgenii Krasnikov, "El'tsin prinial liderov 'Grazhdanskogo Soiuz'" [Yeltsin received the leaders of 'The Civic Union'], *Nezavisimaia gazeta*, 5 November 1992, p. 1.

64. See Ivan Rodin, "Government 'Sends Troops' Against Parliament to Bar 'Variant Four' of Privatization," *Nezavisimaia gazeta*, 18 February 1993, p. 1, in *Russian Press Digest*, 18 February 1993.

65. Yelena Kotelnikova, "State Property Committee Gains Time," *Kommersant-daily*, 23 February 1993, translated by *BBC Summary of World Broadcasts*, SU/1623 Special Supplement, 26 February 1993, p. C1.

66. Blanchard et al., *Post-Communist Reform,* 148.

67. Markova, Lina, "Direktorskaia privatizatsiia: Kakogo sobstvennika ona porodila" [Managerial privatization: What kind of owner did it create?], *Rossiiskaia Federatsia Obstchestvenno-Politicheskii Zhurnal* 17 (1995).

68. On weak labor organization, see Frank Hoffer, "Reform der sowjetischen gewerkschaften in Russland: Ein schwerer, aber nicht hoffnungsloser fall" [Reform of the Soviet trade unions in Russia: Difficult, but not hopeless], *Bundesinstitut für Ostwissenschaftliche und Internationale Studien* (7 October 1998).

69. For more details on these schemes, see Hilary Appel, "Voucher Privatization in Russia: Structural Consequences and Mass Response in the Second Period of Reform," *Europe-Asia Studies* 49, no. 8 (1997): 1433–49.

70. Interview by author of Mikhail Dmitriev, 17 April 1996, Moscow. Dmitriev, a liberal deputy in the Supreme Soviet serving on the subcommittee on privatization, orchestrated the return of the 1993 program and then accompanied Vasiliev as he traveled throughout Russia to enlist support from regional administrations for the 1993 program. Also, see David Filippov and Geoff Winestock, "Yeltsin Withdraws 1993 Privatization Bill," *Moscow Times,* 25 February 1993, p. 1.

71. See "Privatizatsionnaia strategiia ustroila" [The privatization strategy has been built], *Kommersant',* no. 37, 13–19 September 1993; and Nelson and Kuzes, *Property to the People,* 148–49.

72. See Åslund, *How Russia Became a Market Economy,* 237.

73. On advantages for regional governments in privatization, see Åslund, *How Russia Became a Market Economy,* 237.

74. On changes in the 1994 voucher program, see Aleksandr Privalov and Natal'ia Kalinchenko, "Privatizatsionnye caprichos" [Privatization caprices], *Kommersant',* no. 1, 18 January 1994, pp. 43–45.

75. The 1994 program removed the provision requiring foreigners to get approval to participate in voucher auctions and also eliminated barriers to privatization that had been regionally specific. *Rossiiskaia gazeta,* 4 January 1994, cited in FBIS-SOV-94-003, 5 January 1994, pp. 40–41.

76. An excellent discussion of varying paths of privatization in Russia's regions is found in Darrel Slider's "Privatization in Russia's Regions," *Post-Soviet Affairs* 10, no. 4 (1994): 367–96. Slider enumerates the many instances in which various republics designed their privatization programs independently from the federal program, and in which municipal administrations simply discarded central GKI directives.

77. For comments by Dmitri Vasiliev on regions blocking voucher auctions, see comments in Elisabeth Rubinfien, "Private Russia," *Central European Economic Review* (Summer 1993): 34.

78. See Aleksandr Radygin, "Russian Privatization in 1993: Results and Problems," *Studies on Russian Economic Development* 5, no. 2 (1994): 100. For a discussion of destabilizing factors, see chapter 6, in A. D. Radygin, *Reforma sobstvennosti v Rossii: Na puti iz proshlogo v budeshchee* [Property reform in Russia: From the past to the future] (Moscow: Respublika, 1994).

79. Boycko and Shleifer also write that depoliticization was the "primary objective" to which other goals were subordinated. See Boycko, Shleifer, and Vishny, *Privatizing Russia,* 11.

80. For more on this auction, see the complete text of the press conference with the

first deputy property minister in *Official Kremlin International News Broadcast*, 11 June 1998. On relations between the Duma and GKI, see Natal'ia Kalinichenko, "Duma o privatizatsii" [The Duma on privatization], *Kommersant'*, no. 15, 26 April 1994, p. 37; Aleksandr Privalov and Natal'ia Kalinichenko, "Aprel'skie tezisy" [April thesis], *Kommersant'*, no. 12, 5 April 1994, p. 2–3. On the Duma's opposition to privatization following the December 1995 elections in which Communist Party candidates won the most seats, see *Segodnia*, 22 December 1995, p. 2; *CDPSP* 47, no. 51 (1996): 4. A later example in which the Duma attempted to prevent specific auctions is the case of Rosneft. In this auction, members of the Duma tried to block the auction through a law, which the government claimed would only have the status of a resolution and would have no legal force.

81. See chap. 4 n. 149.

82. This section draws from Hilary Appel, "Voucher Privatization in Russia: Structural Consequences and Mass Response in the Second Period of Reform," *Europe-Asia Studies* 49, no. 8 (1997): 1433–49.

83. For the full text of this press conference, see "Press Conference by Anatoly Chubais, Deputy Prime Minister," *Official Kremlin International News Broadcast*, 21 August 1992.

84. Dmitry Vokhrintsev and Natatalya Kalinichenko, "Chubais Calls Privatization Unstoppable," *Kommersant'*, 29 September 1992, p. 6.

85. On the motivation for participating in privatization, and on expectations of receiving stable dividends, see poll data from "O sotsial'nom aspekte privatizatsii" [On the social aspect of privatization], *Voprosy ekonomiki* 4 (1996): 73–80.

86. Anders Åslund, ed., *Economic Transformation in Russia* (New York: St. Martin's Press, 1994), 1.

87. If Russians did not invest their vouchers in the firms where they worked, they typically chose firms close to where they lived. V. S. Tapilina, T. Bogomolova, and A. Mikheeva, "Kuda idti s vaucherom?" [Where does one go with vouchers?], *Ekonomika i organizatsiia promyshlennogo proizvodstva (EKO)*, no. 1 (1993): 123–36.

88. Katharina Pistor and Andrew Spicer, "Investment Funds in Mass Privatization and Beyond," *Between State and Market: Mass Privatization in Transition Economies*, ed. Ira Lieberman, et al. (Washington, DC: World Bank, 1997), 103–4 .

89. Not surprisingly, it is hard to get a clear picture of the structure of MMM. Mavrodi claims that only its employees can understand its complex structure. One fact is certain: millions of Russians fell prey to Mavrodi's scam and lost everything they invested. On the range of vouchers invested, the *Moscow Times* in late 1994 reports that Russians bought as many as 102 million MMM-Invest shares for vouchers (with one voucher buying ten MMM-Invest shares), whereas the *Economist* in mid-1994 estimates that 3.1 million vouchers were traded for MMM-Invest shares, one-third the estimate found in the first source. Julie Tolkacheva, "MMM-Invest Heads for Foreign Markets," *Moscow Times*, 21 December 1994; "Russian Investing: Back from the Grave," *Economist*, 10 September 1994, p. 88; "More Murk in Moscow," *Economist*, 5 November 1994, p. 77.

90. *Facts on File World News Digest*, 4 August 1994.

91. Sebastian Smith, "Yeltsin Acts to Regulate Wild Russian Securities Market," Agence France Presse, 8 November 1994.

92. Joseph Blasi, Maya Kroumova, and Douglas Kruse, *Kremlin Capitalism: Privatizing the Russian Economy* (Ithaca: Cornell University Press, 1997), 192.

93. On 22 July 1994, Yeltsin signed decree no. 1535 initiating the postvoucher privati-

zation program. For text of law, see "Osnovnie polzheniia gosudarstvennoi programmi privatizatsii gosudarstvennykh i munitsipal'nykh predpriatii v Rossiiskoi Federatsii posle 1 iiulia 1994 goda" [On the main principles of the state program of privatization of state and municipal enterprises in the Russian Federation after 1 July 1994], *Rossiiskie Vesti* 138, no. 562 (1994): 4–5.

94. For Chubais's assessment of the GKI's success in making privatization irreversible, see "O Vlasti i sobstvennosti" [About power and property], *Kommersant'*, 1 November 1994, p. 10.

95. *Moscow Times*, 15 April 1994, p. 8.

96. Interestingly, like in voucher privatization, the Yeltsin government once again declined the option of using privatization as a tool to restructure enterprises in favor of other priorities. During voucher privatization, restructuring individual enterprises (as a goal) lost out to restructuring the economy. In essence, privatization officials expected this to occur eventually and naturally since the new system of private ownership would create incentives for property to be used in its most efficient and beneficial manner.

97. Presidential decree no. 474, "On Measures to Guarantee the Federal Budget Revenues from Privatization," 11 May 1995.

98. ITAR-TASS, 25 June 1998.

99. On earlier popular expectations of receiving stable dividends, see polling data from "O sotsial'nom aspekte privatizatsii" [On the social aspect of privatization], *Voprosy ekonomiki*, no. 4 (1996): 73–80.

100. This explanation is credited to former Russian state Duma deputy Nadezhda Bikalova; interview with author, Washington, DC, 20 August 1999.

101. This qualifier is important for reasons discussed in the chapter.

102. Alfred Kokh served as acting chairman of GKI in 1995, when the real chairman was running for a seat in the Duma. Kokh was appointed chairman of GKI 12 September 1996 and resigned 13 August 1997 amid scandal.

103. Juliet Johnson, *A Fistful of Rubles: The Rise and Fall of the Russian Banking System* (Ithaca: Cornell University Press, 2000), 113–14.

104. Åslund, *Building Capitalism*, 243.

105. Kokh mentions many of these problems in explaining his inability to meet revenue targets. Kokh, *The Selling of the Soviet Empire*, 90–94.

106. Auctions were held for the following enterprises: metals—Norilsk Nickel, Novolipetsky, and Mechel; energy—Lukoil, SIDANKO, Surgutneftegaz, YUKOS, Nafta-Moskva, and Sibneft; sea transport—Severo Zapadnoye Parokhodstvo and Morskoye Parokhodstvo.

107. The loans-for-shares program is signed into law through Yeltsin's 31 August 1995 decree (no. 889) "On the Procedure for Pledging Stock Held in Federal Ownership for the Year 1995." An earlier decree that freed up more property (previously deemed too strategic to sell) for privatization was the 11 May 1995 presidential decree "On Measures to Ensure the Flow of Receipts from Privatization into the Federal Budget." This latter decree provided a legal basis for including oil enterprises in the collateral auctions.

108. Kokh, *The Selling of the Soviet Empire*, 105.

109. Lieberman et al., *Between State and Market*, 234.

110. On the government's desperate need for budget revenue, see Freeland, *Sale of the Century*, 175. For an account of scandals within the loans-for shares auctions see Freeland, *Sale of the Century*, 169–89, and David E. Hoffman, *The Oligarchs: Wealth and Power in the New Russia* (New York: Public Affairs, 2002), especially 307–20.

111. Due to a liquidity crisis, several banks (including Menatep and Inkombank) in late August reneged on their payment contracts. In response to the banking crisis in the summer of 1995, the government injected 1.6 trillion rubles ($360.8 million) on 24 August 1995 and then 869 billion rubles (almost $200 million) on 29 August 1995 into numerous troubled banks by buying back Treasury bills in order to stave off a crisis in the interbank currency and loans market. *Moscow Times*, 29–30 August 1995.

112. M. Stephen Fish, "Roots and Remedies for Russia's Racket Economy," in *The Tunnel at the End of the Light: Privatization, Business Networks, and Economic Transformation in Russia*, edited by Stephen S. Cohen, Andrew Schwartz, and John Zysman (Berkeley: University of California Press, 1998), 86–138; Freeland, *Sale of the Century*; Yoshiko Herrera, "Russian Economic Reform, 1991–1999," in *Russian Politics: Challenges of Democratization*, edited by Zoltan Barany and Robert Moser (New York: Cambridge University Press, 2001): 135–74.

113. Freeland, *Sale of the Century*; Hoffman, *The Oligarchs*. It is difficult to assess the intention to use the collateral auctions to win the bankers' support since they, unlike most people in Russia, had thrived during the Yeltsin years. The increased revenue for the budget in an election year should have outweighed the need to buy off the bankers, since they should have strongly supported the status quo over a Communist victory. After all, even the bankers who lost out in the auctions supported the Yeltsin campaign. Duncan Allan, "Banks and the Loans-for-Shares Auctions," in *Russian Banking: Evolution Problems and Prospects*, edited by David Lane (Northampton, Mass.: Edward Elgar, 2002), 137–59.

114. Quoted by Liam Halligan, "Russia's Banks Grow Up," *Moscow Times*, 7 May 1995.

115. Whitefield and Evans report that 67 percent of Russians surveyed responded in support of the idea that "privatization gives wealth to the rich and well-connected" (with 15 percent opposed and 18 percent unsure or neutral). For more on early attitudes toward privatization and distributional consequences, see Stephen Whitefield and Geoffrey Evans, "The Russian Election of 1993: Public Opinion and the Transitions Experience," *Post-Soviet Affairs* 10, no. 4 (1994): 47–49.

116. For comparative purposes, Gini coefficients for Czech Republic were 21.2 in 1991 and 25.9 in 1997. Gini coefficients reported in EBRD Transition Report 2001, *Economic Transition in Central and Eastern Europe and the CIS* (London: EBRD, 2001).

117. See excerpts of Yeltsin's speech in "Chubais to Blame for Poor Showing for NDR-Yeltsin," *ITAR-TASS Russian News Service*, 19 January 1996.

118. *Moscow Times*, 14 December 1995, p. 1.

119. The significance of the Russian aversion to foreign ownership is complex. In some instances this aversion is driven by nationalism, while in others it was driven by greed. Juliet Johnson shows how the major Russian bankers wanted to keep out foreign bidders in the initial stages of auctions to ensure a murky and partial process but recognized the advantages of foreign ownership at later stages. Johnson, *A Fistful of Rubles*, 188.

120. For more details on the winning and losing oligarchs in privatization auctions, see Paul Klebnikov, *Godfather of the Kremlin: Boris Berezovsky and the Looting of Russia* (New York: Harcourt, 2000), especially 197–205; and Freeland, *Sale of the Century*, 169–89.

121. The details of the auctions described in this paragraph are also based on multiple reports by *ITAR-TASS* and *Inter Press Service*, November and December 1995, December 1996, August 1997.

122. *Deutsche-Presse,* 17 August 1997, and "Russia: Rigged Privatization Row Will Not Die Down," *Inter Press Service,* 20 August 1997.

123. Although the bid was 80 percent above the starting price ($140.8 million), the company's market capitalization was $1.4 billion, leading analysts to estimate its market value at $500–$750 million. The second round auction proceeded, despite calls for delays by leading political figures including Premier Chernomyrdin, Duma Speaker Gennadii Selezniov, and Economics Minister Yevgeny Yasin. They objected to Oneximbank's attempts to prevent other bidders from participating. See "Teaching the Privatizers an Expensive Lesson," *Inter Press Service,* 20 August 1997.

124. *Kommersant-daily,* 5 December 1997, p. 2.

125. Yeltsin stated in a television broadcast on NTV "Such work will not do. . . . The scandal around Svyazinvest and Norilsk Nickel is connected to the fact that some banks are evidently closer to Kokh's soul." Translated by Agence France Presse, 15 August 1997. Also, see Yeltsin's public accusation of unfair privileging of Oneximbank, see Associated Press, 12 September 1997.

126. Former first deputy property minister Alexander Braverman in 1998 unequivocally expressed his disapproval: "I am no believer in loan-for-shares schemes." Quoted in *Official Kremlin International News Broadcast,* 11 June 1998.

127. *Intercom Daily Report on Russia,* 5 February 1996; *Segodnia,* 7 September 1996, p. 2.

128. Quoted in *Moscow Times,* 19 March 1996, p. 1.

129. Ira Lieberman and Robi Veimetra, "The Rush for State Shares in the 'Klondyke' of Wild East Capitalism: Loans-for-Shares Transactions in Russia," *George Washington Journal of International Law and Economics* 29, no. 3 (1996): 738, quoted in Nellis, "Time to Rethink Privatization," p. 8.

130. Lynn Berry, "Minister's Nationalization Plan 'Goes Further' than Communists," Associated Press, 14 February 1996.

131. Elena Medvedeva, "Goskomimushchestvo priznaet vse, krome biudzhetnogo zadaniya," ["GKI admits to everything except the budget"] *Kommersant-daily,* 5 April 1996, p. 6. Aleksandr Bekker, 'GKI vstupaet v konkurentsiyu s kommunistami: privatizatsionnoe vedomstvo gotovit zakon o natsionalizatsii," [GKI enters the competition with the communists: The privatization institution prepares a nationalization law"] *Segodnia,* 21 March 1996.

132. During the campaign, Yeltsin criticized Chubais, publicly stating, he "sold off big industry for next to nothing; we cannot forgive this." Quoted by Janet Gultsman, "Yeltsin Says Still Pro-Reform, Scathing on Chubais," Reuters Financial Service, 19 January 1996.

133. *Kommersant-daily,* 5 December 1997.

134. Interfax, 6 April 1999.

135. Author's interview with Vyacheslav Kuznetsov, chairman of the Subcommittee on Corporate Securities and Privatization, State Duma, Moscow, 7 May 1996.

136. Anatoly Chubais, *Privatizatsiia po-Rossiiski* (Moscow: Vagrius, 1999). See *ITAR-TASS,* 14–20 November 1997; *ITAR-TASS,* 2 October 1997; and Associated Press, 1 October 1997.

137. Quotes from the *Jamestown Foundation Daily Monitor,* 31 July 2000. For more see *ITAR-TASS,* 30 July 2000.

138. The nationalization of Yukos may prove to be an exception to the general trend of honoring the results of Yeltsin-era privatization auctions. *Financial Times,* 10 November 1999, p. 1.

139. On the requirement for a more thorough presale preparation of enterprises to be privatized to avoid accusations of insider favoritism, see government spokesperson's comments in Agence France Presse, 27 January 1998; the complete text of press conference by first deputy minister of state property Alexander Braverman, Official Kremlin International News Broadcast, 11 June 1998.

140. However, the slowdown of privatization sales began even prior to the Russian 1996 presidential elections. That is, the privatization of large companies had already ground to a halt during the first half of 1996. Both the success of the Communist Party during the Duma elections in December 1995 and the projections of a Communist victory in the presidential elections discouraged foreign investment.

141. See chap. 2 n. 14.

142. For example, in 1998 the government twice attempted to sell a 75 percent-plus-one stake in Rosneft to no avail, despite lowering the asking price from $2.1 billion to $1.6 billion. Likewise, the late 1997 and early 1998 tenders for 19.7 percent stake in Slavneft failed to attract a buyer, despite lowering the price from $1.9 billion to $1.5 billion; Interfax, 15 July 1999. An auction for a 34 percent stake in Eastern Oil Company (VNK) was canceled due to lack of interest in November 1997; Associated Press, 25 November 1997.

143. Deutsche Presse-Agentur, 17 August 1998. It is reported as well that Soros joined Potanin in June 1997 to pay $1.9 billion for participation in the purchase of the 25 percent stake in Svyazinvest. Agence France Presse, 20 April 1998.

144. *Kommersant-daily,* 23 August 2000, p. 1.

145. For a list of fifty-four additional companies that the Russian government approved for privatization, see *What the Papers Say (Russia),* Section Credits and Investments, 14 September 2001.

146. Deutsche Presse-Agentur, 18 December 2002; *Moscow Times,* 22 December 2001.

147. *Financial Times,* 20 September 2000; *Moscow Times,* 10 October 2001, 22 October 2001; *Russian Press Digest,* 7 August 2003; *Vedomosti,* no. 39, p. B1; *Petroleum Economist,* 10 June 2003, p. 41.

148. Most academic studies are critical of Russian privatization. See chapter 1, note 4, for numerous examples. There are important exceptions, however. For example, Anders Åslund, *Russia's Economic Transformation in the 1990s* (London: Pinter, 1997); Andrei Shleifer and Daniel Treisman, *Without a Map: Political Tactics and Economic Reform in Russia* (Cambridge, Mass.: MIT Press, 2000), especially chaps. 1–2. Also see Boycko, Shleifer, and Vishny, *Privatizing Russia.* Joseph Blasi et al., *Kremlin Capitalism: The Privatization of the Russian Economy* (Ithaca: Cornell University Press, 1997). Ognian Hishow, "Russlands wirtschaftstransformation—Ergebnisse und aussichten" [Russia's economic transition—Outcomes and prospects], *Bundesinstitut für Ostwissenschaftliche und Internationale Studien,* 12 July 2000.

149. Interfax Russian News Agency, 7 July 2000, 3 October 1998.

150. As noted above, the Gini coefficients for Russia nearly doubled in six years. See chap. 4 n. 116.

151. EBRD 2001 Transition Report.

152. Johanna Bockman and Gil Eyal, "Eastern Europe as a Laboratory for Economic Knowledge: The Transnational Roots of Neo-Liberalism," *American Journal of Sociology* 108, no. 2 (September 2001): 310–52.

Chapter 5. The Beliefs of Leaders and the Content of Reform

1. David Weimer, ed., *The Political Economy of Property Rights: Institutional Change and Credibility in the Reform of Centrally Planned Economies* (New York: Cambridge University Press, 1997), 5.

2. Jan Winiecki, *Resistance to Change in the Soviet Economic System* (New York: Routledge, 1991); North, *Structure and Change.*

3. Voucher privatization was the primary means of privatization in Czech Republic, Latvia, Lithuania, Russia, Moldova, Armenia, Georgia, Kazakhstan, Kyrgyzstan, and the secondary means in Poland, Slovakia, Bulgaria, Ukraine. *EBRD Transition Report 1997* (London: EBRD, 1997), 90.

4. John Nellis, senior manager of the World Bank's Enterprise Reform and Privatization Unit, noted in reference to the Czech privatization program. "Initially we had some reservations. We were worried about the efficiency outcomes. That is, where would corporate governance come from?" John Nellis interview, Washington, DC, 11 November 1999.

5. Frydman and Rapaczynski, *Privatization in Eastern Europe.* Roman Frydman et al., "Investing in Insider Dominated Firms: A Study of the Russian Voucher Privatization Funds," in *Corporate Governance in Eastern Europe and Russia,* edited by Roman Frydman et al. (London: CEU Press, 1996), 187–241.

6. Janos Kornai, *The Road to a Free Economy: Shifting from a Socialist System: The Example of Hungary* (New York: W.W. Norton, 1990), 91.

7. Gehard Pohl et al., "Privatization and Restructuring in Central and Eastern Europe: Evidence and Policy Options," World Bank Technical Paper No. 368 (Washington, DC: World Bank, 1997).

8. Boycko, Shleifer, and Vishny, *Privatizing Russia,* 94.

9. Ibid., 12.

10. Václav Klaus and Dušan Tříska, "Review Article of Janos Kornai's "The Socialist System: The Political Economy of Communism," in *Dismantling Socialism, An Interim Report: A Compendium of Texts from the Years 1992–1994,* Prague, September 1994. Also published in the Hungarian journal *Buksz* (Winter 1994).

11. Leszek Balcerowicz writes about a window of opportunity in the Polish context, or a so-called period of extraordinary politics, in which a population is willing to support difficult austerity programs. While no one from the Czech reform team expected voucher privatization to be painful or difficult for the population, the members were concerned that various groups in the population may discover that their interests could be better served by an alternative scheme. Leszek Balcerowicz, *Socialism, Capitalism, and Transformation* (New York: Central European University Press, 1995).

12. Orenstein, *Out of the Red,* 111.

13. Ibid., 50.

14. Dušan Tříska, interview by author, Prague, 13 February 1996.

15. Dmitri Vasiliev, "Rossiiskaia programma privatizatsii i perspectivy ee realizatsii" [The Russian privatization program and the prospects for its realization], *Voprosy ekonomiki,* no. 9 (1992): 11–17.

16. Jeffrey Sachs, "Accelerating Privatization in Eastern Europe: The Case of Poland" (paper prepared for the World Bank Annual Conference on Development Economics, 25–26 April 1991), 1; quoted in Stephen Cohen and Andrew Schwartz, "Deeper into the

Tunnel," in *The Tunnel at the End of the Light: Privatization, Business Networks, and Economic Transformation in Russia*, edited by Stephen S. Cohen, Andrew Schwartz, John Zysman (Berkeley: University of California Press, 1998), 7.

17. David Donaldson and Dileep Wagle, *Privatization: Principles and Practice* (Washington, DC: World Bank/IFC, 1995), 22.

18. While voucher privatization for the majority of citizens meant placing their vouchers in voucher privatization funds rather than participating directly in the bidding process, the privatizers had not foreseen the popularity of investment funds and had fully expected individuals to be personally involved in the repeated bidding process.

19. Martin Kupka, "Transformation of Ownership in the Czech Republic," *Soviet Studies* 44, no. 2 (1992): 309.

20. William Riker and David Weimer, "The Economic and Political Liberalization of Socialism: The Fundamental Problem of Property Rights," *Social Philosophy and Policy* 10, no. 2 (1993): 79–102.

21. See discussion of Gaidar's comments in John Litwack, "Three Issues of Credible Commitment and Russian Privatization," in *The Political Economy of Property Rights*, edited by David Weimer (New York: Cambridge University Press, 1997), 109.

22. Boycko, Shleifer, and Vishny, *Privatizing Russia;* Litwack, "Three Issues of Credible Commitment and Russian Privatization"; and Timothy Frye, "Russian Privatization and Credible Commitment," in *The Political Economy of Property Rights*, edited by David Weimer (New York: Cambridge University Press, 1997). Stefan Hedlund, "Property without Rights: Dimensions of Russian Privatisation," *Europe-Asia Studies* 53, no. 2 (2001): 213–38.

23. Frye sums up his argument succinctly "by distributing vouchers and encouraging their concentration in investment funds, the government sought to raise the political costs of altering privatization. The voucher is an inefficient means of distributing assets due to high transaction costs and weak corporate governance, but the government weighted these losses against . . . constraining current and future governments" (Frye, "Russian Privatization and the Limits of Credible Commitment," 92, 93).

24. Hedlund, "Property without Rights," 215.

25. Quotes from speech given by Klaus at the fourth annual meeting of the Central and Eastern Europe Privatization Network (CEEPN). The proceedings of the meeting were published in *Privatization in Central and Eastern Europe 1993*, edited by Andrea Bohm and Marko Simoneti (Ljubljana: CEEPN Annual Conference Series, 1993), 18.

26. Robert Holman, Klaus's adviser, interview by author, Prague, 29 November 1995.

27. Quotes from speech given by Klaus in Bohm and Simoneti, *Privatization in Central and Eastern Europe 1993.*

28. Dušan Tříska interview, Prague, 13 February 1996.

29. Ibid.

30. Dušan Tříska, "Political, Organizational, and Legislative Aspects of Mass Privatization—Czechoslovakia," in *Privatization in Central and Eastern Europe, 1993*, and cited in Orenstein, *Out of the Red.*

31. *ČTK*, 19 October 1990.

32. See extensive interview with Ježek in Petr Husák, "Co liberál netoleruje" [What a liberal does not tolerate], *Lidové noviny,* 13 December 1991, p. 6.

33. Sokol states, "Ježek is a preacher of Hayek, it is almost a religion for him: Privatization as a salvation." Jan Sokol, interview by author, Prague, 30 January 1996.

34. Boycko, Shleifer, and Vishny, *Privatizing Russia*, 11.

35. Although no more than a curious aside, the Czech privatization minister Tomás Ježek frequently boasted of his 1980s *samizdat* translations of Hayek into Czech while, at the same time, Chubais, Russia's privatization chief expressed his nostalgia for his past study of liberal thinkers, reminiscing, "[I spent] the happiest days of my life, reading Hayek in the library late at night." For Chubais quote, see "Russia's Emerging Market Survey," *Economist*, 8 April 1995, 5.

36. Note the description of economic adviser Anders Åslund of Gaidar's reform team (including the privatizers), which reveals his impression of their ideological orientation as well as his own: "The Russian transformation has been a manifestation of idealism by those who believed in building a better society—one characterized by individual freedom, democracy, a market economy, widespread private ownership and the rule of law. The ruling spirit during the first two years of Russian transformation was indeed ideological and idealistic. Later on, the idealists lost out; but they had already laid the foundation for a free economy and a free society" (Åslund, *How Russia Became a Market Economy*, 312).

37. Viktor Nekipilov, deputy director of the Institute for International Economic and Political Research and consultant to the Duma on privatization, interview by author, Moscow, 14 May 1996.

38. See interview with Šik, "Záporů bude víc než kladů: Ota Šik kritizuje kupónovou privatizaci," *Rudé právo*, 23 January 1992. On the resistance by Šik and others, see Kotrba, "Privatization Process in Czech Republic: An Overview" and "Privatization Process in the Czech Republic: Players and Winners."

39. Václav Klaus, "Jde vlna za vlnou: Proč právě kupónová privatizace" [One wave comes after another: Why voucher privatization], *Hospodářské noviny*, 2 September 1991.

40. Mertlík became the Czech minister of finance in 1999. Pavel Mertlík, "The Cooperative Movements, Labor Managed Firms and Property Rights," *Oeconomica* 1 (1992): 40.

41. Pavel Mertlík, "Czechoslovakian Economic Reform: Perspectives for Cooperation," in *What Markets Can and Cannot Do*, edited by Milan Soyka (Prague: Nova Spes International Press, 1992), 171.

42. In a speech reviewing the results of voucher privatization, Chubais unequivocally stated, "We were strongly against various attempts to divide the property between the workers. . . . We particularly were against the establishment of the so-called closed joint stock companies." See Official Kremlin News Broadcast, 1 July 1994.

43. Ibid.

44. See Chubais's diatribe against employee ownership in "Darovaia sobstvennost' ne sdelaet cheloveka khoziainom" [Property given away will not make a man an owner], *Izvestiia*, 26 February 1992, p. 2. For further discussion of the privatization officials and their view of employee ownership, see Berger, "Privatizatsii ugrozhaet diktatura proletariata," 2.

45. For example, liberal economist and cochairman of the Economic Freedom Party Svyatoslav Fyodorov justifies his opposition to majority worker ownership by stating, "we shall have another Yugoslavia on our hands," in "Press Conference of Economic Freedom Party," Official Kremlin International News Broadcast, 19 June 1992. On the response of economic adviser Andrei Shleifer to proposals for ESOPs, see Shleifer's comments in "Gospodin Simmons iskazhaiet pravdu" [Mr. Simmons distorts the truth],

Rossiiskaia gazeta, 11 June 1992. Also see Åslund, *How Russia Became a Market Economy,* 233.

46. Examples of the government's association of ESOP with past command structures are abundant. Chubais's deputy, Piotr Mostovoi (who later served as the director of GKI), links employee ownership to the past system: "Experience shows employee ownership is almost as ineffective as state ownership" (G. Chazan, "Russian Privatization Program Threatened, Minister Says," United Press International, June 1992). On Chubais's claims that employee share ownership schemes will entrench former industrial nomenklatura, see *Guardian,* 17 April 1993, p. 34. On privatization and ESOP in Russia, see Jon Simmons and Jon Loge, "Trinadtsat' mifov rossiiskoi privatizatsii" [The thirteen myths of Russian privatization], *Izvestiia,* 1 April 1992, p. 5; and on Shleifer's views on ESOP, see Andrei Shleifer, "Gospodin Simmons iskazhaiet pravdu" [Mr. Simmons distorts the truth], *Rossiiskaia gazeta,* 11 June 1992.

47. It is easy to be skeptical about the idealism of former Communist *apparatchiks* appearing to have found liberalism at the most convenient moment possible. One of the most glaring and comical examples of this that I have confronted in the field was the director of the Liberalni Institut (a Western-funded, right-wing liberal think tank), who was a member of the Communist elite before the Velvet Revolution.

48. On the "unwarranted assumptions about the uniformity of convictions" among members of an ideological group, see Schull, "What Is Ideology? Theoretical Problems and Lessons from Soviet-Type Societies," *Political Studies* 40 (December 1992): 728–31. Thomas Hansen notes the tensions created by the "multiplicity of meanings inscribed in most ideological constructions. This tension may be expressed as the tension between the conceptual grammar of a discourse and the connotative domain within which it is articulated." Thomas Hansen, *The Saffron Wave: Democracy and Hindu Nationalism in Modern India* (Princeton, N.J.: Princeton University Press, 1999), 25.

49. An insightful essay by Joseph Schull notes that it would be a mistake to "put a premium on the genuiness of an agent's state beliefs," since "one's actions will be shaped by an ideology in so far as one must conform to its conventions"; one need not "believe in the ideology . . . one must be committed to it. The required attitude is respect, not faith." For this reason, Schull suggests that ideologies are better understood as a discourse rather than a belief system.

50. In fact, Schull recommends that the term *ideology* be replaced with the term *discourse* in instances where an ideas system is not actually "believed in" but constrains the policy debate nonetheless.

51. Bruce Ackerman, *Private Property and the Constitution* (New Haven: Yale University Press, 1977).

52. Orenstein, *Out of the Red.*

53. Václav Klaus, interview by author, Los Angeles, 18 January 2001.

Chapter 6. Power, Interests, and the Ideological Context

1. Gabriel Almond and Sidney Verba, *The Civic Culture* (Boston: Little, Brown, 1964), 12–13.

2. Ibid., 500.

3. For an analysis of political culture as the product of the gradual historical accu-

mulation of meanings and patterns of behavior pervading multiple layers of the society and the polity, see Thomas Hansen, *The Saffron Wave*, 27.

4. On the culture-ideology distinction as representing stasis-change dichotomy in the work of Clifford Geertz, Ann Swidler, and others, see Rhys Williams, "Religion as a Political Resource: Culture or Ideology?" *Journal for the Scientific Study of Religion* 35 (December 1996): 368–78.

5. See Jim Granto, Ronald Inglehart, David Leblang "Cultural Values, Stable Democracy and Economic Development: A Reply," *American Journal of Political Science* 40, no. 3 (1996): 680–96.

6. Schmitter and Karl, "What Democracy Is and Is Not," 83–84.

7. Richard Pipes, *Survival Is Not Enough: Soviet Realities and America's Future* (New York: Simon and Schuster, 1984), and idem, "The Communist System," in *The Soviet System in Crisis*, edited by Alexander Dallin and Gail Lapidus (Boulder: Westview Press, 1991), 18.

8. David Laitin developed a theory of political culture where culture has two faces: the first face of culture defined the identities of people, whereas the second face served as a means to political power. In this instance, self-interest and rational calculation lead political leaders to highlight certain cultural identities in order to avoid resistance to the realization of a political project. David Laitin, *Hegemony and Culture: Politics and Religious Change among the Yoruba* (Chicago: University of Chicago Press, 1986).

9. On the revival of the study of political culture in the second half of the 1980s, see Ronald Inglehart, "The Renaissance of Political Culture," *American Political Science Review* 82, no. 4 (1988): 1203–30. More recently, see Richard Wilson, *Compliance Ideologies: Rethinking Political Culture* (New York: Cambridge University Press, 1992), as well as Laitin's analysis of political culture in "Compliance Ideologies," *American Political Science Review* (March 1995): 168. Additionally, see Larry Diamond, *Political Culture and Democracy in Developing Countries* (Boulder: Lynne Rienner Publishers, 1994), especially the introductory chapter. On Eastern Europe, see *Political Culture and Civil Society in Russia and the New States of Eurasia,* edited by Vladimir Tismaneanu (Armonk, NY: M. E. Sharpe, 1995).

10. Although there are many components considered, this chapter emphasizes the beliefs of actors in society. The aggregate sum of mass and elite beliefs creates an ideological context within a given political space.

11. Eurobarometer surveys report consistent support for joining the European Union among a majority of Czechs over time, not to mention Poles, Hungarians, and others. Central and Eastern Europe Eurobarometer, *Brussels: European Commission, 1990–1998,* nos. 1–8.

12. Boycko, Shleifer, and Vishny, *Privatizing Russia.*

13. Hilary Appel, "Justice and the Reformulation of Property Rights in the Czech Republic," *East European Politics and Societies* 9, no. 1 (1995): 22–40.

14. Frydman, Rapaczynski, and Earle, *The Privatization Process in Central Europe,* 82.

15. For a discussion of the selection of projects, see Joshua Charap and Alena Zemplinerová, "Management Buy-outs in the Privatisation Programme of the Czech Republic," in *Management and Employee Buy-outs in the Context of Privatization,* OECD Special Report 1, no. 3 (1994).

16. Author's interview with Eva Klvačová, former economist in the Ministry of Privatization and editor of *EKONOM,* 2 November 1995, Prague. This form of government pressure is an issue returned to later in the chapter.

17. On the controversy over making the process of submitting privatization projects competitive, see "Další kolo konfliktů Klaus-Ježek," *Rudé právo*, 16 November 1991, pp. 1, 2. Also see the interview with former Czech Privatization Minister Tomáš Ježek in "Pochod Údolím Smrti" [March through the Valley of Death], *Mladý svět*, no. 47, 28 October 1991, pp. 10–11.

18. See Charap and Zemplinerová, "Management Buy-outs." For comparisons between first and second waves of voucher privatization, see Michael Mejstřík et al., "Privatization and the Opening of the Capital Market in the Czech and Slovak Republics," CERGE-EI Working Papers, Prague, April 1994; and Roland Egerer, "Investment Funds and Corporate Governance in Emerging Markets: An Assessment of the Top Ten Voucher Funds in the Czech Republic," Draft World Bank Report, mimeo, December 1994.

19. On the Finance Ministry's interactions with management, the former minister of industry and trade explained that he had "started discussions with Fiat and Mercedes about joint ventures [with Tatra Kopřivnice] and these discussions lasted about four or five months. And when the discussions were almost concluded [deputy minister of finance Dušan] Tříska went there and told them [the managers] explicitly that they should submit the whole firm to vouchers because then they would have many unorganized owners and they would be uncontrolled. The result was they took Tříska's advice and now they are almost bankrupt." Author's interview with former minister of industry and trade, Jan Vrba, 16 January 1996, Prague.

20. Dušan Tříska, interview by author, 29 February 1996, Prague.

21. Karla Brom and Mitchell Orenstein, "The Privatised Sector in the Czech Republic: Government and Bank Control in a Transitional Economy," *Europe-Asia Studies* 6, no. 4 (1995): 907–8.

22. Jarko Fidrmuc and Ming Xie, "The Slovak Republic: New Country, Old Problems," mimeo, p. 19.

23. Jiří Nosal, Patria Finance (Czech investment company), interview by author, 7 November 1995, Prague.

24. Åslund, *Building Capitalism*, 275.

25. The first variant was the default variant that did not require the approval of two-thirds of the worker collective. In brief, the first variant offered employees 25 percent of nonvoting shares for free. The second variant allowed managers and workers to buy 51 percent of the voting shares for a price that was also negligible since it similarly was unadjusted for near hyperinflation. According to the third variant, managers or a small group of employees could buy 20 percent of the voting shares at the nominal price; however, this variant included several conditions rendering it more or less irrelevant.

26. Andrei Shleifer and Dmitry Vasiliev, "Management Ownership and Russian Privatization" (paper prepared for the World Bank Conference on Corporate Governance in Central Europe and Russia, Washington, DC, 15 December 1994), 9. Andrei Shleifer and Dmitry Vasiliev, "Management Ownership and Russian Privatization," in *Corporate Governance in Central Europe and Russia,* edited by Roman Frydman, Cheryl Gray, and Andrzej Rapaczynski (Budapest: Central European University Press, 1996), 2:62–77.

27. Blanchard et al., *Post-Communist Reform*, 148.

28. Joseph Blasi, Maya Kroumova, and Douglas Kruse, *Kremlin Capitalism: Privatizing the Russian Economy* (Ithaca: Cornell University Press, 1997), 193, Table 5. On the difficulty of quantifying managerial ownership see 61–67.

29. Ibid., 193. Note that these figures do not indicate the group that takes the place of the rank-and-file workers, since management figures are cited separately.

30. These findings are reported in Igor Gurkov, "Popular Response to Russian Privatization: Surveys in Enterprises," *Studies in Public Policy* 245 (1995): 1–62, especially 20–21.

31. Paul Klebnikov offers many egregious examples in his *Forbes* articles and in *Godfather of the Kremlin: Boris Berezovsky and the Looting of Russia* (New York: Harcourt, 2000).

32. Figures are taken from Lieberman et al., *Between State and Market*, 242–47.

33. Åslund, *How Russia Became a Market Economy*, 158.

34. Václav Klaus, "Hlavní překážky rychlé ekonomické přeměny ve východní Evropě: Československý pohled" [The principle barriers to rapid economic reform in Eastern Europe: A Czechoslovak perspective], *TOP*, 3 October 1990.

35. Orenstein, *Out of the Red*, 105; See Ales Capek and Pavel Mertlík, "Organizational and Financial Restructuring in Czech Manufacturing Enterprises, 1990–1995," in *Privatization in Post-Communist Countries*, edited by Barbara Blaszcyk and Richard Woodward (Warsaw: Center for Social and Economic Research, 1996), 270.

36. Milan Matějka interview, 16 January 1996, Prague.

37. Dušan Tříska interview, 13 February 1996, Prague.

38. Ibid.

39. See "Reinventing Trade Unions," unpublished survey by the *Central European University Privatization Project*, Fall 1994.

40. Igor Pleskot, "Czech and Slovak Trade Union Movement in the Period of Transformation to a Civil Democratic Society," *World Bank*, mimeo, April 1994.

41. Ibid.

42. See Kotrba, "The Privatization Process in the Czech Republic: Players and Winners," 164–65.

43. For proclamations by trade union leaders that parliamentary deputies were intentionally taking antiunion stands, see *ČTK*, 6 December 1990. On the difficulties of finding support from the center of parliament (including from Civic Forum) on labor issues, see *ČTK*, 4 December 1990. For further details of the trade unions' position on privatization, see *Práce*, 6 November 1990. On the ideologization of debate over worker rights in privatization, see comments by Mertlík in "Czechoslovakian Economic Reform," 30. Difficulties of labor to find support in Parliament also repeated in interviews with members of the first post-Communist Federal Assembly (such as with Jan Kavan, interview with the author, 7 February 1996, Prague).

44. For Vrba's views on privatization as a means to gain access to Western capital and technology, see "Podnikatelům chybí kapitál" [Entrepreneurs are lacking capital], *Lidová demokracie*, 20 February 1991, p. 1; "Reforma versus politika" [Reform versus politics], *Svobodné slovo*, 10 October 1991; "Weighing up the Ways and Means of Privatisation," *Times*, 12 August 1991.

45. Tomáš Ježek, interview by author, 1 March 1996, Prague.

46. Jan Vrba, interview by author, 16 January 1996, Prague.

47. *ČTK*, 7 August 1991.

48. See speech given by Klaus at the fourth annual meeting of the CEEPN. The proceedings of the meeting were published in Bohm and Simoneti, *Privatization in Central and Eastern Europe 1993*, 18.

49. See comments by Tříska in "In Defence of Vouchers," *Financial Times*, 3 July 1991. On the shortage of voucher booklets and the Finance Ministry's expectations, see *Wall Street Journal*, 21 January 1992.

50. On the allocation of shares to vouchers versus other methods, see Charap and Zemplinerová, "Management Buy-outs." For comparisons between first and second waves of voucher privatization, see M. Mejstřík et al., "Privatization and the Opening the Capital Market in the Czech and Slovak Republics," CERGE-EI, April 1994, Prague; and Egerer, "Investment Funds and Corporate Governance in Emerging Markets."

51. Of those companies participating in the first wave of privatization, 63 percent of shares were devoted to vouchers, whereas of those enterprises participating in the second wave, 44 percent of shares were privatized through vouchers. Roman Ceska, "Three Years of Privatization in the Czech and Slovak Republics," in *Privatization Newsletter of the Czech Republic and Slovakia,* 1993. It should be noted that there is some disagreement over the reasons for the drop in percentage of shares devoted to vouchers. Interviews with former employees of the Ministry of Privatization reveal consistently that this ministry was under less pressure to choose projects with high percentages of shares. However, government officials instead account for the difference by pointing to changes in the supply of projects, noting that managers were less willing to devote shares to vouchers in the second wave of privatization, after realizing from the results of the first wave that this would not lead to dispersed ownership and unbridled freedom for managers after all, but the concentrated control of major stakes by large voucher privatization funds. Much to the surprise of managers, concentration was substantial, since voucher privatization funds, which function like mutual funds, collected 72 percent of vouchers from participating citizens in the first wave. Furthermore, of the hundreds of privatization funds established, fourteen controlled 77 percent of the voucher points. *Kupónová privatizace,* no. 21, December 1992.

52. Jan Vrba, interview by author, 29 February 1996, Prague.

53. Ibid.

54. Jan Sokol, interview by author, 30 January 1996, Prague.

55. Throughout the 1990s, no party has deemed the Czech Communist Party (KSCM) an acceptable partner in forming a coalition government. Its parliamentary representatives thus have not held leading posts in the legislature or participated in the government. While coalition support is not an issue in Russia, the Communist Party of Russia (KPRF) has performed well in parliamentary elections and has controlled key posts as a result. The KPRF won more votes than any other party in the 1995 Duma elections (22.3 percent) and was just shy of winning the most votes in the 1999 Duma elections (with 24.3 percent).

56. Paul Lazarsfeld Society, Vienna, New Democracies Barometer III, data reported in Richard Rose, William Mishler, and Christian Haerpfer, *Democracy and Its Alternatives: Understanding Post-Communist Societies* (Baltimore: Johns Hopkins University Press, 1998), 196.

57. Richard Rose, *A Decade of New Russia Barometer Surveys* (Studies in Public Policy no. 360, University of Strathclyde, 2002), 48. In 1993, 75 percent of Russians responded approvingly to the socialist economic system (51).

58. Rose, Mishler and Haerpfer, *Democracy and Its Alternatives,* 111.

59. Yuri Levada, "All-Russian Center for the Study of Public Opinion (VTsIOM)," 17 January 2001, http://www.polit.ru (accessed 30 April 2003).

60. Rose, *A Decade of New Russia Barometer Surveys,* 17.

61. William Miller, Stephen White, and Paul Heywood, *Values and Political Change in Postcommunist Europe* (New York: St. Martin's Press, 1998), 85.

62. Ibid., 88.

63. In the New Soviet Citizen Survey in 1991, 47.5 percent of Russians surveyed responded positively to the Supreme Soviet of the RSFSR, and only 18.6 percent responded negatively (with 33.8 percent defining themselves as neutral). Arthur Miller, William Reisinger, and Vicki Hesli, "New Soviet Citizen Survey, 1991: Monitoring Institutional Change," Inter-university Consortium for Political and Social Research 6521, May 1999.

64. On the ideological makeup of the highest political organs from a pro-government perspective, see Al'bert Plutnik, "Atakuia pravitel'stvo, oppozitsiia boitsia uspekha reform" [Attacking the government, the opposition fears the success of reform], *Izvestiia,* 9 April 1992, pp. 1–2. Also see estimates of the percentage (87 percent) of members of the Supreme Soviet in 1992 believed to be former Communists in *Finansovaia Izvestiia,* 18 November 1992, p. i.

65. Giulietto Chiesa and Douglas Northrop, *Transition to Democracy: Political Change in the Soviet Union, 1987–1991* (Hanover, NH: University Press of New England, 1993), chap. 2. Yitzhak Brudny, "Neoliberal Economic Reform and the Consolidation of Democracy in Russia: Or Why Institutions and Ideas Might Matter More than Economics," in *The International Dimension of Post-Communist Transition in Russia and the New States of Eurasia,* edited by Karen Dawisha (Armonk, NY: M. E. Sharpe, 1997), 304–5.

66. On the early tensions between the legislature and the government, see Ivan Elistratov and Sergei Chubaev, "Pravitel'stvo vozvrashchaetsia" [The government returns], *Izvestiia,* 15 April 1992, p. 1. Also see Lynn Nelson and Irina Kuzes. "Coordinating the Russian Privatization Program." *RFE/RL Research Report* 3, no. 20 (1994): 15–27.

67. *Izvestiia,* 14 January 1992, p. 1.

68. As the president of the Association of Employers Unions, Michal Lach explained, "the privatization philosophy assumed by the government has been formulated jointly [with the Employers Unions]." *Slovenská Republika,* 21 June 1995, as cited in Miklos, "Economic Transition and the Emergence of Clientalist Structures in Slovakia," 65.

69. The Association of Employers Unions (AZZZ) exercised influence through a number of mechanisms. Informally, every Minister of the Economy from the June 1992 elections to the present day has been a member of AZZZ. This includes not only Vladimír Mečiar's ministers but also those appointed by the opposition, Peter Magvasi (March–December 1994) and Ludovit Cernak (June 1992–March 1993; October 1998–present). Political opponents to Mečiar analysts provide specific evidence highlighting AZZZ's role as a strong "industrial lobby" with "enormous influence over the economic and privatization policy of the Mečiar coalition and government" that was crucial in gaining its leading members favorable treatment in privatization decisions. For further recent evidence, see Ivan Miklos, "Privatizacia," in *Slovensko, 1997: Súhrnná správa o stave spoločnosti a trendoch na rok 1998* [The summary report of the state of society and trends in the year 1998], edited by Martin Butora and Michal Ivantysin (Bratislava: Institut pre Verejné Otazky, 1998), 418–20; Ivan Miklos, "Privatization Process in Slovakia: Backstage Interests," *Mapping and Promoting Privatization in Slovakia,* Seminar Bulletin 9, Center for Economic Development, Bratislava, 12 December 1995, p. 7.

70. Until the tripartite meetings were abandoned by the Mečiar government, AZZZ represented employers' interests in tripartite meetings with the government and the peak labor organization, KOZ. AZZZ, "5. Výročie AZZZ SR, 1991–1996" [Anniversary AZZZ SR, 1991–1996], *Spravodaj AZZZ Extra,* March 1996, Bratislava; John Gould's interview with Ludovit Černak, 2 April 1997, Bratislava.

71. In Ira Lieberman, Stilpon Nestor, and Raj Desai, eds., *Between State and Market Mass Privatization in Transition Economies* (Washington, DC: World Bank, 1997), 239.

72. Several theorists seeking to explain both political and economic differences point to economic conditions, whether trying to explain institutional development or relative economic performance after initial reforms, etc. On the latter, see Mertlík, "Czechoslovakian Economic Reform," 165–80. For this approach in Polish economic reform, see Leszek Balcerowicz, *Socialism, Capitalism, Transformation* (Budapest: CEU Press, 1995), 97. On economic conditions and political institutional development, see Herbert Kitschelt, "Formation of Party Cleavages in Post-Communist Democracies," *Party Politics* 1, no. 2 (1995), 447–72. On Slovak managers, see a more in-depth discussion in Appel and Gould, "Identity Politics and Economic Reform," 111–32.

73. Slovak unemployment reached 10.4 percent, while in the Czech lands it remained at 2.7 percent.

74. See Appel and Gould, "Identity Politics and Economic Reform," 117–19, for more extensive discussion.

75. Zora Butorova et al., *Aktuálne problemy Česko-Slovensko, januar 1992: Záverečna sprava zo sociologického prieskumu* [Current problems in Czechoslovakia, January 1992: The final report from the sociological study] (Bratislava: Centrum pre socialnu analyzi, 1992), appendix 2.

76. See data reported in Appel and Gould, "Identity Politics and Economic Reform."

77. Ibid.

78. See John Gould and Sona Szomolanyi, "Elite Division and Convergence," in *Elites After State Socialism,* edited by John Higley and Gyorgy Lenyel (Boulder: Rowman and Littlefield, 1999), 47–70.

79. Two good histories of the events covered here include Carol Skalnik Leff, *National Conflict in Czechoslovakia: The Making and Remaking of a State, 1918–1987* (Princeton: Princeton University Press, 1988); H. Gordon Skilling, *Czechoslovakia's Interrupted Revolution* (Princeton: Princeton University Press, 1976).

80. On Slovak sentiment toward the Communist past, see Kevin Krause, "Accountability and Political Party Competition in Slovakia and the Czech Republic" (Ph.D. diss., University of Notre Dame, 2000).

81. John Gould, "Beyond Creating Owners: Privatization and Democratization in the Slovak and Czech Republics, 1990–1998" (Ph.D. diss., Columbia University, 2000).

82. Petr Pithart, "Toward a Shared Freedom," and Sharon Wolchik, "The Politics of Transition and the Break-up of Czechoslovakia," in *The End of Czechoslovakia,* edited by Jiří Musil (Budapest: CEU Press, 1995); Krause, "Accountability and Political Party Competition."

83. Paul Lazarsfeld Society, Vienna, New Democracies Barometer III, data reported in Rose, Mishler, and Haerpfer, *Democracy and Its Alternatives,* 196. Moreover, 7 percent of Czechs and 16 percent of Slovaks agreed with the statement "we should return to Communist rule" (111).

84. See David Begg, "Economic Reform in Czechoslovakia: Should We Believe in Santa Klaus?" *Economic Policy* 14 (1991), 243–86. Interview by John Gould with Mikuláš Sedlak, president, Association of Independent Economists of Slovakia (NEZES), Bratislava, 12 March 1997.

85. Hence, managers supported Mečiar's creation of a separate Slovak foreign policy apparatus to represent particular Slovak cultural and economic interests abroad.

86. On this point, see Abby Innes, "The Breakup of Czechoslovakia: The Impact of Party Development on the Separation of the State," *East European Politics and Societies* 11, no. 3 (1997): 393–435.

87. Miklos, "Economic Transition and the Emergence of Clientalist Structures in Slovakia," 60.

88. John Gould, "Beyond Creating Owners: Privatization and Democratization in the Slovak and Czech Republics, 1990–1998" (Ph.D. diss., Columbia University, 2000).

89. KDH, "Alternativy dealšecho postupu ekonomické reformy" [The alternatives to further economic reform], *Hospodářské noviny,* 19 March 1991, p. 4.

90. NEZES, whose founders soon joined Mečiar in founding his new party, Movement for a Democratic Slovakia (HZDS), demanded that the Slovak parliament "immediately declare economic sovereignty" and called upon Slovak experts to defend citizens "against the asocial and irritating federal concept of a transition to a market economy." NEZES, "NEZES k reforme a hospodářskéj nezavislosti Slovenska" [NEZES on the economic reform and independence of Slovakia], *Hospodářské noviny,* 19 March 1991, p. 3.

91. "Slovak Meeting Studies Economic Problems," *FBIS,* 17 August 1990.

92. Innes, "The Breakup of Czechoslovakia"; Miklos, "Economic Transition and the Emergence of Clientalist Structures in Slovakia," 65.

93. The government boasted of privatizing only to domestic businessmen in order to create a national entrepreneurial class that would be more likely to conduct business in the interests of Slovakia. Miklos, "Privatizacia," 405–32.

94. On pro-European sentiment throughout the 1990s, see the Eurobarometer surveys. Central and Eastern Europe Eurobarometer, *Brussels: European Commission, 1990–1997,* nos. 1–7. Polish anti-Communist sentiment, although less studied, appears in various surveys in multiple forms. In the New Democracies Barometer, 38 percent of Poles offer a positive rating of a Communist regime, whereas 69 percent approve of the "current" (1993) political regime. Similarly, in response to the question "Was the fall of Communism worthwhile, 67 percent of Poles responded favorably (22 percent unfavorably). Jan Culik, "Evaluating a Decade: Poland, Hungary and the Czech Republic: People's Situation Has Worsened Since the Fall of Communism," in *Central Europe Review* 1, no. 22 (1999); data from New Democracies Barometer III are cited in Rose, Mishler, and Haerpfer, *Democracy and Its Alternatives,* 106.

95. Biuletyn nr. 41/X Kadencja, Komisja Polityki Gospodarczej, Budzetu I Finansow, Kancelaria Sejmu, 8 September 1989, 5–6; cited and translated in Agnieszka Paczynska, "Historical Legacies and Policy Choice: Labor and Public Sector Reform in Poland, Egypt, Mexico and the Czech Republic" (Ph.D. diss., University of Virginia, 2001), 5–6, chap. 2.

96. The OPZZ was the former official trade union confederation established during martial law. The PZPR, the United Polish Workers' Party, was the formerly dominant, Communist-era party with 65 percent of the reserved Sejm seats. It was later renamed the Social Democratic Alliance (SLD). The Employers Association (Konfederacja Pracodawcow) and the organizations within the Worker Self-Management Coalition (such as the Gdansk Self-Management club and the Instytut Badawczy Samorzadu Zalogi) similarly supported employee ownership.

97. In deference to his to pro-labor opposition, Lis agreed to reserve 20 percent of enterprise shares for workers. Paczynska, "Historical Legacies and Policy Choice," chap. 5.

98. Hanley explains that initially workers' councils expected higher wages if their

firms were privatized due to the imposition of the wage tax on state-owned firms. However, once it was realized that wage differentials did not emerge, incentives for workers' councils to approve privatization lost any potency. Eric Hanley, "Cadre Capitalism in Hungary and Poland: Property Accumulation among Communist-Era Elites," *East European Politics and Societies* 14, no. 1 (2000): 156–57.

99. The program works as follows: Each of the fifteen funds owns a controlling stake in approximately thirty enterprises (thereby serving as the lead fund for that enterprise) and a residual share in the remaining enterprises. Shares in NIFs are listed on the Warsaw stock exchange and are the most highly valued securities in Poland. NIFs, run by foreign and local firms, are paid 15 percent of the fund's worth in fees over ten years, with bonuses depending on performance (about $3 million per year). Approximately 95 percent of Poles bought certificates in July 1995 for twenty zlotys (seven to eight dollars). The value of these certificates went up tenfold by the end of the decade, with foreigners holding about half.

100. Mark Kramer, "The Changing Economic Complexion of Eastern Europe and Russia: Results and Lessons of the 1990s," *SAIS Review* 19, no. 2 (1999). Similar figures are found in Orenstein, *Out of the Red*, 111.

101. During the same period, though, the Czech, Russian, Slovak, and Hungarian private sectors showed even greater transformation. The Czech private sector as a percentage of GDP increased 5 percent to 80 percent; Russia's private sector GDP increased 5 percent to 70 percent; Slovakia's private sector GDP increased 5 percent to 75 percent; and Hungary's private sector GDP increased 20 percent to 80 percent. Estimates are based on World Bank 1997 figures and EBRD 1999 figures.

102. The same can be said for China, where the growth of the private sector as a share of GDP stems primarily from the growth of new private start-ups rather than from newly "privatized" large enterprises. Nicholas Lardy, *China's Unfinished Economic Revolution* (Washington, DC: Brookings Institution Press, 1998); Jean C. Oi and Andrew G. Walder, eds., *Property Rights and Economic Reform in China* (Stanford, Calif.: Stanford University Press, 1999).

103. Paczynska, "Historical Legacies and Policy Choice," 21.

104. *Polityka*, 12 December 1998. Cited in and translated by Paczynska, "Historical Legacies and Policy Choice," 23.

105. Paczynska cites survey research to justify worker attitudes toward privatization. For example, Juliusz Gardawski, *Poland's Industrial Workers on the Return to Democracy and Market Economy* (Warsaw: Friedrich Ebert Stiftung, 1996); Paczynska, "Historical Legacies and Policy Choice," 9.

106. Juliusz Gardawski and Tomasz Zukowski, *Rabotnicy 1993—Wybory ekonomiczne I polityczne* (Warszawa: Fundacja im. Friedricha Eberta w Polsce, 1994).

107. On evaluating the role of Polish labor in the early transformation, see Zbigniew Drag and Jerzy Indraszkiewicz, "Employee Consciousness and Reforms of Government System in Poland," Economic and Social Policy Series, no. 20 (Berlin: Friedrich-Ebert Foundation, 1992); Kazimierz Kloc, "Polish Labor in Transition (1990–1992)," *Telos* 92 (Summer 1992): 139–48; and Andrew Newell and Mieczyslaw Socha, "Wage Distribution in Poland: The Roles of Privatization and International Trade, 1992–1996," *Economics of Transition* 6, no. 1 (1998): 47–65.

108. Mark Kramer, "Polish Workers and the Post-Communist Transition, 1989–1993," *Europe-Asia Studies* 47, no. 4 (1995): 704.

109. Åslund distinguishes Polish privatization as a program geared especially toward labor, whereas other insider privatization programs tended to privilege management (Åslund, *Building Capitalism,* 275).

110. Steven Levitsky and Lucan Way, "Between a Shock and a Hard Place: The Dynamics of Labor-Backed Adjustments in Poland and Argentina," *Comparative Politics* 30, no. 2 (1998): 178.

111. As rapid privatization is one of the three pillars of shock therapy (along with liberalization and stabilization), was labor's influence over privatization an exception? The short answer is no, because macroeconomic stabilization and liberalization began earlier. These occurred during what Balcerowicz refers to as the period of extraordinary politics. Polish workers later did begin to resist macroeconomic stabilization. Once the pain of shock therapy became too great, Solidarity lost the support of its core members—that is, the rank-and-file workers. This caused instability in the government and the swift resignation of a series of prime ministers. Having lost faith in the ability of Solidarity to represent the interests of ordinary workers in the early 1990s, labor actively opposed reforms that appeared to have immediate and pressing consequences for labor, with the advancement of privatization being the case in point.

Chapter 7. The Ideological Foundations of Building Compliance

1. Ralf Dahrendorf, *Reflections on the Revolution in Europe* (New York: Random House, 1990); Adam Przeworski, *Democracy and the Market* (Cambridge: Cambridge University Press, 1991); Joel Hellman, "Winners Take All: The Politics of Partial Reform in Post-communist Transitions," *World Politics* 50, no. 2 (1998): 203–34.

2. Leszek Balcerowicz, "Understanding Post-communist Transitions," *Journal of Democracy* 5, no. 4 (1995): 75–89.

3. Frye, "Russian Privatization and the Limits of Credible Commitment." Irreversibility is a common theme of post-Communist privatization. See Boycko, Shleifer, and Vishny, *Privatizing Russia;* Åslund, *How Russia Became a Market Economy.*

4. See especially Daniel Diermeier et al., "Credible Commitment and Property Rights: The Role of Strategic Interaction between Political and Economic Actors," in *The Political Economy of Property Rights,* ed. David Weimer (Cambridge: Cambridge University Press, 1997); Frye, "Russian Privatization and the Limits of Credible Commitment."

5. Ibid.

6. North, *Structure and Change,* 50–52.

7. In noting that slavery was still profitable when it was abolished, North asserts that this "major institutional change . . . was the consequence of the growing abhorrence on the part of civilized human beings of one person owning another person." Douglass North, *Institutions, Institutional Change and Economic Performance* (Cambridge: Cambridge University Press, 1990), 85. North acknowledges the centrality of ideology for institutional development in Arthur Denzau and Douglass North, "Shared Mental Models: Ideologies and Institutions," *KYKLOS* 47 (1994): 3–31.

8. This is especially true for the work that privileges the state as an actor promoting a particular property rights arrangement. For example, William Riker and Itai Sened, "A Political Theory of Property Rights: Airport Slots," *American Journal of Political Science* 35 no. 4 (1991): 951–69; Fred McChesney, "Government as Definer of Property Rights: Indian Lands, Ethnic Externalities, and Bureaucratic Budgets," *Journal of Legal Studies* 19,

no. 2 (1990): 297–335. Even in interest group analyses of property rights, ideology is absent. For example, Libecap, *Contracting for Property Rights;* Demsetz, "Toward a Theory of Property Rights," 347–59.

9. In "Mentalities, Political Cultures and Collective Frames, Constructing Meaning through Action" (in *Frontiers in Social Movement Theory,* edited by Aldon Morris and Carol McClurg Mueller [New Haven: Yale University Press, 1992]), Sidney Tarrow explores how "leaders' ideological messages are formulated and communicated to target groups" (174) as part of a larger examination of how "societal mentalities, political cultures and collective action frames may be linked together in understanding how meaning is constructed in social movements" (176).

10. The term *frame* is attributed to Erving Goffman, who described it as a "schemata of interpretation" that enables individuals "to locate, perceive, identify and label" life occurrences; Goffman, *Frame Analysis* (Cambridge, Mass.: Harvard University Press, 1974).

11. David Snow and Robert Bedford, "Ideology, Frame Resonance and Participant Mobilization," in Bert Klandermans, Hanspeter Kriesi, and Sidney Tarrow, *International Social Movement Research: From Structure to Action Comparing Social Movement Research across Cultures*" (London: JAI Press, 1988), 1:198.

12. Ibid., 214 n. 3. In addition to analyzing "motivational framing," the authors examine "diagnostic framing," which "involves identification of a problem and the attribution of blame or causality" (200), and "prognostic framing," which "suggest[s] solutions to the problem but also to identify strategies, tactics, and targets" (201).

13. Tversky and Kahneman in Cook and Levi, *The Limits of Rationality,* 60–89.

14. Zald defines strategic framing as "an active process of framing and definition of ideology, of symbols, of iconic events by moral entrepreneurs . . . [who] attempt to define the issues, invent metaphors, attribute blame, define tactics. Both cultural breaks and cultural contradictions lead to action and policy imperatives only as they are defined in an active process of cultural and movement construction"; Mayer Zald, "Culture, Ideology, and Strategic Framing," in *Comparative Perspectives on Social Movements: Political Opportunities, Mobilizing Structures, and Cultural Framings,* edited by Doug McAdam, John McCarthy, and Mayer Zald (New York: Cambridge University Press, 1996), 269.

15. Doug McAdam, John McCarthy, and Mayer Zald, "Introduction: Opportunities, Mobilizing Structures, and Framing Processes—Toward a Synthetic, Comparative Perspective on Social Movements," in *Comparative Perspectives on Social Movements: Political Opportunities, Mobilizing Structures, and Cultural Framings,* edited by Doug McAdam, John McCarthy, and Mayer Zald (New York: Cambridge University Press, 1996), 16.

16. Broader targets enumerated in David Snow, E. Burke Rochford Jr., Steven Worden, and Robert Bedford, "Frame Alignment Processes, Micromobilization, and Movement Participation," *American Sociological Review* 51 (August 1986): 465 n. 2.

17. Zald, "Culture, Ideology, and Strategic Framing," 269.

18. Amitai Etzioni, *A Comparative Analysis of Complex Organizations: On Power, Involvement and Their Correlates* (New York: The Free Press, 1961), 4–22. See the discussion of (and extension of) the three reinforcing mechanisms in Ian Lustick, "Hegemony and the Riddle of Nationalism: The Dialectics of Political Identity in the Middle East" (working paper 1997-01, Christopher H. Browne Center for International Politics, University of Pennsylvania, 1997).

19. For a discussion of the dependence of normative compliance mechanisms on material incentives and coercion potential, see Levi, *Of Rule and Revenue*, 68.

20. Jerry Hough and Merle Fainsod, *How the Soviet Union Is Governed* (Cambridge, Mass.: Harvard University Press, 1980), 148–52.

21. See the speech by Klaus at G-30 conference in Vienna on 24 April 1993, "The Czech Republic's Prospects," published in *Telegraf*, 4 May 1993. Cited in "Klaus Hands Down 'Ten Commandments' for Reform," FBIS-EEU 93-087, 7 May 1993, pp. 7, 9.

22. Ibid.

23. Ibid.

24. Zdenka Mansfeldová, "Justice as an Ethic Legitimacy of Economic Reform" (paper presented at the conference Normative Foundations of the Polity: Conceptual Approaches in East and Central Europe, 20–22 January 1995, Bremen).

25. For example, see Klaus's remarks when forming the Interparliamentary Group of the Democratic Right Wing, a subgroup of Civic Forum, and declaring the fundamental principles of the organization (*ČTK Czech Newswire*, 31 October, 1990). Also, see Peter Rutland on Klaus's pro-European posturing in "Thatcherism, Czech-style," *Telos* 94 (Winter 1992): 103–29.

26. Similarly, in building a new, post-Communist identity, political leaders resorted to similar appeals to history, citing the Masaryk period in particular, to support the "naturalness" of democracy in the Czech lands. For development of this theme, see Ladislav Holy, *The Little Czech and the Great Czech Nation* (Cambridge: Cambridge University Press, 1996). Ivo Bayer and Jiri Kabele, "Politische kultur der Tschechischen Republik und ihre transformation" [The political culture of the Czech Republic and its transformation], *Bundesinstitut für Ostwissenschaftliche und Internationale Studien*, 28 May 1996.

27. Although Klaus has repeated this numerous times, this quotation can be found in Reuters, 31 May 1990.

28. *ČTK*, 8 December 1990. Examples of Klaus's reach to history in public speeches abound. Note Klaus's historical references when he founded Civic Democratic Party (ODS) and announces the programmatic principles of the party. According to the Czech national news agency, Klaus explained that ODS would "follow the traditions of European Christian civilization, the humanistic and democratic traditions of the pre-Munich republic (1918–1938) and the experience of the present Western democracies. It resolutely and entirely rejects Marxist and Leninist ideology, and all trends toward Socialization and Collectivization in the economy and politics are alien to it." Applicants to be members of the ODS would have to state whether they had been members of the Communist Party, and the ODS rejects the applications of former members of the People's Militia and collaborators with the former secret police. *ČTK*, 1 March 1991.

29. Quoted from Klaus, "Hlavní Překážky Rychlé Ekonomické Přeměny ve Východní Evropě," 70–71. Also see Klaus's portrayal of the 1968 reform Communists in his speeches: Václav Klaus, "Budeme podniky privatizovat, anebo sanovat?" [Will we privatize or restructure?], *Nemám rád katastrofické scénáře* (Ostrava: Sagit Press, 1991), 43–49.

30. See Snow and Bedford, "Ideology, Frame Resonance and Participant Mobilization," 204.

31. Jan Kavan, interview by author, 7 February 1996, Prague.

32. Ibid.

33. Valeš is an interesting example of a politician who had suffered under the Communist period of normalization (fired as a government minister and incarcerated for

three years) but still faced accusations of Communist collaboration. For Havel's comments, see *ČTK*, 17 September 1991.

34. Moreover, he would have antagonized virtually all the employees of his ministry, who, as past Ministry of Finance employees, would have necessarily been members of the party during the Communist period. Klaus needed their cooperation to execute his reform programs and could never have replaced an entire staff. Furthermore, Tomáš Ježek, the former minister of privatization, who by no means has been a defender of Klaus's character, insists that Klaus was never against people because they were Communists. Ježek explains: "Klaus was 'anti-' the communist system. . . . And he was 'anti' certain people, but because they disagreed with him, not because they had been communists." Ježek interview, 1 March 1996, Prague.

35. Examples abound of such name-calling. See Klaus's portrayal of the 1968 reform Communists in his speeches: "Budeme Podniky Privatizovat, Anebo Sanovat?" and "Hlavní Překážky Rychlé Ekonomické Přeměny ve Východní Evropě."

36. Official press conference with Anatoly Chubais, Official Kremlin International News Broadcast, 30 July 1992.

37. "Speech of Anatoly Chubais to Congress of People's Deputies," Official Kremlin International News Broadcast, 8 April 1992.

38. This work concluded that Russians were as much "economic beings" as Americans were. Robert Shiller, Maxim Boycko, and Vladimir Korobov's "Hunting for Homo Sovieticus: Situational versus Attitudinal Factors in Economic Behavior," *Brookings Papers on Economic Activity,* no. 2 (1993): 139–81. (Boycko was a key player in Russian property reforms, holding numerous positions in the privatization process, including director of the Russian Privatization Center and briefly chairman of the State Property Committee [GKI]). Other survey research reported that Muscovites held similar views as New Yorkers toward fairness, income inequality, and economic incentives; and they shared similar understandings of the functioning of markets. Robert Shiller, Maxim Boycko, and Vladimir Korobov, "Popular Attitudes Toward Free Markets: The Soviet Union and the United States Compared," *American Economic Review* 81, no. 3 (1991).

39. See *Nezavisimaia gazeta*, 27 March, 1992, quoted by Shlapentokh, "Privatization Debates in Russia," 19–32.

40. Peter Rutland, "Mission Impossible? The IMF and the Failure of the Market Transition," *Review of International Studies*, Fall 1999, 187.

41. On the reformers' self-perception as macroeconomic technocrats and indifference to popularity ratings, see "Egor Gaidar i v bezbykhodnykh situatsiiakh nado iskat' vykhod" [Egor Gaidar in a hopeless situation must search for an exit], *Izvestiia*, 5 July 1992, pp. 1, 3.

42. Yeltsin, *The View from the Kremlin*, 159.

43. *TASS*, 6 October 1992, quoted in George Breslauer and Catherine Dale, "Boris Yel'tsin and the Invention of the Russian Nation-State," *Post-Soviet Affairs* 13, no. 4 (1997): 316.

44. See A. Chereshnia, "Protivniki reform—Takoe zhe grazhdane Rossii, kak i ikh storonniki" [Reform opponents—such are the Russian citizens and their supporters] *Izvestiia*, 10 April, 1992, p. 7.

45. See Peter Reddaway's analysis of the Russian backlash against the West and its institutions in "Visit to Maelstrom," *New York Times*, 10 January 1994.

46. Excerpts taken from a published collection of essays and newspaper interviews of

Ziuganov from the previous five years: Gennadii Ziuganov, *Za gorizontom* [Beyond the Horizon] (Orel: Veshnie Vody, 1995). Quoted in "Gennadii Ziuganov in His Own Words [trans. Susan Kennedy Orttung], in *Transition* 2, no. 11 (1996): 17.

47. Quoted in Nelson and Kuzes, *Property to the People*, 81, from "Pravitel'stvo meniat' poka rano, no programmu reform nado korrektirovat," *Delovoi mir*, no. 225, 21 November 1992, p.2.

48. *Independent* (London), 16 August 1992, p. 10.

49. Interview with Volsky translated in "Volskiy on Privatization, Other Issues," FBIS-SOV-92-196. p. 30, from *La Republica*, 3 October, 1992 p. 19.

50. Sergei Chugayev, "By Attacking the Government, the Opposition Is Trying to Score Points," *Izvestiia*, 23 September 1992, pp. 1–2; *CDPSP* 44, no. 38 (1992): 8. By way of further example of this sentiment, one outspoken nationalist writes, "The principles of our society's social organization must differ fundamentally from the principles of the Anglo-Saxon liberal model. In our type of society, the destruction of state forms for the organization of society, the economy, culture, and ideology is ruinous and will inevitably result in the total and irreversible collapse of society itself. . . . We categorically reject [that Russia must undergo a harsh transformation to capitalism] which is aimed at the destruction of its identity. . . . Whether it is called Marxism or economic determinism in the spirit of the 'Harvard School,' that model can only destroy Russian reality." Sergei Kurginyan, the president of the Experimental Creative Center Corporation, published these statements in *Nash Sovremenik*, No. 7, July 1992, pp. 3–15; *CDPSP* 44, no. 40 (1992): 13. Also see Georgii Arbatov, "Neo-Bolsheviks of the IMF," *New York Times*, 7 May 1992.

51. Ivan Troitsyn, "How Today's Yeltsin Differs from Former One," *VEK*, 9 August 1996, no. 31, p. 1. Translated by Russica, *Russian Press Digest*.

52. For comments by Alexander Voronin, the deputy minister for nationalities at the time see ITAR-TASS, 18 February 1997.

53. Anna Ostapchuk and Yevgeny Krasnikov, "An Idea Visits the Kremlin," *Moskovskiie novosti*, no. 38, 21–28 September 1997, pp. 6–7; *CDPSP* 49, no. 38 (1997): 10.

54. The winner of the prize for the new Russian idea writes that "The Russian national character is not based on market activity. That is the root of the principal difference of the (Russian) spiritual makeup." For a discussion of the midterm winner of the prize, Gurii Sudakov, a regional politician from Vologda region, and his patriotic idea as a "rejection of Western individualist money-oriented mentality," see Viktoria Mitlyng, "Russia Asks: What Is the Big Idea," *Moscow Times*, 17 January 1997.

55. Anna Ostapchuk and Yevgeny Krasnikov, "An Idea Visits the Kremlin," *Moskovskiie novosti*, no. 38, 21–28 September 1997, pp. 6–7; *CDPSP* 49, no. 38 (1997): 10.

56. Indeed, such efforts could have little effect on the legitimacy of property reform after the widely publicized corruption and collusion within in the loans-for-shares program.

57. On redefining Russia's relationship with Europe and the West in the post–cold war context, see S. Neil MacFarlane, "Russian Conceptions of Europe," *Post-Soviet Affairs* 10 no. 3 (1994): 234–69.

58. See Aleksandr Tsipko, *Nezavisimaia Gazeta*, 9 November 1995, p. 5; *CDPSP* 47, no. 45 (1995): 4.

59. See Chereshnia, "Protivniki reform," p. 7. This interesting op-ed piece, written by a Russian academic, criticizes the government as early as April 1992 for caring more about how the reforms appear to the West than to the Russian people and for ignoring

the symbolic importance of reforms and the people's need for national symbols. Furthermore, the author chastises the government for not finding a language that has meaning for ordinary people.

Chapter 8. The Ideological Fit and the Cost of Compliance

1. See Max Weber, "The Protestant Ethic and the Spirit of Capitalism," in *Weber Selections in Translation,* edited by W. G. Runciman and translated by Eric Matthews (Cambridge: Cambridge University Press, 1978), especially, pp. 173–74. For a discussion of Weber in relation to the materialist (Marxian especially) theories of his time, see Reinhard Bendix, *Max Weber: An Intellectual Portrait* (Berkeley: University of California Press, 1977), chap. 3, especially 50–55. As an alternative perspective on Weber's famous essay, see Randall Collins, "Weber's Last Theory of Capitalism," *American Sociological Review* 45 (December 1980): 925–42.

2. John Stewart Mill, "The Claims of Labour," *Essays on Economics and Societies,* vol. 4, 1845, in *The Collected Works of John Stewart Mill* (Toronto: University of Toronto Press, 1963), 370.

3. The notion of ideas "fitting" or "resonating" in a given context is found in the works of many influential contributors to the ideas of literature in one form or another. See Peter Hall, *The Political Power of Economic Ideas: Keynesianism across Nations* (Princeton: Princeton University Press, 1989); Kathryn Sikkink, *Ideas and Institutions: Developmentalism in Argentina and Brazil* (Ithaca: Cornell University Press, 1991); John Odell, *U.S. International Monetary Policy: Markets, Power, and Ideas as a Source of Change* (Princeton: Princeton University Press, 1982); and Ikenberry, "Creating Yesterday's New World Order."

4. Peter Hall, *The Political Power,* 370–71, 383–84.

5. See Snow and Bedford, "Ideology, Frame Resonance and Participant Mobilization," 204.

6. An ideological campaign, in my formulation, would have enabled the benefits for employees to remain much closer to the original preferences of those designing privatization, and certainly not reaching the 51 percent of enterprise shares ultimately made available for nearly three-quarters of those firms involved in mass privatization. In other words, an ideological campaign would have meant, for example, that the privatizers would have found ways to privilege rhetorically and symbolically the significance of a much lower level of employee transfers.

7. While Central Europeans often assert their European identity, Russians' attitudes are much more mixed. The New Russia Barometers reaffirm this Russian ambivalent relationship toward Europe. In 1994, the majority of Russians surveyed responded that they "rarely or never" think of themselves as European, whereas less than one-third think of themselves as European "often or sometimes." Richard Rose and Christian Haerpfer, *New Russia Barometer III: The Results* (University of Strathclyde Studies in Public Policy, no 228, 1994), 43.

8. On the "unwarranted assumptions about the uniformity of convictions" among members of an ideological group, see Joseph Schull, "What Is Ideology? Theoretical Problems and Lessons from Soviet-Type Societies," *Political Studies* 40 (December 1992): 728–31. Thomas Hansen also notes the tensions created by the "multiplicity of meanings inscribed in most ideological constructions." See Hansen, *The Saffron Wave,* 25.

9. Hall, *Political Power of Economic Ideas,* 366–67.

10. On the insulation of technocratic elites, see Stephen Haggard and Robert Kaufman, eds., *The Politics of Adjustment: International Constraints, Distributive Conflicts, and the State* (Princeton: Princeton University Press, 1992).

11. On the "cosmopolitaness of technocrats," see Thomas Callaghy, "Vision and Politics in the Transformation of the Global Political Economy: Lessons from the Second and Third Worlds," in *Global Transformation and the Third World,* edited by Robert Slater, Barry Schultz, and Steven Dorr (Boulder: Lynn Rienner, 1993), 161–257.

12. Most strikingly, see Stiglitz's diatribe against the Western advisers in "Whither Reform" (paper prepared for the Annual Bank Conference on Development Economics, Washington, DC, 28–30 April 1999).

13. In *Building Capitalism,* Åslund speaks to this point: "Initially, privatization was an intellectual and idealistic exercise, which bred the many voucher schemes, for instance. Next privatization became the art of the possible, as powerful forces were less interested in the effects on society than in their own fortunes" (279).

Bibliography

Abdelal, Rawi. *National Purpose in the World Economy: Post-Soviet States in Comparative Perspective*. Ithaca: Cornell University Press, 2001.

Ackerman, Bruce. *Private Property and the Constitution*. New Haven: Yale University Press, 1977.

Adam, Jan. *Economic Reforms in the Soviet Union and Eastern Europe since the 1960s*. New York: St. Martin's Press, 1991.

———. "Transformation to a Market Economy in the Former Czechoslovakia." *Europe-Asia Studies* 45 (1993): 627–45.

Aghion, Philippe, Olivier Blanchard, and Wendy Carlin. "The Economics of Enterprise Restructuring in Central and Eastern Europe." CEPR Discussion Paper, No. 1058. London: Centre for Economic Policy Research, 1994.

Allan, Duncan. "Banks and the Loans-for-Shares Auctions." In *Russian Banking: Evolution Problems and Prospects*, edited by David Lane, 137–59. Northampton, Mass.: Edward Elgar, 2002.

Allison, Graham T., and Grigory Yavlinsky. *Window of Opportunity: The Grand Bargain for Democracy in the Soviet Union*. New York: Pantheon Books, 1991.

Almond, Gabriel. *A Discipline Divided: Schools and Sects in Political Science*. Newbury Park, Calif.: Sage Publications, 1990.

Almond, Gabriel, and Sidney Verba. *The Civic Culture: Political Attitudes and Democracy in Five Nations: An Analytic Study*. Boston: Little, Brown, 1965.

Anderson, Terry, and Peter Hill. "The Evolution of Property Rights: A Study of the American West." *Journal of Law and Economics* 18 (1975): 163–79.

Appel, Hilary. "The Ideological Determinants of Liberal Economic Reform: The Case of Privatization." *World Politics* 52 (2000): 520–49.

———. "Justice and the Reformulation of Property Rights in the Czech Republic." *East European Politics and Societies* 9 (1995): 22–40.

———. "Voucher Privatization in Russia: Structural Consequences and Mass Response in the Second Period of Reform." *Europe-Asia Studies* 49 (1997): 1433–49.

Appel, Hilary, and John Gould. "Identity Politics and Economic Reform: Examining Industry-State Relations in the Czech and Slovak Republics." *Europe-Asia Studies* 52 (2000): 111–32.

Artemiev, Igor, and Gary Fine. "Albania." In *Between State and Market: Mass Privatization in Transition Economies*, edited by Ira Lieberman, Stilpon Nestor, and Raj Desai, 177–80. Washington, DC: World Bank, 1997.

Åslund, Anders. *Building Capitalism: The Transformation of the Former Soviet Bloc.* New York: Cambridge University Press, 2002.

———. *Gorbachev's Struggle for Economic Reform.* Ithaca: Cornell University Press, 1991.

———. *How Russia Became a Market Economy.* Washington, DC: Brookings Institution, 1995.

———. *Russia's Economic Transformation in the 1990s.* London: Pinter, 1997.

Balcerowicz, Leszek. *Socialism, Capitalism, and Transformation.* New York: Central European University Press, 1995.

———. "Understanding Post-communist Transitions." *Journal of Democracy* 5, no. 4 (1995): 75–89.

Bayer, Ivo, and Jiri Kabele. "Politische kultur der Tschechischen Republik und ihre transformation" [The political culture of the Czech Republic and its transformation]. *Bundesinstitut für Ostwissenschaftliche und Internationale Studien,* 28 May 1996.

Begg, David. "Economic Reform in Czechoslovakia: Should We Believe in Santa Klaus?" *Economic Policy* 13 (1991): 243–86.

Bendix, Reinhard. *Max Weber: An Intellectual Portrait.* Berkeley: University of California Press, 1977.

Berman, Sheri. *The Social Democratic Moment: Ideas and Politics in the Making of Interwar Europe.* Cambridge, Mass.: Harvard University Press, 1998.

Black, Bernard, Reinier Kraakman, and Anna Tarassova. "Russian Privatization and Corporate Governance: What Went Wrong." *Stanford Law School John Olin Program in Law and Economics.* Working Paper No. 178, Stanford Law School, Palo Alto, Calif., September 1999.

Blanchard, Olivier J., Maxim Boycko, Marek Dabrowski, Rudiger Dornbusch, Richard Layard, and Andrei Shleifer. *Post-Communist Reform: Pain and Progress.* Cambridge: MIT Press, 1993.

Blasi, Joseph, Maya Kroumova, and Douglas Kruse. *Kremlin Capitalism: Privatizing the Russian Economy.* Ithaca: Cornell University Press, 1997.

Blyth, Mark. *Great Transformations: Economic Ideas and Institutional Change in the Twentieth Century.* New York: Cambridge University Press, 2002.

Bockman, Johanna, and Gil Eyal. "Eastern Europe as a Laboratory for Economic Knowledge: The Transnational Roots of Neo-Liberalism." *American Journal of Sociology* 108, no. 2 (2001): 310–52.

Boettke, Peter. *Why Perestroika Failed: The Politics of Socialist Transformation.* New York: Routledge, 1993.

Bohm, Andrea, and Marko Simoneti, eds. *Privatization in Central and Eastern Europe 1993.* Ljubljana: CEEPN Annual Conference Series, 1993.

Boycko, Maxim, Andrei Shleifer, and Robert Vishny. *Privatizing Russia.* Cambridge: MIT Press, 1995.

Breslauer, George, and Catherine Dale. "Boris Yel'tsin and the Invention of the Russian Nation-State." *Post-Soviet Affairs* 13 (1997): 303–32.

Broadman, Harry. "Ownership and Control of Russian Industry." OECD Conference on Corporate Governance in Moscow, 31 May–2 June 1999.

Brom, Karla, and Mitchell Orenstein. "The Privatised Sector in the Czech Republic: Government and Bank Control in a Transitional Economy." *Europe-Asia Studies* 46, no. 4 (1994): 893–928.

Brudny, Yitzhak. "The Dynamics of 'Democratic Russia,' 1990–1993." *Post-Soviet Affairs* 9 (1993): 141–70.

————. "Neoliberal Economic Reform and the Consolidation of Democracy in Russia: Or Why Institutions and Ideas Might Matter More than Economics." In *The International Dimension of Post-Communist Transition in Russia and the New States of Eurasia,* edited by Karen Dawisha, 297–321. Armonk, NY: M. E. Sharpe, 1997.

Bundesinstituts für Ostwissenschaftliche und Internationale Studien, ed. *The Soviet Union, 1988–1989: Perestroika in Crisis?* Boulder: Westview Press, 1990.

Burawoy, Michael, and Katherine Verdery. *Uncertain Transition: Ethnographies of Change in the Post-Socialist World.* Lanham, Md.: Rowman and Littlefield, 1999.

Butorova, Zora, et al. *Aktualne problemy Cesko-Slovensko, januar 1992: Zaverecna sprava zo sociologickeho prieskumu.* Bratislava: Centrum pre socialnu analyzi, 1992.

Callaghy, Thomas. "Vision and Politics in the Transformation of the Global Political Economy: Lessons from the Second and Third Worlds." In *Global Transformation and the Third World,* edited by Robert Slater, Barry Schultz, and Steven Dorr, 161–257. Boulder: Lynne Rienner Publishers, 1993.

Capek, Ales, and Pavel Mertlik. "Organizational and Financial Restructuring in Czech Manufacturing Enterprises, 1990–1995." In *Privatization in Post-Communist Countries,* edited by Barbara Blaszczyk and Richard Woodward. Warsaw: Center for Social and Economic Research, 1996.

Cepl, Vojtech. "Lustration in the CSFR." *East European Constitutional Review* 1 (1992): 24–26.

Češka, Roman. "Three Years of Privatization in the Czech and Slovak Republics." *Privatization Newsletter of the Czech Republic and Slovakia* (1993).

Charap, Joshua, and Alena Zemplinerova. "Management Buy-outs in the Privatisation Programme of the Czech Republic." In *Management and Employee Buy-outs in the Context of Privatization, OECD Special Report* 1, no. 3 (1994).

Checkell, Jeffrey. *Ideas and International Political Change: Soviet/Russia Behavior and the End of the Cold War.* New Haven: Yale University Press, 1997.

Chiesa, Giulietto, and Douglas Northrop. *Transition to Democracy: Political Change in the Soviet Union, 1987–1991.* Hanover, NH: University Press of New England, 1993.

Chubais, Anatoly. *Privatizatsiia po-Rossiiski.* Moscow: Vagrius, 1999.

Clarke, Simon. "Privatisation: The Politics of Capital and Labour." In *Developments in Russian and Post-Soviet Politics,* edited by Stephen White, 162–86. Durham: Duke University Press, 1994.

Cohen, Benjamin. "Balance of Payments Financing: Evolution of a Regime." In *International Regimes,* edited by Stephen Krasner, 315–36. Ithaca: Cornell University Press, 1982.

Cohen, Stephen, and Andrew Schwartz. "Deeper into the Tunnel." In *The Tunnel at the End of the Light: Privatization, Business Networks, and Economic Transformation in Russia,* edited by Stephen S. Cohen, Andrew Schwartz, and John Zysman, 1–23. Berkeley: University of California Press, 1998.

Collins, Randall. "Weber's Last Theory of Capitalism." *American Sociological Review* 45 (1980): 925–42.

Cook, Karen Schweers, and Margaret Levi, eds. *The Limits of Rationality.* Chicago: University of Chicago Press, 1990.

Cooper, Lee. *Soviet Reform and Beyond.* New York: St. Martin's Press, 1991.

Culik, Jan. "Evaluating a Decade: Poland, Hungary and the Czech Republic: People's Situation Has Worsened since the Fall of Communism." *Central Europe Review,* 22 November 1999, http://www.ce-review.org/99/22/culik22.html (accessed 22 April 2003).

Dabrowski, J. *Przedsiebiorstwa Panstwowe w Roku 1990—Wyniki Badan*. Warsaw: Instytut Badan nad Gospodarka Rynkowa I Prawami Wlasnosciowymi, 1991.

Dahrendorf, Ralf. *Reflections on the Revolution in Europe*. New York: Random House, 1990.

Debardeleben, Joan. "Attitudes towards Privatization in Russia." *Europe-Asia Studies* 51 (1999): 447–65.

Demsetz, Harold. "Towards a Theory of Property Rights." *American Economic Review* 57 (1967): 347–59.

Denzau, Arthur, and Douglass North. "Shared Mental Models: Ideologies and Institutions." *KYKLOS* 47 (1994): 3–31.

Desai, Padma. *Perestroika in Perspective: The Design and Dilemmas of Soviet Reform*. Princeton: Princeton University Press, 1989.

Desai, Raj, and Mitchell Orenstein. "Business Associations and the State in the Czech Republic." *Emergo* 3 (Spring 1996): 29–43.

Desai, Raj, and Vladena Plockova. "The Czech Republic." In *Between State and Market: Mass Privatization in Transition Economies*, edited by Ira Lieberman, Stilpon Nestor, and Raj Desai, 190–96. Washington, DC: World Bank, 1997.

Diamond, Larry. *Political Culture and Democracy in Developing Countries*. Boulder: Lynne Rienner Publishers, 1994.

Diermeier, Daniel, Joel Ericson, Timothy Frye, and Steven Lewis. "Credible Commitment and Property Rights: The Role of Strategic Interaction between Political and Economic Actors." In *The Political Economy of Property Rights*, edited by David Weimer, 84–108. Cambridge: Cambridge University Press, 1997.

Dolowitz, David, and David Marsh. "Who Learns What from Whom: A Review of the Policy Transfer Literature." *Political Studies* 44 (1996): 343–57.

Donaldson, David, and Dileep Wagle. *Privatization: Principles and Practice*. Washington, DC: World Bank and IFC, 1995.

Drag, Zbigniew, and Jerzy Indraszkiewicz. "Employee Consciousness and Reforms of Government System in Poland." *Economic and Social Policy Series*, No. 20. Berlin: Friedrich-Ebert Foundation, 1992.

Dyba, Karel, and Jan Svejnar. "Czechoslovakia: Recent Economic Developments and Prospects." *American Economic Review Papers and Proceedings* 81 (1991): 185–90.

"Eastern Europe Report." *American Banker Bond Buyer* 1, no. 22 (1991): 7.

EBRD Transition Report 2001. *Economic Transition in Central and Eastern Europe and the CIS*. London: EBRD, 2001.

EBRD Transition Report 2002. *Economic Transition in Central and Eastern Europe and the CIS*. London: EBRD, 2002.

Egerer, Roland. "Investment Funds and Corporate Governance in Emerging Markets: An Assessment of the Top Ten Voucher Funds in the Czech Republic." *World Bank Report*, mimeo, December 1994. Draft.

Eggertsson, Thrainn. *Economic Behavior and Institutions*. Cambridge: Cambridge University Press, 1990.

Ellerman, David. "Lessons from Eastern Europe's Voucher Privatization." *Challenge* 44, no. 4 (2001): 14–37.

———. "Voucher Privatization with Investment Funds: An Institutional Analysis." World Bank Policy Research Paper, No. 1924. Washington, DC: World Bank, 1998.

Ellman, Michael. "Russia: The Economic Program of the Civic Union." *RFE/FL Research Report* 2, no. 11 (1993): 34–45.

Etzioni, Amitai. *A Comparative Analysis of Complex Organizations: On Power, Involvement and Their Correlates.* New York: Free Press, 1961.

European Commission. "PHARE Publications." *Enlargement,* 15 September 2003, http://europa.eu.int/comm/enlargement/pas/phare/publist.htm (accessed 28 October 2003).

Evans, Mark, and Jonathan Davies. "Understanding Policy Transfer: A Multi-level, Multi-disciplinary Perspective." *Public Administration* 77, no. 2 (1999): 361–86.

Evans, Peter. "The State as Problem and Solution: Predation, Embedded Autonomy, and Structural Change." In *The Politics of Economic Adjustment: International Constraints, Distributive Conflicts, and the State,* edited by Stephen Haggard and Robert Kaufman, 139–81. Princeton: Princeton University Press, 1992.

Feigenbaum, Harvey, and Jeffrey Henig. "The Political Underpinnings of Privatization: A Typology." *World Politics* 46, no. 2 (1994): 185–208.

Fidrmuc, Jarko, and Ming Xie. "The Slovak Republic: New Country, Old Problems." *World Bank* 19 (1998). Mimeo.

Fish, M. Steven. "The Determinants of Economic Reform in the Post-Communist World." *East European Politics and Societies* 12, no. 1 (1998): 31–78.

———. "Roots and Remedies for Russia's Racket Economy." In *The Tunnel at the End of the Light: Privatization, Business Networks, and Economic Transformation in Russia,* edited by Stephen S. Cohen, Andrew Schwartz, and John Zysman, 86–138. Berkeley: University of California Press, 1998.

Freeland, Chrystia. *Sale of the Century: Russia's Wild Ride from Communism to Capitalism.* New York: Random House, 2000.

Frydman, Roman, and Andrzej Rapaczynski. *Privatization in Eastern Europe: Is the State Withering Away?* London: Central European University Press, 1994.

Frydman, Roman, Katharina Pistor, and Andrzej Rapaczynski. "Investing in Insider Dominated Firms: A Study of the Russian Voucher Privatization Funds." In *Corporate Governance in Eastern Europe and Russia,* edited by Roman Frydman, Cheryl Gray, and Andrzej Rapaczynski, 187–241. London: Central European Press, 1996.

Frydman, Roman, Andrzej Rapaczynski, and John Earle. *The Privatization Process in Central Europe.* Central European University Privatization Reports, No.1. London: Central European University Press, 1993.

Frye, Timothy. "Russian Privatization and the Limits of Credible Commitment." In *The Political Economy of Property Rights,* edited by David Weimer, 84–108. Cambridge: Cambridge University Press, 1997.

Gaidar, Egor. *Dni porazhenii i pobed* [Days of defeat and victory]. Moscow: Vargrius, 1997.

———. "Kak nomenklatura 'privatizirovala' svoiu vlast" [How the nomenklatura "privatized" its power]. *Literaturnaia gazeta,* 9 November 1994, 10.

Gardawski, Juliusz. *Poland's Industrial Workers on the Return to Democracy and Market Economy.* Warsaw: Friedrich Ebert Stiftung, 1996.

Gardawski, Juliusz, and Tomasz Zukowski. *Rabotnicy 1993—wybory ekonomiczne I polityczne.* Warsaw: Fundacja im. Friedricha Eberta w Polsce, 1994.

Garton Ash, Timothy. "Prague: Inside the Magic Lantern." In *We the People: The Revolu-*

tion of '89 Witnessed in Warsaw, Budapest, Berlin and Prague. Cambridge: Granta Books, 1990.

———. "The Prague Advertisement." In *The Uses of Adversity: Essays on the Fate of Central Europe.* Cambridge: Granta Books, 1989.

Geertz, Clifford. "Ideology as a Cultural System." In *The Interpretation of Cultures,* 193–233. New York: Basic Books, 1973.

"Gennadii Ziuganov in His Own Words." Translated by Susan Kennedy Orttung. *Transition* 2, no. 11, 31 May 1996, http://www.tol.cz (accessed 20 April 2003).

Goffman, Erving. *Frame Analysis.* Cambridge: Harvard University Press, 1974.

Goldman, Marshall. *The Piratization of Russia: Russian Reform Goes Awry.* New York: Routledge, 2003.

Goldstein, Judith. "The Impact of Ideas on Trade Policy: The Origins of U.S. Agricultural and Manufacturing Policies." *International Organization* 43, no. 1 (1989): 31–71.

Goldstein, Judith, and Robert Keohane. "Ideas and Foreign Policy: An Analytical Framework." In *Ideas and Foreign Policy: Beliefs, Institutions, and Political Change,* edited by Judith Goldstein and Robert Keohane. Ithaca: Cornell University Press, 1993.

Gorbachev, Mikhail. *Perestroika: New Thinking for Our Country and the World.* New York: Harper and Row, 1987.

Gould, John. "Beyond Creating Owners: Privatization and Democratization in the Slovak and Czech Republics, 1990–1998." Ph.D. diss., Columbia University, 2000. Abstract in *Digital Dissertations.*

Gould, John, and Sona Szomolanyi. "Elite Division and Convergence." In *Elites after State Socialism,* edited by John Higley and Gyorgy Lenyel, 47–70. Boulder: Rowman and Littlefield, 1999.

Granto, Jim, Ronald Inglehart, and David Leblang. "Cultural Values, Stable Democracy and Economic Development: A Reply." *American Journal of Political Science* 40, no. 3 (1996): 680–96.

Gray, Cheryl. "In Search of Owners: Privatization and Corporate Governance in Transition Economies." *World Bank Research Observer* 11, no. 2 (1996): 179–98.

Green, Donald, and Ian Shapiro. *Pathologies of Rational Choice Theory: A Critique of Applications in Political Science.* New Haven: Yale University Press, 1994.

Gurkov, Igor. "Popular Response to Russian Privatization: Surveys in Enterprises." *Studies in Public Policy* 245 (1995): 1–62.

Hadjiisky, Magdalena. "The Failure of Participatory Democracy in the Czech Republic." *West European Politics* 24, no. 3 (2001): 55–56.

Haggard, Stephen, and Robert Kaufman, eds. *The Politics of Adjustment: International Constraints, Distributive Conflicts, and the State.* Princeton: Princeton University Press, 1992.

Hall, Peter. *The Political Power of Economic Ideas: Keynesianism across Nations.* Princeton, N.J.: Princeton University Press, 1989.

Hall, Peter, and Rosemary Taylor. "Political Science and the Three New Institutionalisms." *Political Studies* 4, no. 5 (1996): 936–57.

Halpern, Nina. "Creating Socialist Economies: Stalinist Political Economy and the Impact of Ideas." In *Ideas and Foreign Policy: Beliefs, Institutions, and Political Change,* edited by Judith Goldstein and Robert Keohane, 87–110. Ithaca: Cornell University Press, 1993.

Hamilton, Malcolm. "The Elements of the Concept of Ideology." *Political Studies* 35 (1987): 18–38.

Hanley, Eric. "Cadre Capitalism in Hungary and Poland: Property Accumulation among Communist-Era Elites." *East European Politics and Societies* 14 (Winter 2000): 143–78.

Hansen, Thomas. *The Saffron Wave: Democracy and Hindu Nationalism in Modern India.* Princeton: Princeton University Press, 1999.

Havrylyshyn, Oleh, and Donal McGettigan. "Privatization in Transition Countries." *Post-Soviet Affairs* 16, no. 3 (2000): 257–86.

Hedlund, Stefan. "Property without Rights: Dimensions of Russian Privatisation." *Europe-Asia Studies* 53 (March 2001): 213–38.

Heinrich, Ralph. "Corporate Governance." In *Privatization, Corporate Governance and the Emergence of Markets,* edited by Eckehard Rosenbaum, Frank Bonker, and Hans-Jurgen Wagener, 83–97. New York: St. Martin's Press, 2000.

Hellman, Joel. "Winners Take All: The Politics of Partial Reform in Post-communist Transitions." *World Politics* 50, no. 2 (1998): 203–34.

Henig, Jeffrey, C. Hammett, and Harvey Feigenbaum. "The Politics of Privatization: A Comparative Perspective." *Governance* 1, no. 4 (1988): 442–68.

Herrera, Yoshiko. "Russian Economic Reform, 1991–1999." In *Russian Politics: Challenges of Democratization,* edited by Zoltan Barany and Robert Moser, 135–74. New York: Cambridge University Press, 2001.

Hishow, Ognian. "Makroökonomische politik und reformfortschritte im ostlichen Europa: Differenzierung durch unterschiedliche transformations-konzepte" [Macroeconomic policies and reform progress in Eastern Europe: Distinguishing between the different transformation paths]. *Bundesinstituts für Ostwissenschaftliche und Internationale Studien* 25 (1997).

———. "Russlands wirtschaftstransformation—Ergebnisse und aussichten." [Russia's economic transition—Outcomes and prospects]. *Bundesinstitut für Ostwissenschaftliche und Internationale Studien,* 12 July 2000.

Hoffer, Frank. "Reform der Sowjetischen gewerkschaften in Russland. Ein schwerer, aber nicht hoffnungsloser fall" [Reform of the Soviet trade unions in Russia. Difficult, but not hopeless]. *Bundesinstitut für Ostwissenschaftliche und Internationale Studien,* 7 October 1998.

Hoffman, David E. *The Oligarchs: Wealth and Power in the New Russia.* New York: Public Affairs, 2002

Holy, Ladislav. *The Little Czech and the Great Czech Nation.* Cambridge: Cambridge University Press, 1996.

Hough, Jerry, and Merle Fainsod. *How the Soviet Union Is Governed.* Cambridge: Harvard University Press, 1980.

Howlett, Michael. "The Lessons of Learning: Reconciling Theories of Policy Learning and Policy Change." *Policy Sciences* 25, no. 3 (1992): 275–94.

Ikenberry, John. "Creating Yesterday's New World Order: Keynesian 'New Thinking' and the Anglo-American Postwar Settlement." In *Ideas and Foreign Policy: Beliefs, Institutions and Political Change,* edited by Judith Goldstein and Robert Keohane, 57–86. Ithaca: Cornell University Press, 1993.

———. "The International Spread of Privatization Policies: Inducements, Learning, and 'Policy Bandwagoning.'" In *The Political Economy of Public Sector Reform and Privatization,* edited by Ezra Suleiman and John Waterbury, 88–110. Boulder: Westview Press, 1990.

Inglehart, Ronald. "The Renaissance of Political Culture." *American Political Science Review* 82, no. 4 (1988): 1203–30.

Innes, Abby. "The Breakup of Czechoslovakia: The Impact of Party Development on the Separation of the State." *East European Politics and Societies* 11, no. 3 (1997): 393–435.

"International Organization: Knowledge, Power and International Policy Coordination." Special edition, edited by Peter Hass, *International Organization* 46, no. 1 (1992).

Jackson, Robert. "The Weight of Ideas in Decolonization: Normative Change and International Relations." In *Ideas and Foreign Policy: Beliefs, Institutions and Political Change,* edited by Judith Goldstein and Robert Keohane, 111–38. Ithaca: Cornell University Press, 1993.

Jacobsen, John. "Much Ado about Ideas: The Cognitive Factor in Economic Policy." *World Politics* 47, no. 2 (1995): 283–310.

Johnson, Juliet. *A Fistful of Rubles: The Rise and Fall of the Russian Banking System.* Ithaca: Cornell University Press, 2000.

Katz, Barbara G., and Joel Owen. "The Impact of Voucher Privatization on Efficiency." *World Bank,* 2000. Mimeo.

———. "The Investment Choices of Voucher Holders and Their Impact on Privatized Firm Performance." New York University Stern School of Business Working Paper, EC-96-08, New York University, 1996.

Katzenstein, Peter. *Cultural Norms and National Security.* Ithaca: Cornell University Press, 1996.

Kelley, Stanley. "Rational Choice: Its Promises and Limitations." *Critical Review* 9 (Winter 1995): 95–106.

Kitschelt, Herbert. "Formation of Party Cleavages in Post-Communist Democracies." *Party Politics* 1 (1995): 447–72.

Klaus, Václav. "Budeme podniky privatizovat, anebo sanovat?" [Will we privatize or restructure?]. In *Nemám Rád Katastrofické Scénáře.* Ostrava: Sagit Press, 1991.

———. *Czechoslovakia at the Crossroads.* Prague: Lidové noviny, 1990.

———. "Hlavní Překážky rychlé ekonomické přeměny ve východní Evropě: Československý pohled" [The principle barriers to rapid economic reform in Eastern Europe: A Czechoslovak perspective]. *TOP* 13 (1990).

Klaus, Václav, and Dušan Tříska. "Review Article of Janos Kornai's 'The Socialist System: The Political Economy of Communism.'" In *Dismantling Socialism, An Interim Report: A Compendium of Texts from the Years 1992–1994.* Prague, 1994.

Klebnikov, Paul. *Godfather of the Kremlin: Boris Berezovsky and the Looting of Russia.* New York: Harcourt, 2000.

Kloc, Kazimierz. "Polish Labor in Transition (1990–1992)." *Telos* 92 (Summer 1992): 139–48.

Koh, Byung Chol. *Japan's Administrative Elite.* Berkeley: University of California Press, 1989.

Kokh, Alfred. *The Selling of the Soviet Empire.* New York: Liberty Publishing House, 1998.

Komárek, Valtr. *Prognoza a Program.* Prague: Academia Publishers, 1990.

Kornai, Janos. *The Road to a Free Economy: Shifting from a Socialist System: The Example of Hungary.* New York: W. W. Norton, 1990.

Kotrba, Josef. "Privatization Process in Czech Republic: An Overview." *World Bank,* December 1993, mimeo.

———. "The Privatization Process in the Czech Republic: Players and Winners." In *The*

Czech Republic and Economic Transition in Eastern Europe, edited by Jan Svejnar, 159–98. San Diego: Academic Press, 1995.

Kramer, Mark. "The Changing Economic Complexion of Eastern Europe and Russia: Results and Lessons of the 1990s." *SAIS Review* 19, no. 2 (1999): 16–45.

———. "Polish Workers and the Post-Communist Transition, 1989–1993." *Europe-Asia Studies* 47, no. 4 (1995): 669–712.

Krasner, Stephen. "Approaches to the State." *Comparative Politics* 16, no. 2 (1984): 223–46.

Krause, Kevin. "Accountability and Political Party Competition in Slovakia and the Czech Republic." Ph.D. diss., University of Notre Dame, 2000.

Kupka, Martin. "Transformation of Ownership in the Czech Republic." *Soviet Studies* 44, no. 2 (1992): 297–311.

Laitin, David. "The Civic Culture at 30." *American Political Science Review* 89, no. 1 (1995): 168–73.

———. *Hegemony and Culture: Politics and Religious Change among the Yoruba.* Chicago: University of Chicago Press, 1986.

Lardy, Nicholas. *China's Unfinished Economic Revolution.* Washington, DC: Brookings Institution Press, 1998.

Larrain, Jorge. *The Concept of Ideology.* London: Hutchinson, 1979.

Leeds, Eva Marikova. "Voucher Privatization in Czechoslovakia." *Comparative Economic Studies* 35, no. 3 (1993): 19–38.

Leff, Carol Skalnik. *National Conflict in Czechoslovakia: The Making and Remaking of a State, 1918–1987.* Princeton: Princeton University Press, 1988.

Levada, Yuri. "All-Russian Center for the Study of Public Opinion (VTsIOM)," 17 January 2001, http://www.polit.ru (accessed 30 April 2003).

Levi, Margaret. *Of Rule and Revenue.* Berkeley: University of California Press, 1988.

Levitsky, Steven, and Lucan Way. "Between a Shock and a Hard Place: The Dynamics of Labor-Backed Adjustments in Poland and Argentina." *Comparative Politics* 30, no. 2 (1998): 171–92.

Libecap, Gary. *Contracting for Property Rights.* Cambridge: Cambridge University Press, 1989.

———. "The Political Allocation of Mineral Rights: A Reevaluation of Teapot Dome." *Journal of Economic History* 44 (1984): 381–91.

———. "Property Rights in Economic History: Implications for Research." *Explorations in Economic History* 23, no. 3 (1986): 227–52.

Libecap, Gary, and Steven Wiggins. "Contractual Responses to the Common Pool, Prorationing of Crude Oil Production." *American Economic Review* 74, no. 1 (1984): 87–98.

Lieberman, Ira W., Stilpon S. Nestor, Raj M. Desai, and Carol Gabyzon, eds. *Between State and Market: Mass Privatization in Transition Economies.* Washington, DC: World Bank, 1997.

Lieberman, Ira, and Robi Veimetra. "The Rush for State Shares in the 'Klonkyke' of Wild East Capitalism: Loans-for-Shares Transactions in Russia." *George Washington Journal of International Law and Economics* 29, no. 3 (1996): 737–68.

Litwack, John. "Three Issues of Credible Commitment and Russian Privatization." In *The Political Economy of Property Rights,* edited by David Weimer, 109. Cambridge: Cambridge University Press, 1997.

Lohr, Eric. "Arkadii Volsky's Political Base." *Europe-Asia Studies* 45, no. 5 (1993): 811–29.

Lustick, Ian. "Hegemony and the Riddle of Nationalism: The Dialectics of Political Identity in the Middle East." Christopher H. Browne Center for International Politics, Working Paper 1997-01. Philadelphia: University of Pennsylvania, 1997.

MacFarlane, S. Neil. "Russian Conceptions of Europe." *Post-Soviet Affairs* 10, no. 3 (1994): 234–69.

Mansbridge, Jane, ed. *Beyond Self-Interest.* Chicago: University of Chicago Press, 1990.

Mansfeldová, Zdenka. "Justice As an Ethic Legitimacy of Economic Reform." Paper presented at "The Normative Foundations of the Polity: Conceptual Approaches in East and Central Europe" conference, Bremen, Germany, 20–22 January 1995.

———. "Professional and Political Strategies in Economic Discourses." Mimeo, August 1994.

Markova, Lina. "Direktorskaia privatizatsiia: Kakogo sobstvennika ona porodila" [Managerial privatization: What kind of owner did it create?]. *Rossiiskaia Federatsia Obstchestvenno-Politicheskii Zhurnal* 17 (1995).

McAdam, Doug, John McCarthy, and Mayer Zald. "Introduction: Opportunities, Mobilizing Structures, and Framing Processes—Toward a Synthetic, Comparative Perspective on Social Movements." In *Comparative Perspectives on Social Movements: Political Opportunities, Mobilizing Structures, and Cultural Framings,* edited by Doug McAdam, John McCarthy, and Mayer Zald, 1–22. Cambridge: Cambridge University Press, 1996.

McChesney, Fred. "Government as Definer of Property Rights: Indian Lands, Ethnic Externalities, and Bureaucratic Budgets." *Journal of Legal Studies* 19, no. 2 (1990): 297–335.

McDermott, Gerald. *Embedded Politics: Industrial Networks and Institutional Change in Postcommunism.* Ann Arbor: University of Michigan Press, 2002.

McManus, John. "An Economic Analysis of Indian Behavior in the North American Fur Trade." *Journal of Economic History* 32, no. 1 (1972): 36–53.

McNamara, Kathleen. *The Currency of Ideas: Monetary Politics and the European Union.* Ithaca: Cornell University Press, 1998.

Megginson, William, and Jeff Netter. "From State to Market: A Survey of Empirical Studies on Privatization." Paper presented to the Global Equity Markets Conference, Paris, December 1998.

Mejstrik, M., R. Lastovicka, A. Marcincin, and D. Semetillo. "Privatization and the Opening the Capital Market in the Czech and Slovak Republics." CERGE-EI Working Papers, Prague, November 1993.

Mejstrik, M., A Dervis, and A. Zemplinerova. *The Privatization Process in East-Central Europe, Evolutionary Process of Czech Privatizations.* Boston: Kluwer Academic Publishers, 1997.

Mertlík, Pavel. "The Co-operative Movements, Labor Managed Firms and Property Rights." *Acta Oeconomica* 1 (1992): 39–50.

———. "Czechoslovakian Economic Reform: Perspectives for Cooperation." In *What Markets Can and Cannot Do,* edited by Milan Soyka, 165–80. Prague: Nova Spes International Press, 1992.

Miklos, Ivan. "Economic Transition and the Emergence of Clientalist Structures in Slovakia." In *Slovakia: Problems of Democratic Consolidation and the Struggle for the Rules of the Game,* edited by Sona Szomolányi and John Gould. New York: Columbia University Press, 1997, CIAONet, February 1998.

———. "Privatizacia." In *Slovensko, 1997: Suhrnna sprava o stave spolocnosti a trendoch na rok 1998* [Slovakia, 1997: The summary report of the state of society and trends in the year 1998], edited by Martin Butora and Michal Ivantysin, 6–70. Bratislava: Institut pre Verejne Otazky, 1998.

———. "Privatization Process in Slovakia: Backstage Interests." *Mapping and Promoting Privatization in Slovakia,* Seminar Bulletin IX, Center for Economic Development, Bratislava, 12 December 1995.

Miller, Arthur, William Reisinger, and Vicki Hesli. "New Soviet Citizen Survey, 1991: Monitoring Institutional Change." *Inter-university Consortium for Political and Social Research,* No. 6521, May 1999. Ann Arbor: University of Michigan.

Miller, William, Stephen White, and Paul Heywood. *Values and Political Change in Postcommunist Europe.* New York: St. Martin's Press, 1998.

Nellis, John. "Time to Rethink Privatization in Transition Economies?" *International Finance Corporation,* Discussion Paper 38. Washington, DC: World Bank, 1999.

Nelson, Joan. "The Politics of Economic Transformation: Is Third World Experience Relevant in Eastern Europe?" *World Politics* 45, no. 3 (1995): 433–63.

Nelson, Lynn, and Irina Kuzes. "Evaluating the Russian Voucher Privatization Program." *Comparative Economic Studies* 36 (Spring 1994): 55–67.

———. *Property to the People: The Struggle for Radical Reform in Russia.* London: M. E. Sharpe, 1994.

Newell, Andrew, and Mieczyslaw Socha. "Wage Distribution in Poland: The Roles of Privatization and International Trade, 1992–1996." *Economics of Transition* 6, no. 1 (1998): 47–65.

North, Douglass. "A Framework for Analyzing the State in Economic History." *Explorations in Economic History* 16 (1979): 249–59.

———. *Institutions, Institutional Change and Economic Performance.* Cambridge: Cambridge University Press, 1990.

———. *Structure and Change in Economic History.* New York: W. W. Norton, 1981.

North, Douglass, and Robert Thomas. "The First Economic Revolution." *Economic History Review* 30, no. 2 (1977): 229–41.

———. *The Rise of the Western World: A New Economic History.* Cambridge: Cambridge University Press, 1973.

Odell, John. *U.S. International Monetary Policy: Markets, Power, and Ideas as a Source of Change.* Princeton: Princeton University Press, 1982.

Oi, Jean C., and Andrew G. Walder, eds. *Property Rights and Economic Reform in China.* Palo Alto, Calif.: Stanford University Press, 1999.

Orenstein, Mitchell. *Out of the Red: Building Capitalism and Democracy in Post-Communist Europe.* Ann Arbor: University of Michigan Press, 2001.

"O sotsial'nom aspekte privatizatsii" [On the social aspect of privatization]. *Voprosy ekonomiki* 4 (1996): 73–80.

Paczynska, Agnieszka. "Historical Legacies and Policy Choice: Labor and Public Sector Reform in Poland, Egypt, Mexico and the Czech Republic." Ph.D. diss., University of Virginia, 2001.

Palmer, Robert C. "The Origins of Property in England." *Law and History Review* 3 (1985): 1–50.

Pipes, Richard. "The Communist System." In *The Soviet System in Crisis,* edited by Alexander Dallin and Gail W. Lapidus. Boulder: Westview Press, 1991.

———. *Survival Is Not Enough: Soviet Realities and America's Future.* New York: Simon and Schuster, 1984.

Pistor, Katharina, and Andrew Spicer. "Investment Funds in Mass Privatization and Beyond." In *Between State and Market: Mass Privatization in Transition Economies*, edited by Ira Lieberman, Stilpon Nestor, and Raj Desai, 96–106. Washington, DC: World Bank, 1997.

Pithart, Petr. "Toward a Shared Freedom." In *The End of Czechoslovakia*, edited by Jiří Musil. Budapest: CEU Press, 1995.

Pleskot, Igor. "Czech and Slovak Trade Union Movement in the Period of Transformation to a Civil Democratic Society." *World Bank*, April 1994, mimeo.

Pohl, Gehard, et al. "Privatization and Restructuring in Central and Eastern Europe: Evidence and Policy Options." *World Bank Technical Paper*, No. 368. Washington, DC: World Bank, 1997.

Przeworski, Adam. *Democracy and the Market.* Cambridge: Cambridge University Press, 1991.

Radygin, Alexander. "Ownership and Control of the Russian Industry." Paper given at the Conference on Corporate Governance in Russia, OECD, Moscow, 31 May–2 June 1999.

———. *Reforma sobstvennosti v Rossii: Na puti iz proshlogo v budeshchee* [Property reform in Russia: From the past to the future]. Moscow: Respublika, 1994.

———. "Russian Privatization in 1993, Results and Problems." *Studies on Russian Economic Development* 5, no. 2 (1994): 100–108.

"Reinventing Trade Unions." Unpublished Survey by the Central European University Privatization Project, Prague, Fall 1994.

Riker, William, and Itai Sened. "A Political Theory of the Origins of Property Rights: Airport Slots." *American Journal of Political Science* 35, no. 4 (1991): 951–69.

Riker, William, and David Weimer. "The Economic and Political Liberalization of Socialism: The Fundamental Problem of Property Rights." *Social Philosophy and Policy* 10, no. 2 (1993): 79–102.

Róna-Tas, Ákos. "The Czech Third Wave: Privatization and the New Role of the State in the Czech Republic." *Problems of Post-Communism* 44, no. 6 (1997): 53–62.

Rose, Richard. "A Decade of New Russia Barometer Surveys." *Studies in Public Policy,* no. 360 (2002). University of Strathclyde, Glasgow.

Rose, Richard, and Christian Haerpfer. "New Russia Barometer III: The Results." *Studies in Public Policy,* no. 228 (1994). University of Strathclyde, Glasgow.

Rose, Richard, William Mishler, and Christian Haerpfer. *Democracy and Its Alternatives: Understanding Post-Communist Societies.* Baltimore: Johns Hopkins University Press, 1998.

Rubinfien, Elizabeth. "Private Russia." *Central European Economic Review* (Summer 1993).

"Russian Federation, Letter of Development Policy for the Third Structural Adjustment Loan." Mimeo provided by the World Bank, 1999.

Rutland, Peter. "The Economy: The Rocky Road from Plan to Market." In *Developments in Russian and Post-Soviet Politics*, edited by Stephen White, 131–61. Durham: Duke University Press, 1994.

———. "Mission Impossible? The IMF and the Failure of the Market Transition." *Review of International Studies* 25 (Fall 1999): 1–18.

———. "Privatisation in Russia: One Step Forward Two Steps Back?" *Europe-Asia Studies* 46, no. 7 (1994): 1109–31.

————. "Thatcherism, Czech-style." *Telos* 94 (Winter 1992): 103–29.

Sachs, Jeffrey. "Accelerating Privatization in Eastern Europe: The Case of Poland." Paper prepared for the World Bank Annual Conference on Development Economics, 25–26 April 1991.

Schmitter, Phillipe, and Terry Karl. "What Democracy Is and Is Not." *Journal of Democracy* 2, no. 3 (1991): 75–88.

Schneider, Christopher. "Western Assistance to Central and Eastern European Countries in their Transition to Market Systems." Economic Transitions and Integration Project, Working Paper 94-006, International Institute for Applied Systems Analysis, Laxenburg, Austria, February 1994.

Schroeder, Gertrude. "Crisis in the Consumer Sector: A Comment." *Soviet Economy* 6, no. 1 (1990): 56–64.

Schull, Joseph. "What Is Ideology? Theoretical Problems and Lessons from Soviet-Type Societies." *Political Studies* 40 (1992): 728–31.

Schusselbauer, Gerhard. "Privatization and Restructuring in Economies in Transition: Theory and Evidence Revisited." *Europe-Asia Studies* 51, no. 1 (1999): 65–83.

Schwartz, Andrew. "The Czech Approach to Residual Share Management." In *Between State and Market: Mass Privatization in Transition Economies,* edited by Ira Lieberman, Stilpon Nestor, and Raj Desai, 70–79. Washington, DC: World Bank, 1997.

Shiller, Robert, Maxim Boycko, and Vladimir Korobov. "Hunting for Homo Sovieticus: Situational Versus Attitudinal Factors in Economic Behavior." *Brookings Papers on Economic Activity,* no. 2. Washington, DC: Brookings Institution, 1993.

————. "Popular Attitudes toward Free Markets: The Soviet Union and the United States Compared." *American Economic Review* 81, no. 3 (1991): 385–400.

Shlapentokh, Vladimir. "Privatization Debates in Russia: 1989–1992." *Comparative Economic Studies* 35, no. 2 (1993): 19–32.

Shleifer, Andrei, and Daniel Treisman. *Without a Map: Political Tactics and Economic Reform in Russia.* Cambridge: MIT Press, 2000.

Shleifer, Andrei, and Dmitry Vasiliev. "Management Ownership and Russian Privatization." Paper presented at the World Bank Conference on Corporate Governance in Central Europe and Russia, Washington, DC, 15 December 1994.

Shleifer, Andrei, and Robert Vishny. *The Grabbing Hand: Government Pathologies and Their Cures.* Cambridge, Mass.: Harvard University Press, 1999.

Sikkink, Kathryn. *Ideas and Institutions: Developmentalism in Brazil and Argentina.* Ithaca: Cornell University Press, 1991.

Siklova, Jirina. "Lustration or the Czech Way of Screening." *East European Constitutional Review* 6, no. 1 (1996): 57–62.

Skilling, H. Gordon. *Czechoslovakia's Interrupted Revolution.* Princeton: Princeton University Press, 1976.

Skocpol, Theda. "Bringing the State Back In: Strategies and Analysis of Current Research." In *Bringing the State Back In,* edited by Peter Evans, Dietrich Rueschemeyer, and Theda Skocpol, 3–43. Cambridge: Cambridge University Press, 1985.

Slider, Darrel. "Privatization in Russia's Regions." *Post-Soviet Affairs* 10, no. 4 (1994): 367–96.

Snow, David, and Robert Bedford. "Ideology, Frame Resonance and Participant Mobilization." In *International Social Movement Research: From Structure to Action Comparing Social Movement Research across Cultures,* edited by Bert Klandermans,

Hanspeter Kriesi, and Sidney Tarrow, 197–218. London: JAI Press, 1988.

Snow, David, E. Burke Rochford Jr., Steven Worden, and Robert Bedford. "Frame Alignment Processes, Micromobilization, and Movement Participation." *American Sociological Review* 51 (August 1986): 464–81.

Steinmo, Sven. "A Political Economy of Policy Ideas: Tax Policy in the 20th Century." Manuscript, November 2001.

Steinmo, Sven, Kathleen Thelen, and Frank Longstreth, eds. *Structuring Politics: Historical Institutionalism in Comparative Analysis.* New York: Cambridge University Press, 1992.

Stiglitz, Joseph. "Knowledge for Development: Economic Science, Economic Policy and Economic Advice." Paper prepared for the Annual Bank Conference on Development Economics, World Bank, 1998.

———. "Whither Reform? Ten Years of the Transition." Paper presented at the World Bank Annual Conference on Development Economics, Washington, DC, 28–30 April 1999.

Stone, Randall. *Lending Credibility: The International Monetary Fund and the Post Communist Transition.* Princeton: Princeton University Press, 2002.

———. "Russia and the IMF: Reputation and Unrestricted Bargaining." Paper presented at the APSA annual meeting, 14–17 November 1996.

Šulc, Zdislav. " Stručné dějiny ekonomických reformem v Československu (České republice), 1945–1995" [A brief history of economic reforms in Czechoslovakia (Czech Republic), 1945–1995]." *Studie Národohospodářského ústavu* 3 (3 December 1996): 62–70.

Supyan, Victor B. "Privatization in Russia: Phases and Effects." In *Transitions to Capitalism and Democracy in Russia and Central Europe: Achievements, Problems Prospects,* edited by M. Donald Hancock and John Logue, 11–28. Westport: Praeger 2000.

Svejnar, Jan. "A Framework for the Economic Transformation of Czechoslovakia." *PlanEcon Report* 5, no. 52 (1989): 1–18.

Tarrow, Sidney. "Mentalities, Political Cultures and Collective Frames, Constructing Meaning through Action." In *Frontiers in Social Movement Theory,* edited by Aldon Morris and Carol McClurg Mueller, 174–202. New Haven: Yale University Press, 1992.

Tismaneanu, Vladimir, ed. *Political Culture and Civil Society in Russia and the New States of Eurasia.* Armonk: M. E. Sharpe, 1995.

Tříska, Dušan. "Political, Organizational and Legislative Aspects of Mass Privatization—Czechoslovakia." In *Privatization in Central and Eastern Europe, 1991,* edited by Marko Simoneti and Andreja Bohm. Ljubljana: Central and East European Privatization Network, 1992.

Tversky, Amos, and Daniel Kahneman. "Rational Choice and the Framing of Decisions." In *The Limits of Rationality,* edited by Karen Schweers Cook and Margaret Levi, 60–89. Chicago: University of Chicago Press, 1990.

U.S. Congress. Senate. Committee on Banking, Housing and Urban Affairs. *Impact of IMF/World Bank Policies toward Russia and the Russian Economy,* 103d Cong., 2d sess., 8 February 1994, 1–3.

Vasiliev, Dmitri. "Rossiiskaia programma privatizatsii i perspectivy ee realizatsii" [The Russian privatization program and the prospects for its realization]. *Voprosy ekonomiki* 9 (1992): 11–17.

Wade, Robert. "East Asia's Economic Success: Conflicting Perspectives, Partial Insights, Shaky Evidence." *World Politics* 44, no. 2 (1992): 270–320.

Weber, Max. "The Protestant Ethic and the Spirit of Capitalism." In *Weber Selections in Translation,* edited by W. G. Runciman and translated by Eric Matthews, 138–73. Cambridge: Cambridge University Press, 1978.

Wedel, Janine. *Collision and Collusion: The Strange Case of Western Aid to Eastern Europe, 1989–1998.* New York: St. Martin's Press, 1998.

Weimer, David. *The Political Economy of Property Rights: Institutional Change and Credibility in the Reform of Centrally Planned Economies.* New York: Cambridge University Press, 1997.

Weiss, Andrew, and Georgiy Nikitin. "Effects of Ownership by Investment Funds on the Performance of Czech Firms." In *Designing Financial Systems in Transition Economies: Strategies for Reform in Central and Eastern Europe,* edited by Anna Meyendorff and Anjan Thakor. Cambridge, Mass.: MIT Press, 2002.

Whitefield, Stephen, and Geoffrey Evans. "The Russian Election of 1993: Public Opinion and the Transitions Experience." *Post-Soviet Affairs* 10, no. 4 (1994): 47–49.

Williams, Rhys. "Religion as a Political Resource: Culture or Ideology?" *Journal for the Scientific Study of Religion* 35 (December 1996): 368–78.

Wilson, Richard. *Compliance Ideologies: Rethinking Political Culture.* New York: Cambridge University Press, 1992.

Winiecki, Jan. *Resistance to Change in the Soviet Economic System.* New York: Routledge, 1991.

Wolchik, Sharon. "The Politics of Transition and the Break-up of Czechoslovakia." In *The End of Czechoslovakia,* edited by Jiří Musil. Budapest: CEU Press, 1995.

"World Bank/IMF Agenda." *Transition Newsletter,* June 1997, http://www.worldbank.org/html/prddr/trans/mayjun97/art12.htm (accessed 10 November 2003).

Yavlinsky, G., B. Fedorov, S. Shatalin, N. Petrakov, S. Aleksashenko, A. Vavilov, L. Grigoriev, M. Zadornov, V. Machits, A. Mikhailov, and E. Yasin. *500 Days Transition to the Market.* Translated by David Kushner. New York: St. Martin's Press, 1991.

Yee, Albert. "The Causal Effects of Ideas on Policies." *International Organization* 50, no. 1 (1996): 69–108.

Yeltsin, Boris. *The View from the Kremlin.* London: Harper Collins, 1994.

Zald, Mayer. "Culture, Ideology, and Strategic Framing." In *Comparative Perspectives on Social Movements: Political Opportunities, Mobilizing Structures, and Cultural Framing,* edited by Doug McAdam, John McCarthy, and Mayer Zald, 261–74. Cambridge: Cambridge University Press, 1996.

Ziuganov, Gennadii. *Za gorizontom.* Orel: Veshnie Vody, 1995.

Index

academic communities, 38–40, 42, 48, 72–73, 76–78, 80, 83
Academy of Sciences (Czechoslovakia), 39–40, 48
"Accelerating Privatization of State-Owned and Municipal Enterprises" (Russia), 81–82
Ackerman, Bruce, 124
Act 92/1991 Coll. (Czech large-scale privatization law), 54–55, 138, 191n36
Act 173/1988 Coll. (Czech joint venture law), 41
Act 403/1990 Coll. (Czech restitution law), 54, 173
Act 427/1990 Coll. (Czech small-scale privatization law), 54
Act of the Privatization of State-Owned Enterprises (1990, Poland), 152
advisers, foreign. *See* consultants/foreign advisers
Agrobanka (Czechoslovakia), 64
Alfa Bank (Russia), 98–99
All-Russian Center for Public Opinion Research (VTsIOM), 104
Almond, Gabriel, 127–28
anti-Communism: in Czechoslovakia/Czech Republic, 17–20, 44–45, 51, 53, 135–42, 148–49, 155–56, 160, 162–65, 173; as ideology, 9, 129; labor unions and, 136–37; in Poland, 150–51, 155; Russian lack of, 17–18, 142–45, 156, 173; in Slovakia, 148–49
Armenia, 23, 206n3
Åslund, Anders, 10, 134, 208n36
asset stripping, 4, 66, 112, 132
Association of Employers Unions (AZZZ, Slovakia), 146
Association of Entrepreneurs (Czechoslovakia), 58
automobile industries, 100, 139

Aven, Piotr, 167
AWS (Akcja Wyborcza "Solidarność"), 153
Azerbaijan, 23

Balcerowicz, Leszek, 113, 151–53, 177
banking industries: Czech, 61–66, 69; Russian, 95, 96–102, 110
Baránek, Rudolf, 58
"Basic Provisions for Fundamental Perestroika of Economic Management" (1987, Soviet Union), 71
"Basic Provisions of the State Program for Privatization of State and Municipal Enterprises" (1991-92, Russia), 81–82
Bedford, Robert, 158, 174
Belarus, 23, 32
Blitzer, Mark, 97–98
Bogomolov, Oleg, 72
Boycko, Maxim, 10, 29, 78, 90, 101, 112, 120, 129, 132, 166–67
Braverman, Alexander, 204n126
Brazil, 178
Breslauer, George, 167
Brezhnev, Leonid, 41
Broadman, Harry, 5
Bulgaria, 15, 28, 32, 206n3
Burbulis, Gennadii, 77

capital flight, 95
Carnegie Corporation of New York, 30
Center for Economics Research and Graduate Education (Czech Republic), 30
Central and Eastern Europe Privatization Network (CEEPN), 33, 60
Central European University (Hungary), 30
Česká spřitelná banka, 69 [Česká spořitelná banka]

Československá obchodní banka (ČSOB, Czechoslovakia), 63, 65, 69
Chara (Russian investment fund), 92
Chernomyrdin, Viktor, 80
Christian Democratic Movement (KDH, Slovakia), 150
Chubais, Anatoly: background of, 77–78, 80; book contract advance scandal and, 102; compliance mechanisms used by, 166, 169, 174–77; dismissal of, 101; ESOPs and, 122–23, 132; ideological beliefs/context and, 105, 120–21, 123–24; international funding for, 29; privatization and, 81–86, 88–91, 94–95, 98, 105, 116; revenue extraction and, 94–95; securities regulation and, 92; speed of privatization and, 83–85, 93, 118
citizen participation, 55, 60, 82, 85–86, 90, 114–15
Civic Democratic Alliance (ODA, Czech), 63
Civic Democratic Party (ODS, Czech), 63, 68–69, 220n28
Civic Forum, 42–43, 50–53, 162
Civic Union (Russia), 87, 197n30
coal industries, 64, 103
coercive compliance mechanisms, 18, 23–26, 31, 159–60
Čokoládovny (Czech firm), 67, 139
collateral auctions, 82, 110. See also loans-for-shares program (Russia)
collectivization, Soviet, 160
Communist Party (Czechoslovakia/Czech Republic), 40, 43, 69, 136, 142
Communist Party (SDL, Slovakia), 150
Communist Party (Soviet Union/Russia), 71–74, 142–43
Communist Secret Police (St.B., Czechoslovakia), 135
compliance mechanisms, 7, 18–21; coercive, 18, 23–26, 31, 159–60; cost of, 172–79; ideological, 9, 17–20, 44–45, 51, 53, 129, 135–45, 148–51, 155–56, 160–65, 169–70, 173, 175–77; ideological foundations of, 157–71; remunerative, 18–19, 159–60, 165–67, 175, 177
conferences, international, 32–33
consultants/foreign advisors, 5, 15–16, 28, 32, 34–35; Czech privatization and, 54, 63; Russian privatization and, 100, 105
corporate governance structures, 66, 70, 110–13, 129
corruption, 3; in Czech privatization, 67–68, 70, 129; in Russian privatization, 83, 87–88, 91–92, 98–102, 133, 169

Credit Anstalt (Czech firm), 65
Croatia, 23
Crystalex (Czech firm), 67
ČSOB. See Československá obchodní banka
ČSSD. See Social Democratic Party, Czech
currency devaluations, 66, 94–95, 149
Czech and Slovak Confederation of Trade Unions (ČSKOS), 136–37
Czechoslovakia: anti-Communism in, 17–20, 44–45, 51, 53, 135–42, 148, 155–56, 160, 162–65, 173; dissident movement in, 42–44; dissolution of, 60–61; economic conditions in, 43–44, 146–47; educational reforms in, 30, 39–40; GDP in, 15, 39, 44. See also Czech Republic; Slovakia
Czechoslovak Peoples Party, 56, 121
"Czech Plan," 49–50
Czech Republic, 14–15; economic conditions in, 66–67, 147; ESOPs, absence of, in, 13, 69, 121–22; GDP in, 67, 194n73; Gini coefficients in, 203n116; international loans/funding in, 24–25, 35; labor unions in, 13, 17, 136–37, 156; national identity/nationalism in, 19–20, 162, 167, 175. See also Czechoslovakia

Dale, Catherine, 167
dekulakization, Soviet, 160
Democratic Party of Russia, 87
Democratic Russia movement, 76, 80
demonstration effect. See policy emulation
Demsetz, Harold, 11
Dlouhý, Vladimír, 42, 191n30
Dmitriev, Mikhail, 200n70
donor organizations, Western, 23, 29–36
Dubček, Alexandr, 190n17
Dyba, Karel, 42, 191n30

East Germany, 119
EBRD. See European Bank for Reconstruction and Development
economic efficiency theory, 12, 110–12, 118–21
Economics Education and Research Consortium (EERC), 30
Economy Ministry (Slovak), 146
educational reforms, 23, 29–30, 39–40
Eggertsson, Thrainn, 184n35
elective affinity, 172–73
Ellerman, David, 5
employee rights, 18, 87, 143–44
employee shareownership programs (ESOPs): absence of, in Czech Republic, 13, 56, 69,

121–22, 130, 137; in Poland, 152; in Russia, 13, 18, 112, 122–23, 132–33; in Ukraine, 133
Employers Association (Poland), 152
energy industries, 70, 103
enterprise restructuring/valuation, 4; Czech, 47–50, 55, 62, 64, 66, 119; Russian, 104, 202n96
epistemic communities, 33–34
Erste Bank (Austria), 69
Estonia, 23, 26
Etzioni, Amitai, 18–19, 159
European Bank for Reconstruction and Development (EBRD), 23, 26–27
European Community (EC), 24
European Union (EU), 27–28, 129
European University at St. Petersburg, 30
Evans, Geoffrey, 203n115

Federal Assembly (Czechoslovakia), 47–50, 53
Federal Property Fund (Russia), 89
Fedorov, Boris, 73
Feigenbaum, Harvey, 183n27
fellowships, 29–30
Finance Ministry (Czech), 45, 54, 57, 61, 65, 130–31, 139
financial institutions, international, 5, 15–16, 23–36, 95, 178. See also International Monetary Fund; World Bank
"500 Days Program" (Soviet Union), 73–74, 79–80
FOM (Fund for Public Opinion, Russia), 104
Ford Foundation, 30
foreign debt, 43, 101
foreign investment: in Czechoslovakia/Czech Republic, 41, 55–56, 69, 139, 149; in Hungary, 111; in Russia, 75, 98, 103, 112, 205n140
foundations. See donor organizations, Western
framing, 158–61, 163, 165
Freedom Union (Czech Republic), 69
Freedom Union (Poland), 153
Free Russia People's Party, 87
Frye, Timothy, 116–17
Fund for Public Opinion (FOM, Russia), 104

Gaidar, Egor, 76–81, 86, 116
Garton Ash, Timothy, 43, 190n17
Gazprom (Russian firm), 24, 103
Gekht, Yurii, 87
Georgia, 23, 206n3
Gerashchenko, Viktor, 94–95
Germany, 25, 28
Gini coefficients, 98, 205n150

GKI. See State Property Committee (GKI, Russia)
GKOs (Russian treasury bonds), 95–96, 103
glasnost, 40, 195n1
Goffman, Erving, 219n10
Gorbachev, Mikhail, 41, 71–74, 79
Gould, John, 146, 148
Gramsci, Antonio, 174
Great Britain, 3
Grégr, Miroslav, 138
gross domestic/national product (GDP/GNP): in Czechoslovakia, 15, 39, 44; in Czech Republic, 67, 194n73; in Poland, 15, 67, 153; in Soviet Union, 15
Group of Seven (G-7), 25

Hall, Peter, 173, 176
Hamilton, Malcolm, 8–9
Hanley, Eric, 152
Harvard Capital and Consulting (Czechoslovakia), 62
Harvard Institute for International Development (HIID), 29, 170
Havel, Václav, 42, 50, 52–53, 149, 164
Havlová, Olga, 51
Henig, Jeffrey, 183n27
Heywood, Paul, 143
Higher Economic School (Russia), 30
HIID. See Harvard Institute for International Development
holding companies, 66
hostile takeovers, 65
Hranice Cement Company (Czech Republic), 139
Hungary, 15, 26, 30, 67, 111, 119, 145
Husák, Gustav, 40
HZDS (Movement for a Democratic Slovakia), 150

ideas, theory of, 8–9, 36, 44, 174
ideological compliance mechanisms, 177; anti-Communism as, 9, 17–20, 44–45, 51, 53, 129, 135–45, 148–51, 155–56, 160, 162–65, 173; historical appropriateness as, 19, 161–63, 175; pro-Europeanism as, 19–20, 129, 148, 160–63, 169–70, 173; Russia and, 175–76
ideology/ideological contexts, 7–9, 14, 127–30; change or politics as usual and, 115–18; compliance mechanisms and, 7, 18–21, 157–79; elective affinity and, 172–73; framing and, 158–61, 163, 165; of policy makers, 16–19, 33–36, 105, 123–26, 176; sincerity of, 123–26

Imperial (Russian bank), 99–100
Industrial Union (Russia), 87
Industry and Trade Ministry (Czech), 138–39
inflation, 4, 43, 94–95
Inkombank (Russia), 98–99, 203n111
Institute for Economic Forecasting (Czech), 39–40, 42, 48
interest group theory, 11, 13
international community. *See* consultants/foreign advisors; lenders/lending institutions, international
International Monetary Fund (IMF), 23–26, 28, 32, 35–36, 100, 103, 178
International Renaissance Foundation, 30, 188n44
Investiční a poštovní banka (IPB, Czechoslovakia), 63
investment privatization funds, 61–62, 64–66, 111–12, 131
IVVM (Czech polling firm), 68, 70

Jakeš, Miloš, 41
Japan Bank for International Cooperation, 28
Ježek, Tomáš, 54–55, 57–60, 65, 120, 139, 191n30, 191n39, 221n34
Johnson, Juliet, 203n119
joint stock companies, 66, 72, 74, 81–82, 84, 133
joint ventures, 41, 75, 139–40

Kahneman, Daniel, 158
Karlovarská-Becherovka (Czech firm), 67
Kasianov, Mikhail, 102
Kavan, Jan, 163–64
Kazakhstan, 23, 132, 206n3
Kazakov, Alexander, 101
KBC Bank (Belgium), 69
KDH (Christian Democratic Movement, Slovakia), 150
Khasbulatov, Ruslan, 83, 85, 87–88, 144, 198n44
Khopyor (Russian firm), 92
Klaus, Václav: anti-communism and, 51, 53, 141, 160, 162–65; bank privatization and, 62–63, 66; Civic Forum and, 42–45, 50–53, 77, 120; compliance mechanisms used by, 160–63, 169, 175–77; corruption awareness of, 68; currency devaluation and, 66, 149; education/scholarly background of, 40; and Finance Ministry, appointment to, 45, 47, 53; ideological beliefs/context and, 19, 52, 58–59, 105, 118–20, 124–26, 140; international funding programs and, 35; on managerial interests, 135–36; national identity and, 19, 162,

173; "97+3 Proposal" and, 56–57; political fortunes/power of, 42, 50–52, 140–41; "Programmatic Principles" and, 43, 45, 161; restitution programs and, 58; speed of privatization and, 46–47, 55–56, 58–59, 83, 113, 135; voucher privatization and, 50, 53–61, 70, 131, 138–40
Klímová, Rita, 42
Kliuchnikov, Vitalii, 87
Know How Fund (Great Britain), 28
Kočárnik, Ivan, 191n30
Kožený, Viktor, 62
Kokh, Alfred, 26, 95, 102
Komárek, Valtr, 39–40, 42, 44–48, 78
Komerční banka (Czech Republic), 65, 69
Kornai, Janos, 111
Kramer, Mark, 154
KSČM. *See* Communist Party (Czechoslovakia/Czech Republic)
Kučera, Petr, 51
Kurashvili, Boris, 72
Kuzbassugol (Russian firm), 103
Kyrgyzstan, 206n3
Kysilka, Pavel, 41

labor unions, 10; in Czech Republic, 13, 17, 136–37, 156; in Poland, 152, 154–56
Laitin, David, 210n8
land ownership, 89–90
large-scale privatization, Czech: assessment of, 60–70, 116; citizen participation in, 55, 60; corruption and, 67–68, 70, 129; design of, 53–60; employee participation in, 13, 56, 69, 121–22, 130, 137; enabling legislation for, 54–55, 191n36; government dissolution and, 60–61; investment privatization funds and, 61–62, 64–66, 111–12, 131; manager participation in, 13, 17, 59, 114, 129–32, 134–36, 139, 145, 156; residual state ownership and, 61–64; speed of, 46–47, 55–56, 58–59, 66, 83, 113, 134–35; submission of proposals and, 54, 57–59, 130–31. *See also* voucher privatization programs
large-scale privatization, Russian, 73, 81–106; citizen participation in, 82, 85–86, 90; collective ownership and, 83; corruption in, 83, 87–88, 91–92, 98–102, 133, 169; employee participation in, 13, 18, 82–85, 87–88, 90, 98, 112, 122–23, 132–33, 175; enabling legislation/decrees for, 81–82, 84–85; investment/mutual funds and, 91–92; irreversibility of, 93–94, 102, 105, 116–17; loans-for-shares program

and, 26, 96–103, 105, 110, 117–18; manager participation in, 84, 87, 90, 132–34, 144–45, 175; monetary programs and, 93–106, 133; *nomenklatura* privatization and, 82; public opinion of, 90–91, 94, 98, 104–5; regional governments and, 88–90; speed of, 82–85, 93, 97, 102, 117—8; variants of, 84, 132. *See also* voucher privatization programs

Latvia, 23, 206n3

Law on Cooperatives (1998, Soviet Union), 72

Law on Enterprises and Entrepreneurial Activity (1990, Russian Republic), 75

Law on Foreign Investment (1991, Russian Republic), 75

Law on Privatization of State and Municipal Enterprises in the Russian Federation (1991), 75–76, 81–82

Law on Property (1990, Soviet Union), 72

Law on State Enterprises (1987, Soviet Union), 71–72

Law on the Principles of Destatization and Privatization of Enterprises (1991, Soviet Union), 74

leasing programs, 72, 74, 133

Left Alternative (Czechoslovakia), 52

legitimacy, state, 3, 18, 143–44, 158, 169

lenders, international. *See* financial institutions, international

lending conditionality, 23–26, 31, 103

Levi, Margaret, 11–12

Levitsky, Steven, 154

Lewandowski, Janusz, 152

Libecap, Gary, 11

Lidové noviny, 42

Lieberman, Ira, 100

Lis, Krzysztof, 151–52

Lithuania, 24, 32, 206n3

Lizner, Jaroslav, 67

loans-for-shares program (Russia), 26, 96–103, 105, 110, 117–18

Lobov, Vladimir, 197n29

Lukoil (Russian firm), 24, 99–100, 103

Lula da Silva, Luiz Inácio, 178

lustration laws, 17, 129, 135, 144, 149

Luzhkov, Yuri, 100

Macedonia, 23

managers, 10; Czech, 13, 17, 59, 114, 129–32, 134–36, 139, 145, 156; lustration laws and, 17, 129, 135, 144, 149; Russian, 13, 18, 82, 84, 87, 129, 132–34, 144–45, 175; Slovak, 145–46, 149,

156; tunneling and, 66, 129. *See also nomenklatura* elites

Mansfeldová, Zdenka, 46

Marxist economics, 17, 118

Matějka, Milan, 135

material incentives. *See* remunerative compliance mechanisms

Matrosov Mine (Russia), 103

Mavrodi, Sergei, 91–92

Mazowiecki, Tadeusz, 151, 153

Mečiar, Vladimír, 61, 146, 149–50, 162

media coverage: in Czechoslovakia/Czech Republic, 46–47, 48, 52, 56, 65, 136–37; in Soviet Union/Russia, 73, 83, 168

Menatep (Russian bank), 99, 203n111

Mertlík, Pavel, 121–22

Mikhailov, Aleksei, 73

Miklos, Ivan, 149

Mill, John Stuart, 172

Miller, William, 143

Ministry of. *See specific ministries (e.g.,* Finance Ministry*)*

Mlčoch, Lubomír, 41, 46

MMM (Russian investment firm), 91–92

Moldova, 23, 132, 206n3

monetary privatization programs, 93–106, 133, 152, 153

Montblanc (Russian bank), 99

Morningstar, Richard, 29

Mostovoi, Petr, 102

Motoinvest (Czech firm), 65

Movement for a Democratic Slovakia (HZDS), 150

mutual funds, 91–92, 112, 152

national identity/nationalism, 19–20, 148–50, 162, 166–71, 174–75

National Investment Funds Privatization Law (1993, Poland), 152

National Property Fund (Czech), 48–50, 55, 61

Nekipilov, Victor, 120–21

Nellis, John, 5–6, 206n4

Nemtsov, Boris, 169

neoliberalism, 16, 31–33, 109, 119

New Democracies Barometer, 142, 149

New Economic School (Russia), 30

New Russia Barometers, 143, 223n7

NEZES (Slovak association), 150

"97+3 Proposal" (Czech), 56–57

nomenklatura elites, 4, 10, 55–56, 134

nomenklatura privatization, 82

Norilsk Nickel (Russian firm), 99–101, 204n125

normative compliance mechanisms, 159
Norsi Oil (Russian firm), 103
North, Douglass, 7, 11–12, 158, 186n53
North-Western Shipping Company (Russia), 100

Obroda (Czechoslovakia), 52, 136, 163
ODA (Civic Democratic Alliance, Czech), 63
ODS. *See* Civic Democratic Party
oil industry, Russian, 24, 97, 99–101, 103
oligarchs, Russian, 97–98, 102, 104
Onako (Russian firm), 103
Oneximbank (Russia), 99, 102
Open Society Institute, 30
OPZZ (Polish trade union), 152
Orenstein, Mitchell, 113

Paczynska, Agnieszka, 154
Palouš, Martin, 51, 52
perestroika, 39–40, 71–72
Pew Charitable Trusts, 30
PHARE program, 27
Piiasheva, Larisa, 82
Pipes, Richard, 128
Poland: anti-Communism in, 150–51, 155–56; economics education in, 30; enabling legislation in, 152; GDP in, 15, 67, 153; international loans/funding in, 23–24, 26–28; labor in, 154–56; privatization in, 112–13, 150–55, 206n3; systemic reforms in, 145
policy emulation, 31–33, 60, 84
policy makers, 7, 10; compliance mechanisms used by, 19, 159–60; ideological beliefs/context of, 16–19, 33–36, 105, 123–26, 176; international funding for, 28–29; political fortunes/power of, 12, 29, 115–18; workshops/conferences (international) and, 32–33. *See also individuals by name*
political culture, 127–28
political slogans. *See* rhetoric, use of
polls. *See* public opinion
Popov, Gavriil, 80
Popular Investment Construction Company (Russia), 92
Potanin, Vladimir, 96
power relationships, theories based on, 11–12, 14, 115–18
Prague Economics Institute, 40
predation theory, 11–12, 110
přestavba, 39
Privatization Ministries (Czech, Slovak), 50, 59–61, 130–31, 139

pro-Europeanism, 19–20, 129, 148, 160–63, 169–70, 173
"Programmatic Principles of the Civic Forum" (1989), 43, 45, 161
property rights theories, 10–15, 157–59
Protestant Ethic and the Spirit of Capitalism, The (Weber), 172
pro-Westernism. *See* pro-Europeanism
public opinion, 129; Czech, 52, 60, 68, 70, 142–43, 147, 149; Slovak, 143, 147, 149; Soviet/Russian, 73, 90–91, 94, 98, 104–5, 142–43
Public Opinion Research Institute (IVVM, Czech Republic), 68, 70
Putin, Vladimir, 102
PZPR. *See* United Polish Workers' Party

Radygin, Aleksandr, 89
Rakona (Czech firm), 139
rational choice analysis, 13–14
remunerative compliance mechanisms, 18–19, 159–60, 165–67, 175, 177
re-nationalization, 100–101, 117, 157
residential property privatization, 130
restitution programs, 54, 56, 58, 129, 160, 173
revenue extraction, 4, 12, 93–95, 110. *See also* loans-for-shares program (Russia)
"revolutionary moment" theory, 113–14, 124
rhetoric, use of, 19, 158, 162, 165–66, 169
Riker, William, 11–12, 115
Romania, 15, 23–24
Rosneft (Russian firm), 103, 201n80
Rossiiskaia gazeta, 169
Rossiisky Kredit (Russia), 98–99
Russia, 14–15; anti-Communism, lack of, in, 17–18, 142–45, 156, 173; capital flight in, 95; economic conditions in, 83–84, 94–95, 98, 104; educational reforms in, 30; ESOPs in, 13, 18, 122–23; Gini coefficients in, 98, 205n150; international loans/funding in, 23–26, 28, 35, 95; national identity/nationalism in, 80, 166–71, 174–75
Russian Privatization Center, 28
Russian Union of Industrialists and Entrepreneurs (RSPP), 86
Russki Dom Selenga (Russian firm), 92
Rutland, Peter, 167
Rutskoi, Alexandr, 87

Sachs, Jeffrey, 100, 114, 125
Satarov, Georgy, 169
"Scenario for Economic Reform" (1990, Czechoslovakia), 48–51, 53, 137, 190n22

School of Economics (Czechoslovakia), 40, 48
Schull, Joseph, 123, 176
Schwartz, Andrew, 63–64
screening laws. *See* lustration laws
SDL (Communist Party, Slovakia), 150
securities regulation, 64–66, 92
Sedláček, Vojtech, 51
Segodnia Press (Russia), 102
Sened, Itai, 185n37
Shatalin, Stanislav, 73–74, 78
Shleifer, Andrei, 10, 29, 90, 112, 120, 129, 132
Shmelev, Nikolai, 72
Sibneft (Russian firm), 103
Sidanko (Russian firm), 99
Šik, Ota, 56, 121
Sikkink, Kathryn, 173
Škoda (Czech automaker), 139
Škoda Energo (Czech firm), 139
Slavneft (Russian firm), 103
Slovakia, 15; GDP in, *67*; national identity/nationalism in, 148–50, 162; privatization in, 61, 145–50, 206n3; standby agreements in, 23, 131. *See also* Czechoslovakia
small-scale privatization: Czech, 54, 56, 130; Russian, 78
Smena (Russian political party), 87
Snow, David, 158, 174
Social Democratic Party, Czech (ČSSD), 56, 62, 68–70, 121, 125
social movement theory, 158–59, 163
Sokol, Jan, 51, 141, 189n8
Solidarity (Poland), 151–52, 155, 218n111
Soros, George, 30, 188n44
Soviet Union, 15, 39, 71–76. *See also* Russia
speculators, 55–56, 64
speed of privatization, 5–6, 15, 218n111; Czech, 46–47, 55–56, 58–59, 66, 83, 113, 134–35; "revolutionary moment" theory and, 113–14; Russian, 82–85, 93, 97, 102, 117–18; Soviet, 73
spontaneous privatization, 82
SPT Telecom (Czech firm), 67
standby agreements, 23–24, 26
State Audit Chamber (Russia), 100–101
State Property Committee (GKI, Russia), 18, 81, 83, 85, 87, 97, 101
State Property Fund (Russia), 95
St.B. (Communist Secret Police, Czechoslovakia), 135
Steinmo, Sven, 182n19
Stiglitz, Joseph, 6, 16
Stock Exchange Commission (Czech Republic), 65

Stolichny (Russian bank), 99
Stone, Randall, 25
Štrougal, Lubomír, 40–41
student demonstrations, 137
Suchocka, Hanna, 154
Šulc, Zdislav, 48
Svaz průmyslu (Union of Industry, Czechoslovakia), 49
Švejnar, Jan, 46
Svyazinvest (Russian firm), 24, 101, 103, 204n125
symbols, use of, 19, 158, 166, 168
Szomolanyi, Sona, 148

Tabak Kutna Hora (Czech firm), 139
Tarrow, Sidney, 219n9
Tatra Kopřivnice (Czech automaker), 139
Telemarket (Russian firm), 92
Thatcherism, 125, 164
Tibet (Russian investment fund), 92
Tošovský, Josef, 69
Travkin, Nikolai, 87
Tříska, Dušan, 191n30; ideological beliefs/context and, 119–20, 140; on managerial interests, 114, 135–36; "97+3 Proposal" of, 56–57; as privatization advisor/consultant, 32; speed of privatization and, 55–56, 113; voucher privatization and, 54–57, 60, 131, 139–40
Tsipko, Aleksandr, 170–71
tunneling *(tunelování)*, 66, 129
Turek, Otakar, 48
Tversky, Amos, 158
Tyumen Oil Company (Russia), 101, 103

Uhl, Petr, 52
Ukraine, 15, 23, 25, 28, 30, 132–33, 206n3
unemployment, 43, 146–47
Union of Industry (Czechoslovakia), 49
United Polish Workers' Party (PZPR), 152, 155
Urban, Jan, 42, 80
USAID (United States Agency for International Development), 6, 28–30
UW (Freedom Union party, Poland), 153
Uzbekistan, 23

Valeš, Václav, 51, 138, 164
valuation. *See* enterprise restructuring/valuation
Vasiliev, Dmitri, 78, 82, 85, 93, 114
Veimetr, Rogi, 100
Verba, Sydney, 127–28
Vishny, Robert, 10, 29, 112, 120, 129

Vlasák, František, 48–50

Volsky, Arkadii, 86–88, 168

voucher privatization programs, 4, 32, 206n3; Czech, 32, 48, 53–70, 113, 152–53, 161; economic efficiency theory and, 110–11, 118–21; Hungarian, 111; ideology or politics as usual and, 115–18; policy emulation and, 32–33, 60, 84; as remunerative compliance mechanism, 160–61, 166; "revolutionary moment" theory and, 113–14; Russian, 28, 32, 82, 84–93, 104, 112, 168; Slovak, 61; Ukrainian, 133

Vrba, Jan, 138–41

VTsIOM (All-Russian Center for Public Opinion Research), 104

Warsaw School of Economics, 30

Way, Lucan, 154

Weber, Max, 172

Wedel, Janine, 29

Weimer, David, 11–12, 115

White, Stephen, 143

Whitefield, Stephen, 203n115

Worker Self-Management Coalition (Poland), 152

workshops, international, 32–33

World Bank, 35, 178; assessments of privatization by, 6, 63–64, 114, 116; consultants of, 32, 60; educational reform and, 30; lending conditionality and, 23–26, 103; loans-for-shares programs, assessments of, by, 96–97, 100; support of existing privatizing programs by, 26–28

Yasin, Yevgeny, 73

Yavlinsky, Grigory, 73–74, 78–79

Yeltsin, Boris, 72–76; decrees of, 85–86, 93–94; dissolution of parliament and, 90, 144; economic team of, 76–81; ideological beliefs/context and, 167; loans-for-shares criticized by, 100–101; political fortunes/power of, 26, 76, 95, 97, 117, 169

Yugoslavia, 122, 145

Yukos (Russian firm), 99–100, 204n138

Zadornov, Mikhail, 73

Zald, Mayer, 219n14

Zeman, Miloš, 48, 69, 189n1

Zil (Russian automaker), 100

Ziuganov, Gennadii, 100, 117, 168

Živnostenská banka (Czechoslovakia), 65